4th Workshop on Argument Mining 2017

Copenhagen, Denmark
8 September 2017

ISBN: 978-1-5108-4754-5

EMNLP 2017

Proceedings of the
4th Workshop on Argument Mining

September 8, 2017
Copenhagen, Denmark

Introduction

The goal of this workshop is to provide a follow-on forum to the last three years' Argumentation Mining workshops at ACL and NAACL, the first research forum devoted to argumentation mining in all domains of discourse.

Argument mining (also, "argumentation mining", referred to as "computational argumentation" in some recent works) is a relatively new challenge in corpus-based discourse analysis that involves automatically identifying argumentative structures within discourse, e.g., the premises, conclusion, and argumentation scheme of each argument, as well as argument-subargument and argument-counterargument relationships between pairs of arguments in the document. To date, researchers have investigated methods for argument mining in areas such as legal documents, on-line debates, product reviews, academic literature, user comments on proposed regulations, newspaper articles and court cases, as well as in dialogical domains. To date there are few corpora with annotations for argumentation mining research although corpora with annotations for argument sub-components have recently become available.

Proposed applications of argumentation mining include improving information retrieval and information extraction as well as end-user visualization and summarization of arguments. Textual sources of interest include not only the formal writing of legal text, scientific writing and parliamentary records, but also a variety of informal genres such as microtext, spoken meeting transcripts, product reviews and user comments. In instructional contexts where argumentation is a pedagogically important tool for conveying and assessing students' command of course material, the written and diagrammed arguments of students (and the mappings between them) are educational data that can be mined for purposes of assessment and instruction. This is especially important given the wide-spread adoption of computer-supported peer review, computerized essay grading, and large-scale online courses and MOOCs.

Success in argument mining will require interdisciplinary approaches informed by natural language processing technology, theories of semantics, pragmatics and discourse, knowledge of discourse of domains such as law and science, artificial intelligence, argumentation theory, and computational models of argumentation. In addition, it will require the creation and annotation of high-quality corpora of argumentation from different types of sources in different domains.

We are looking forward to a full day workshop to exchange ideas and present ongoing research on all of the above - see you all in Copenhagen, Denmark at EMNLP 2017!

Organizers:

Ivan Habernal, Technische Universität Darmstadt (chair)
Iryna Gurevych, Technische Universität Darmstadt (chair)
Kevin Ashley, University of Pittsburgh
Claire Cardie, Cornell University
Nancy Green, University of North Carolina Greensboro
Diane Litman, University of Pittsburgh
Georgios Petasis, NCSR Demokritos, Athens
Chris Reed, University of Dundee
Noam Slonim, IBM Research
Vern R. Walker, Maurice A. Deane School of Law at Hofstra University, New York

Program Committee:

Stergos Afantenos, University of Toulouse
Ahmet Aker, University of Duisburg-Essen
Carlos Alzate, IBM Research - Ireland
Katarzyna Budzynska, Polish National Academy of Sciences and University of Dundee
Elena Cabrio, Universite Cote d'Azur, CNRS, Inria, I3S, France
Matthias Grabmair, Carnegie Mellon University
Graeme Hirst, University of Toronto
Jonas Kuhn, University of Stuttgart
Ran Levy, IBM Research
Maria Liakata, University of Warwick
Beishui Liao, Zhejiang University
Marie-Francine Moens, KU Leuven
Smaranda Muresan, Columbia University
Alexis Palmer, University of North Texas
Joonsuk Park, Williams College
Simon Parsons, King's College London
Mercer Robert, University of Western Ontario
Ariel Rosenfeld, Bar-Ilan University, Israel
Patrick Saint-Dizier, IRIT-CNRS
Jodi Schneider, University of Illinois at Urbana-Champaign
Christian Stab, Technische Universität Darmstadt
Benno Stein, Bauhaus-Universität Weimar
Karkaletsis Vangelis, NCSR Demokritos, Athens
Serena Villata, CNRS, France
Henning Wachsmuth, Bauhaus-Universität Weimar
Lu Wang, Northeastern University
Zhongyu Wei, Fudan University
Janyce Wiebe, University of Pittsburgh
Adam Wyner, University of Aberdeen

Table of Contents

Conference Program

Friday, September 8, 2017

8:50–9:50   **Welcome session**

8:50–9:00   *Welcome*
Workshop Chairs

9:00–9:50   *Invited talk*
Christian Kock, Dept. of Media, Cognition and Communication, University of Copenhagen

9:50–10:30   **Paper session I**

9:50–10:10   *200K+ Crowdsourced Political Arguments for a New Chilean Constitution*
Constanza Fierro, Claudio Fuentes, Jorge Pérez and Mauricio Quezada

10:10–10:30   *Analyzing the Semantic Types of Claims and Premises in an Online Persuasive Forum*
Christopher Hidey, Elena Musi, Alyssa Hwang, Smaranda Muresan and Kathy McKeown

10:30–11:00   **Coffee break**

11:00–12:30   **Paper session II**

11:00–11:20   *Annotation of argument structure in Japanese legal documents*
Hiroaki Yamada, Simone Teufel and Takenobu Tokunaga

11:20–11:40   *Improving Claim Stance Classification with Lexical Knowledge Expansion and Context Utilization*
Roy Bar-Haim, Lilach Edelstein, Charles Jochim and Noam Slonim

11:40–12:00   *Mining Argumentative Structure from Natural Language text using Automatically Generated Premise-Conclusion Topic Models*
John Lawrence and Chris Reed

12:00–12:20   *Building an Argument Search Engine for the Web*
Henning Wachsmuth, Martin Potthast, Khalid Al Khatib, Yamen Ajjour, Jana Puschmann, Jiani Qu, Jonas Dorsch, Viorel Morari, Janek Bevendorff and Benno Stein

12:30–14:30   Lunch break

14:30–15:30   Poster session

14:30–15:30   *Argument Relation Classification Using a Joint Inference Model*
Yufang Hou and Charles Jochim

14:30–15:30   *Projection of Argumentative Corpora from Source to Target Languages*
Ahmet Aker and Huangpan Zhang

14:30–15:30   *Manual Identification of Arguments with Implicit Conclusions Using Semantic Rules for Argument Mining*
Nancy Green

14:30–15:30   *Unsupervised corpus–wide claim detection*
Ran Levy, Shai Gretz, Benjamin Sznajder, Shay Hummel, Ranit Aharonov and Noam Slonim

14:30–15:30   *Using Question-Answering Techniques to Implement a Knowledge-Driven Argument Mining Approach*
Patrick Saint-Dizier

14:30–15:30   *What works and what does not: Classifier and feature analysis for argument mining*
Ahmet Aker, Alfred Sliwa, Yuan Ma, Ruishen Lui, Niravkumar Borad, Seyedeh Ziyaei and Mina Ghobadi

200K+ Crowdsourced Political Arguments
for a New Chilean Constitution

Constanza Fierro   **Jorge Pérez**   **Mauricio Quezada**
Department of Computer Science, Universidad de Chile
`{cfierro,jperez,mquezada}@dcc.uchile.cl`

Claudio Fuentes-Bravo
Center for Argumentation and Reasoning Studies, Universidad Diego Portales
`claudio.fuentes@udp.cl`

Abstract

In this paper we present the dataset of 200,000+ political arguments produced in the local phase of the 2016 Chilean constitutional process. We describe the human processing of this data by the government officials, and the manual tagging of arguments performed by members of our research group. Afterwards we focus on classification tasks that mimic the human processes, comparing linear methods with neural network architectures. The experiments show that some of the manual tasks are suitable for automatization. In particular, the best methods achieve a 90% top-5 accuracy in a multiclass classification of arguments, and 65% macro-averaged F1-score for tagging arguments according to a three-part argumentation model.

1   Introduction

The current constitution of Chile was written during Pinochet's dictatorship (Political Constitution of the Republic of Chile, 1980). Since the return to democracy in 1990, there has been an increasing pressure to make changes to this constitution. During 2016, the Chilean government finally decided to begin with a participative process to delineate what a new constitution should consider (Jordán et al., 2016). Several aspects of the Chilean process diverged from a classical way of producing a new constitution. The first phase of the process included small assemblies across the country, big group discussions at the regional level, on-line individual surveys, and so on. All the generated data was uploaded by the participants using a dedicated Web-site: http://unaconstitucionparachile.cl.

One of the most interesting parts of the process was the local participative phase in which small groups join together in a half-day meeting. During the meeting the participants had to agree on which are the most important *constitutional concepts*, writing an argument about why each of these concepts is relevant. The process produced a dataset of 200,000+ political arguments that was openly published in a raw and anonymous form (General Secretariat, Presidency of Chile, 2016).

In this paper we present the curated and tagged dataset of political arguments produced in the local phase of the 2016 Chilean constitutional process, and we analyze it to understand what type of automated reasoning is necessary to classify and tag the components of these arguments. We describe the manual processing and tagging performed by the government officials and then by members of our research group. We consider a three-part argumentation model dividing arguments into *policies* (e.g., "The state should provide free education for all"), *facts* (e.g., "Global warming will threaten food security by the middle of the 21st century"), and *values* (e.g., "The pursuit of economic prosperity is less important than the preservation of environmental quality"). This tagging included the manual parsing, normalization and classification of every single argument in the dataset, and was used as input for the official report of the 2016 process (Baranda et al., 2017).

The effort and resources spent in the manual classification and tagging of arguments was considerable, taking months of work. This motivates us to look for ways to automatize at least parts of these tasks. In particular, one of our motivations is the possibility of adding more arguments from new participant groups, but without the burden of relying on such an expensive and time consuming manual post processing.

We present several baselines on tasks that mimic the human classification and tagging pro-

1

Proceedings of the 4th Workshop on Argument Mining, pages 1–10
Copenhagen, Denmark, September 8, 2017. ©2017 Association for Computational Linguistics

cessing. We consider two tasks. The first task is a multiclass classification problem of arguments according to the constitutional concept that they are referring to. The second task is an automatic tagging of arguments according to our three-part argumentation model. For these tasks, we compare standard methods, in particular, Logistic Regression, Random Forests and Support Vector Machines, with modern neural-network architectures tailored for natural language processing. Our baseline methods achieve a good performance thus showing that some of the manual tasks are suitable for automatization. In particular, our best methods achieve more than 90% top-5 accuracy in the multiclass classification on the first task. Regarding the second task, we obtain a performance of over 65% macro-averaged F1-score.

The data presented in this paper is one of the biggest datasets of arguments written in the Spanish language. Moreover, to the best of our knowledge, it is the only dataset of its characteristics in the Chilean Spanish dialect. We expect that this dataset plus our baselines can be useful for analyzing political arguments in Spanish beyond the specific tasks that we consider in this paper. The full dataset is available at https://github.com/uchile-nlp.

Related work

One particular work that is similar to ours presents a dataset of ideological debates in the English language and the specific task of classifying the stance (e.g. in favor or against) (Somasundaran and Wiebe, 2010). This work deals with controversial topics and the corresponding stances, but not on how relevant the topics are to propose public policies. Another similar corpus is the one regarding suggestions of the future use of a former German airport (Liebeck et al., 2016). This corpus is similar to ours in the sense of having informal arguments about public policies, but differs considerably in size (about 1% of our dataset).

A dataset of political arguments in the English language is presented with the corresponding annotation of sentiment, agreement, assertiveness, etc., obtained from an online forum (Walker et al., 2012; Abbott et al., 2016). The dataset consists of pairs question-answer about different topics. The main differences lay in the informal nature of an online forum and that the opinions are made by individuals. In our corpus, the arguments are made

from collective meetings in a semi-formal setting.

In the Spanish language, a corpus consisting of 468 theses and undergrad proposals was made public in 2015 (González-López and López-López, 2015). The main difference is the formal tone of its contents and the homogeneity of the individuals that produced the texts. Gorrostieta and López-López (2016) perform classification techniques for argument mining on that dataset. Regarding the size of the data, it is roughly 10% of the dataset presented in this work. We did not find any more related datasets in the Spanish language.

2 Background of the 2016 Chilean Constitutional Process

Here we discuss the background of the constitutional process in Chile, and we describe how the data was generated. The process was divided in several steps (Jordán et al., 2016). First, citizens interested in discussing a new constitution were invited to organize themselves in small groups called *Self-convened Local Meetings* (SLMs). Every SLM was composed of 10 to 30 people that had to meet between April and June 2016. From June to August 2016 there were meetings at the municipality level and finally at the regional level, in which bigger groups discussed the output of the previous phases. The whole process was supervised by a *Citizen Council* of 15 members politically independent from the government. In January 2017, considering the output of all the previous phases, the Citizen Council produced the *Citizen Foundations for a New Constitution* (Baranda et al., 2017) in a set of documents that were given to the Chilean president of the time, Michelle Bachelet. The presidency is, at the time of this paper, preparing a bill to be sent to the Congress during late 2017. The decision about the mechanism to produce the constitution is to be decided by the 2018-2022 Congress (Jordán et al., 2016).

The 2016 phase of the process was a success in terms of the number of participating citizens, especially the SLMs phase. The government expected to have at most 3,000 SLMs, but more than 8,000 were successfully completed across the whole country with 106,412 total participants (General Secretariat, Presidency of Chile, 2017). This was 5 times the number of participants in the regional phase. In this paper we focus on the data produced by the SLMs.

SLMs and raw data

SLMs were guided by a form provided by the government (Jordán et al., 2016) which was replicated in the Web site used upload the info after the SLM. The form proposes four **topics** for discussion: Values (**V**), Rights (**R**), Duties (**D**), and Institutions (**I**). Among every topic, the participants should select seven constitutional **concepts**. For example, for the **V** topic they can select concepts such as "Dignity", "Gender Equality" or "Justice", and for the **R** topic they can select concepts such as "Privacy", "Non discrimination", "Right to education" and so on. The form included example concepts for every topic (37 example concepts for **V**, 44 for **R**, 12 for **D**, and 21 for **I**), but the participants can also include their own concepts. In that case they should select the concept "Other" and then write the new concept and its argument. We call them *open concepts*. For every selected constitutional concept, the participants should write an **argument** (in natural language) explaining why this concept should be considered in an eventual future constitution. Table 1 shows examples of (real) **concept-argument** pairs for the **R** topic.

The complete raw dataset of SLMs is composed of 205,357 arguments organized in the four mentioned topics. The total number of words (concept plus arguments) in the complete corpus is 4,653,518, which gives an average of 22.6 words per argument ($\sigma = 13$). Most of the arguments were given for concepts proposed in the SLM form, and only 10.7% were given for open concepts. Nevertheless, since open concepts are freely written by the participants, the data contains an important number of (syntactically) different constitutional concepts (11,568). Table 2 shows a summary of these numbers organized by topics. Table 3 shows the portion of arguments from the total that were given for open concepts.

It should be noticed that SLMs participants were diverse in terms of age, educational level, professional background and so on. As expected, arguments have different styles, and some of them partially lack proper grammatical constructions or correct punctuation (Table 1).

3 Tagging and processing of the corpus

3.1 Concept classification

The initial analysis by the Government officials was a frequency count of constitutional concepts. The main difficulty was that although concepts may be syntactically different, they can represent the same abstract idea (e.g. "Gender equality" and "Equality of rights for men and women"). To cope with this problem, they first tried to classify all the open concepts as one of the 114 initial constitutional concepts proposed in the SLM form. They proceed by classifying inside every topic (e.g., an open concept in topic **V** should only be classified as one of the 37 original **V** concepts). In the classification, every open concept-argument pair was independently classified by two annotators, and discrepancies were solved by the inclusion of a third one. In the published data there are 22,015 arguments with an open concept. Of them, 10,263 were successfully classified as one of the 114 initial concepts, 3,001 were considered as unclassifiable and the remaining 8,751 were clustered to form 47 new constitutional concepts with few arguments each (213 in average).

A total of 18 annotators plus 4 managers participated in the classification; they had a professional background in sociology and completed one day of training. The annotation achieved 87% total agreement and a Cohen's Kappa score of 0.85 (Cortés, 2017). The process was performed by the United Nations Development Program and the Department of Psychology of one of the main universities in the country, and is briefly described in a report prepared by the Constitutional Systematization Committee (2017). The technical details reported here were provided via personal communication (Cortés, 2017).

3.2 Argumentation model and tagging

The model used for the manual analysis of the arguments of the corpus is an adaptation of the criteria of Informal Logic for the detection and analysis of arguments (Hitchcock, 2007), the theory of collective intentionality of Searle (2014) and Tuomela (2013), and the classification of controversial topics in the American academic debate of Snider and Schnurer (2002) and Branham (1991).

Theoretical background

Hitchcock's (2007) account of argument subsumes the possibility that premises and conclusions may be speech acts of different sorts. In particular, it allows a premise to be any communication act which asserts a proposition (such as suggesting, hypothesizing, insulting and boasting), and allows a conclusion to be a request for information, a request

concept	argument	(argument mode)
Equality before the law	There should exist equality before the law for regular people businessmen politicians businessmen and politicians relatives without privileges or benefits.	(policy)
Right to a fair salary	The worst of all inequalities is the salary of the congressmen, Ministers and others with respect to the salary of (CLP)$250,000 of the workers.	(value)
Right to education	It is a fundamental social right, the basis of equality that democratizes access to the construction of thought to develop the potential of the participative citizen.	(fact)

Table 1: Examples of constitutional concepts and arguments for the topic "Rights" produced during a SLM. (Arguments were translated from Spanish trying to preserve their original draft and punctuation.) The final column is the annotation according to the argumentation model.

Topic	words	arguments	open conc.	gov. conc.
V	1,202,629	53,780	1,876	37
R	1,253,300	53,060	3,712	44
D	1,156,644	48,758	2,860	12
I	1,040,945	49,759	3,120	21
Total	4,653,518	205,357	11,568	114

Table 2: Statistics for SLMs raw data with open and government concepts.

	V	**R**	**D**	**I**	Total
#	4,625	6,173	4,596	6,621	22,015
%	8.6%	11.6%	9.4%	13.3%	10.7%

Table 3: Arguments with open concepts.

to do something, a commissive, an expressive, or a declarative. This broadening of the notion of argument is essential to recognize and distinguish the diverse roles that argument and inference play in real-life contexts.

From a pragmatic point of view, we can determine, based on the ideas of Searle (2014) and Tuomela (2013), that the opinions formulated on the arguments that we analyzed reflect different purposes. If the expression analyzed is identified as an assertive speech act (a report of facts, rules or states), then we can reconstruct such reasoning as a factual one ("The production of genetically modified foods is a political problem for Latin America"). If the expression can be identified as a directive speech act, then it is a reasoning of politics ("Chile must be incorporated into the OECD").

Factual and political reasonings follow a propositional pattern that allows one to reconstruct a partial or fragmented enunciative structure. This happened frequently in the arguments of SLMs. Once the arguments were reconstructed, we used the classification proposed by Snider and Schnurer (2002) and Branham (1991) for controversial topics. This classification gathers 150 years of categorization of statements in the tradition of academic debating in the United States which made it a fairly robust strategy for categorizing natural language. With this strategy we classified all the arguments in the corpus using three kinds of propositions: facts, values and policies.

Facts, values and policies

Factual propositions speak of what it "is", "was" or "will be". They are composed of a subject ("the house", "capitalism"), the verbal formula "is", which entails the idea of identity or subduction, and finally, a set of conditions.

Value propositions represent evaluation statements that use abstract binary concepts (such as beautiful vs. ugly, relevant vs. irrelevant, equity vs. inequity), regarding people, places, things or events (Snider and Schnurer, 2002, pp. 88–89). The value propositions are composed, in similar terms of the factual thesis, of a subject (or study case), a verbal form "is", and a set of conditions. Value propositions differ from facts in the presence of a qualificative, consisting of an adjective whose semantic function is to evaluate either positively or negatively. Pragmatical or instrumental qualifications such as "efficient", "useful", and "convenient", are usually considered as value propositions. Nevertheless, it is preferable to treat them as facts if their value depends exclusively on factual situations, e.g., if we say "S is efficient" meaning that it spends the lesser possible resources.

Finally, policies, or political propositions, are formulated according to a question of the type "What should be done?". The political propositions are composed of a deontological modal indicator "it should" (or an equivalent). In general,

Argument mode	Amount	Percentage
policy	135,489	66.0%
fact	37,397	18.2%
value	11,912	5.8%
undefined	11,238	5.5%
blank	9,321	4.5%

Table 4: Distribution of argument modes resulting from human annotators.

the object will be composed of a verbal form that aims towards an illocutive intention (e.g. allow, prohibit, approve, made), and a subject or object. Political debates can be referred as potential actions of the local or national government ("Chile should have free education at all levels").

Every fact, policy and value proposition was normalized to follow the structural pattern *subject–verb–direct object*, having in some cases a complement that comprises indirect objects or other kinds of syntactic complements. This choice of reconstruction allows us to go deeper in a morphosyntactical analysis without forcing the more elemental claims to have a complex construction. With all these ingredients, we consider a tagging scheme in which every argument is normalized identifying the following essential parts: (1) subject, (2) verbal syntagm, (3) nominal syntagm, (4) prepositional syntagm, and (5) argumentative mode (either fact, value or policy). As an example, consider the following sentence in Spanish: "Se debe aceptar el matrimonio homosexual en Chile". Its verbal syntagm is "Se debe aceptar" ("it should be allowed"), the nominal syntagm is "el matrimonio homosexual" ("gay marriage") and the propositional syntagm is "en Chile" ("in Chile"). In this case the subject is implicit, which is a typical form to state policies in Spanish (starting with the form "Se debe"). Given this component identification it is clear that the sentence has a policy mode.

Normalization tagging process

We considered candidate annotators from local undergrad students and professionals in sociology, psychology, political science, linguistics, etc. They were given a 90-minute orientation and then tested in a normalization and tagging task of 50 arguments. Those candidates that achieved at least 80% accuracy (compared to a gold standard of examples previously annotated and corrected by the team) were invited to continue as annotators on an on-site work alongside with research assistants from our group. Every annotator was closely followed by one manager during the first five working days. The manager corrected the annotations along with the annotator and, if needed, re-trained him or her. After those first days, the annotators that achieved a proper standard in the evaluation of the team, processed arguments independently of the manager, but every annotation was inspected for correctness by the manager. Those annotations considered as incorrect were sent back to the pool of unprocessed arguments, to be processed again by a different annotator. More than 120 annotators participated in the process, receiving 0.15 USD per correctly annotated argument. After completing the process, we performed a validation step, by sampling a random set of annotations, which were corrected again by the team. The error estimated by using that procedure was less than 15%. It should be noticed that the quality control procedure used here was a compromise between academic methodologies and the requirements made by the contracting party, which stressed the short time available to complete the analysis of the 200,000+ cases. Table 4 shows the number of arguments tagged in every mode of our argumentation model. As the numbers show, most of the arguments (66%) were tagged as policies.

4   Classification tasks

We consider three main tasks. Task A and Task B are associated to the classification of concepts (Section 3.1) and Task C to the tagging process of arguments according to our argumentation model.

One of our main motivations is to mimic the classification of open concepts described in Section 3.1. Towards this goal, we first define a task that tries to predict to which concept a given argument is referring to. Formally, let C_G be the set of 114 constitutional concepts provided by the Government in the SLMs. Recall that SLMs were divided in four topics, thus C_G can be partitioned in four disjoint sets of concepts, $C_G^{\mathbf{V}}$, $C_G^{\mathbf{R}}$, $C_G^{\mathbf{D}}$, and $C_G^{\mathbf{I}}$, one for each topic. Let D_G be the set of concept-argument pairs (c, a) such that $c \in C_G$ (that is, concept-argument pairs that were explicitly written as one of the 114 government concepts by the SLM participants), and let A_G be the set of all arguments associated to concepts in C_G. Similarly as for C_G, we can partition D_G and A_G into sets D_G^T and A_G^T with $T \in \{\mathbf{V}, \mathbf{R}, \mathbf{D}, \mathbf{I}\}$. We have all the necessary notation to formalize our first task.

Task A. *Fix a topic $T \in \{\mathbf{V}, \mathbf{R}, \mathbf{D}, \mathbf{I}\}$. Given an argument $a^\star \in A_G^T$, predict the concept $c \in C_G^T$ such that $(c, a^\star) \in D_G^T$.*

Notice that Task A is essentially defining four independent classification problems, one for each different topic. We show in the next sections that finding models for Task A proves to be useful in solving a classification problem for open concepts that we next formalize.

Let C_O be the set of open concepts, that is, the set of concepts $c^\star$ such that $c^\star \notin C_G$. Similarly as for the previous task, one can define D_O (the set of pairs with open concepts) and A_O (the set of arguments for open concepts) and their partitions by topics C_O^T, D_O^T and A_O^T with $T \in \{\mathbf{V}, \mathbf{R}, \mathbf{D}, \mathbf{I}\}$.

Task B. *Fix a topic $T \in \{\mathbf{V}, \mathbf{R}, \mathbf{D}, \mathbf{I}\}$. Given a pair $(c^\star, a^\star) \in D_O^T$, determine a concept $c \in C_G^T$ to which $(c^\star, a^\star)$ is most probably referring to.*

Our final task is a prediction of the argumentation mode and is formalized as follows.

Task C. *Given an argument $a^\star \in A_G \cup A_O$, predict the most suitable tag for $a^\star$ according to our argumentation model (policy, fact, value).*

Notice that in our final task we do not make any distinction by topic or whether the argument was given for an open concept or not.

5 Methods

We consider two types of methods to compute (non-trivial) baselines for the above-mentioned tasks: standard linear classifiers, and simple neural-network based methods tailored for natural language processing. We begin by describing the standard classifiers and the features that we consider.

5.1 Standard classifiers

We consider three baseline standard classifiers: Logistic Regression (LR), Random Forests (RF) (Breiman, 2001), and Support Vector Machines (SVM) (Cortes and Vapnik, 1995). The setting involves several combinations of feature sets and normalizations. Feature sets comprise (1) the extraction of *unigrams*, *bigrams*, and unigrams plus bigrams (denoted as *ngram*), and (2) raw tokens (denoted as *raw*) and Part of Speech tagged tokens (denoted as *POS*). Normalizations comprises (1) raw term counts (denoted as *count*), (2) term counts normalized by term frequency (denoted as *tf*), and (3) normalized by term frequency

and inverse document frequency (denoted as *tf-idf*). For all combinations we use the lemma of a token instead of the original token, and stopwords are removed. This ends up in 18 combinations for every one of the three classifiers, resulting in 54 baselines.

5.2 Neural networks classifiers

We consider two methods, fastText (Joulin et al., 2016) and Deep Averaging Networks (Iyyer et al., 2015), that have been proposed as simple yet efficient baselines for text classification. We also consider the use of *word embeddings*.

FastText Joulin et al. (2016) propose a simple two-layer architecture for text classification called fastText. The input for the classifier is a text represented as a bag of words. In the first layer the classifier transforms those words into real-valued vectors that are averaged to produce a hidden-variable vector representation of the text. This representation is fed to a softmax output layer. The model is then trained with stochastic gradient descent. Joulin et al. (2016) show that fastText outperforms competing methods by one order of magnitude in training time, having superior accuracy in a tag prediction task over 300,000+ tags.

Deep averaging networks Iyyer et al. (2015) propose what can be considered as a generalization of the above method; after the first hidden averaging layer, the average is passed trough one or more feed forward layers. The final output layer is also a softmax layer. As in the case of fastText, the authors show a significant performance gain in training time while having a high accuracy in a sentiment analysis task. The resulting family of models is called Deep Averaging Networks (DAN) (Iyyer et al., 2015).

Word embeddings Word embeddings are vector representations for words learned from the contexts in which words appear in large corpora of text (and idea that can be traced back to the distributional semantics hypothesis in linguistics (Harris, 1954)). There are several methods to learn word representations from unlabelled data (Mikolov et al., 2013; Pennington et al., 2014; Bojanowski et al., 2016), and usually, training over more data produces vectors with better semantic characteristics. Word embeddings can be used to check the similarity of two texts by simply averaging the vector representation of the words of each text and then computing a vector similarity measure (such as the cosine similarity).

It has been shown that pre-trained vectors can help when using neural networks for text classification (Kim, 2014). In our experiments we also consider versions of fastText and DAN with pre-trained word-embedding vectors in the first layer.

5.3 Implementation details

The standard classifiers are implemented with Scikit-learn (Pedregosa et al., 2011). For tokenization, lemmatization and Part of Speech tagging, we use FreeLing (Carreras et al., 2004), which supports the Spanish language. For fastText we use the C++ implementation provided by Grave et al. (2016). We implemented DANs using the Keras framework (Chollet et al., 2015). We use pre-trained word embeddings computed from the Spanish Wikipedia by using the method proposed by Bojanowsky et al. (2016).

6 Experiments and results

In the following sections we describe the experiment settings and results for the tasks defined in Section 4.

For Task A and Task B, we compare our methods using accuracy and top-5 accuracy (percentage of cases in which the correct class belongs to the top-5 predictions). Accuracy is useful in our case, given that there are several classes (12 to 44) and the biggest is around 10% of the total instances. The use of top-5 accuracy allows us to evaluate our models in the scenario of helping humans to quickly determine the class an argument is referring to. For Task C we use macro-averaged precision, recall and F1-score as metrics due to the class imbalance.

6.1 Task A

For Task A we consider pairs (c, a) with $c \in C_G$ and such that a was not marked as *blank* in the manual classification process (Section 3.2). This gives us a total of 169,242 pairs. We divide this set into four sets, one for each topic $(\mathbf{V}, \mathbf{R}, \mathbf{D}, \mathbf{I})$, that we use as data for the four instantiations of Task A. In every case we randomly divide the data into 80% train, 10% dev and 10% test sets with a stratified sampling. For the standard models, we use 90% for training (train plus dev), as we do not use the dev set to tune model parameters.

Table 5 reports our results for Task A for each topic. The first row shows a majority baseline as comparison and the last column reports the average over the four topics as an overview of the performance. For the standard classifiers we report only the best-performing configuration for each strategy. All reported results are over the test set.

In almost all topics, fastText with pre-trained word embeddings is the best performing model for (top-1) accuracy, with Logistic Regression being behind by a little margin. For the case of fastText, the use of pre-trained vectors and bigrams gives an average of 2% in gain over plain fastText. For top-5 accuracy, fastText is again the best performing model, however, in contrast to the previous case, the use of bigrams can harm the performance. The best methods achieve over 90% top-5 accuracy for all topics.

In the case of standard models, both Logistic Regression and SVM have competitive performance compared to more complex models. We found that the use of bigrams actually hurts the performance of the linear models, although using them in conjunction with unigrams improve the accuracy in some cases. We believe that this is due to the typical sparsity that the use of bigrams introduce in the models. Using only unigrams and tf-idf gives the best performance at top-5 accuracy in the Logistic Regression.

6.2 Task B

For Task B we consider as test set the 10,263 pairs (c, a) with open concepts that were manually classified as one of the 114 concepts in C_G (as described in Section 3.1). We perform experiments considering as input the string of the concept and also the concatenation of the concept and argument strings, and we feed this input to the same models computed for Task A. That is, we do not re-train our models, instead we use the same trained models for the previous task to solve this new task with a different test set. We consider two additional simple baselines that only compares the strings of the concepts:

- **Edit-distance**: given $(c^\star, a^\star) \in D_O^T$ we compute the edit distance between $c^\star$ and all the elements $c \in C_G^T$, and rank the results.
- **Word-embedding**: given an input $(c^\star, a^\star) \in D_O^T$ we compute the cosine distance between the average word-embedding of (the words in) $c^\star$ and the average word-embeddings of every $c \in C_G^T$, and rank the results.

	Values (37 classes)		Rights (44 classes)		Duties (12 classes)		Institutions (21 classes)		Average	
	Acc	Top-5	Acc	Top-5	Acc	Top-5	Acc	Top-5	Acc	Top-5
Majority	8.5	39.5	12.2	40.7	14.1	60.1	12.6	43.8	11.8	46.0
RF+unigram+raw (tf)	56.1	79.5	62.3	83.0	68.1	90.5	61.7	84.4	62.0	84.3
LR+unigram+raw (tf-idf)	66.3	**91.0**	70.3	91.7	75.5	96.2	69.6	91.6	70.4	92.6
LR+ngram+raw (count)	67.5	90.8	70.7	91.6	76.6	96.1	**70.2**	91.5	71.3	92.5
SVM+ngram+POS (tf-idf)	67.9	-	70.7	-	76.2	-	69.8	-	71.2	-
fastText	65.9	89.4	68.6	90.6	75.1	95.8	68.4	91.1	69.5	91.7
fastText+bigram	64.9	88.2	67.1	89.1	75.9	95.4	68.5	91.0	69.1	90.9
fastText+pre	67.1	90.7	70.8	**92.3**	75.7	**96.4**	69.3	92.5	70.7	**93.0**
fastText+pre+bigram	**68.0**	90.2	**71.1**	91.8	**76.9**	95.8	69.4	**92.7**	**71.4**	92.6
DAN+pre	64.5	89.4	68.2	91.7	73.6	96.2	66.4	91.8	68.2	92.3

Table 5: (Task A) Classification results. Top-1 and top-5 accuracy is reported for each baseline and topic.

	Values (37 classes)		Rights (44 classes)		Duties (12 classes)		Institutions (21 classes)		Average	
	Acc	Top-5	Acc	Top-5	Acc	Top-5	Acc	Top-5	Acc	Top-5
Majority	03.0	22.2	02.8	20.2	10.1	48.6	07.1	25.4	05.8	29.1
Edit-distance (c)	41.2	60.6	30.9	46.7	41.6	64.9	22.7	38.6	34.1	52.7
Word-embeddings (c)	60.2	86.3	58.8	79.1	60.4	80.8	45.5	86.1	56.2	83.1
RF+unigram+POS (tf) (c, a)	50.5	76.8	63.1	84.1	69.9	94.7	46.7	68.1	57.5	80.9
LR+ngram+POS (count) (c, a)	60.4	89.9	71.9	**92.7**	77.6	95.0	56.1	84.8	66.5	**90.6**
SVM+ngram+POS (tf-idf) (c, a)	61.4	-	71.9	-	78.4	-	55.3	-	66.7	-
fastText+pre (c)	61.4	89.0	**73.3**	91.8	79.0	95.3	55.3	86.4	67.2	**90.6**
fastText+pre (c, a)	60.7	89.9	70.6	92.3	75.5	95.5	52.7	83.2	64.9	90.2
fastText+pre+bigram (c)	**62.9**	87.4	72.4	91.0	**79.2**	94.7	**60.2**	**86.7**	**68.7**	90.0
fastText+pre+bigram (c, a)	60.9	89.9	71.1	92.1	76.3	95.4	53.8	81.2	65.5	89.6
DAN+pre (c)	61.6	87.2	70.4	92.6	77.9	**96.3**	55.6	82.3	66.4	89.6
DAN+pre (c, a)	60.4	**91.1**	69.6	92.4	75.0	95.2	51.4	80.8	64.1	89.9

Table 6: (Task B) Classification results. Top-1 and top-5 accuracy are reported for each baseline and topic. After each baseline, (c) indicates that only the concept is used as a test instance, and (c, a) indicates that both the concept and the argument are used.

We report accuracy and top-5 accuracy per topic in Table 6. Regarding (top-1) accuracy, fastText and DAN perform best when only the string of the concept is given as input, a trend that changes for top-5 accuracy in which having the concept plus the argument actually helps to make better predictions (except for topic **I**). In our experiments we observed that the gap in top-k accuracy between using and non-using the argument consistently increases as k increases. On the other hand, we found that the use of the concept plus the argument improves the performance of the linear models. As a final comment, the estimated human accuracy for this task was 87% (Cortés, 2017), and our best method achieves 68.7% in average. This gives an important space for improvement.

	Prec.	Recall	F1
Majority	24.4	33.3	28.2
RF+unigram+POS (tf)	64.1	50.0	53.0
LR+ngram+POS (count)	65.1	54.7	57.9
SVM+ngram+POS (tf-idf)	66.5	55.1	58.3
fastText+pre	69.6	59.7	63.3
fastText+bigram	68.9	62.0	64.8
fastText+pre+bigram	**69.9**	**62.4**	**65.4**
DAN+pre	67.1	59.0	62.1

Table 7: (Task C) Classification results. Values correspond to macro-averaged metrics.

6.3 Task C

For this task we consider the set of all arguments that have been tagged as either policy, fact, or value by the process described in Section 3.2. That is, we do not consider blank or undefined arguments. Thus the dataset is composed of 184,798 arguments from which 73.3% are policies, 20.2% facts and 6.5% values. We split our set into 80% train, 10% dev and 10% test sets. Since our dataset contains clearly unbalanced classes we consider macro-averaged precision, recall and F1-score as our performance metric. Results on the test set are reported in Table 7. FastText with pre-trained vectors and bigrams is the best performing model with 65.4% F1. This model achieves a performance of 81.1% accuracy which is close to the estimated human accuracy of the process (85%).

7 Conclusions

In this paper we have presented the corpus of political arguments produced in the 2016 Chilean Constitutional Process together with several baselines for classification tasks. This corpus is one of the largest tagged datasets of arguments in the Chilean Spanish language.

Our defined tasks and baselines can be useful in applications beyond the ones we analyzed in this paper. In particular, the classification of arguments into concepts could be useful to identify political subject matters in open text in the Spanish language.

Chile is going through an important political discussion. Our natural next step is to use our tools to help in the analysis of new opinions, emphasize the transparency, and foster the repeatability of the process to draw new conclusions.

Acknowledgements

We thank the anonymous reviewers, Camilo Garrido, and Miguel Campusano for their helpful comments. We also thank Pamela Figueroa Rubio from the Ministry General Secretariat of the Presidency of Chile and Rodrigo Marquez from the United Nations Development Program for their help in the analysis process. Fierro, Pérez and Quezada are supported by the Millennium Nucleus Center for Semantic Web Research, Grant NC120004. Quezada is also supported by CONICYT under grant PCHA/Doctorado Nacional 2015/21151445.

References

Rob Abbott, Brian Ecker, Pranav Anand, and Marilyn A. Walker. 2016. Internet Argument Corpus 2.0: An SQL schema for Dialogic Social Media and the Corpora to go with it. In *LREC*.

Benito Baranda, Jean Beausejour, Roberto Fantuzzi, Arturo Fermandois, Francisco Fernandez, Patricio Fernandez, Gaston Gomez, Hernan Larrain, Hector Mery, Salvador Millaleo, Ruth Olate, Juanita Parra, Lucas Sierra, Francisco Soto, and Patricio Zapata. 2017. Final Report on the Participative Phase of the Chilean Constituent Process (in Spanish). Ministry General Secretariat of the Presidency of Chile https://unaconstitucionparachile.cl/ Informe-Final-CCO-16-de-enero-de-2017.pdf.

Piotr Bojanowski, Edouard Grave, Armand Joulin, and Tomas Mikolov. 2016. Enriching word vectors with subword information. *arXiv preprint arXiv:1607.04606* .

Robert James Branham. 1991. *Debate and critical analysis: The harmony of conflict*. Routledge.

Leo Breiman. 2001. Random forests. *Machine learning* 45(1):5–32.

Xavier Carreras, Isaac Chao, Llus Padr, and Muntsa Padr. 2004. Freeling: An open-source suite of language analyzers. In *Proceedings of the 4th International Conference on Language Resources and Evaluation (LREC'04)*.

François Chollet et al. 2015. Keras. https://github.com/fchollet/keras.

Constitutional Systematization Committee. 2017. Self-convened Local Meetings: Quantitative Results (in Spanish). Ministry General Secretariat of the Presidency of Chile http://www.sistematizacionconstitucional.cl/app/ themes/cs/dist/docs/ela_frecuencias.pdf.

Corinna Cortes and Vladimir Vapnik. 1995. Support-vector networks. *Machine Learning* 20(3):273–297.

Flavio Cortés. 2017. *Personal Communication*.

General Secretariat, Presidency of Chile. 2016. *Proceso Constituyente Abierto a la Ciudadanía* [Dataset]. http://datos.gob.cl/dataset/ proceso-constituyente-abierto-a-la-ciudadania.

General Secretariat, Presidency of Chile. 2017. Quantitative Summary of the 2016 Chilean Constituent Process, Participative Phase (in Spanish). Ministry General Secretariat of the Presidency of Chile https://unaconstitucionparachile.cl/sintesis_ de_resultados_etapa_participativa.pdf.

Samuel González-López and Aurelio López-López. 2015. Colección de tesis y propuesta de investigación en TICs: un recurso para su análisis y estudio. In *XIII Congreso Nacional de Investigación Educativa*. page 15.

Jesús Miguel García Gorrostieta and Aurelio López-López. 2016. *Argumentation Identification for Academic Support in Undergraduate Writings*, Springer International Publishing, Cham, pages 98–109.

Edouard Grave, Piotr Bojanowski, Armand Joulin, et al. 2016. fastText. https://github.com/facebookresearch/fastText.

Zellig Harris. 1954. Distributional structure. *Word* 23:146–162.

David Hitchcock. 2007. Informal logic and the concept of argument. In *Philosophy of Logic*. volume 5, Handbook of the Philosophy of Science, pages 101–129.

Mohit Iyyer, Varun Manjunatha, Jordan L. Boyd-Graber, and Hal Daumé III. 2015. Deep unordered composition rivals syntactic methods for text classification. In *Proceedings of the 53rd Annual Meeting of the Association for Computational Linguistics and the 7th International Joint Conference on Natural Language Processing of the Asian Federation of Natural Language Processing, ACL 2015, July 26-31, 2015, Beijing, China, Volume 1: Long Papers*. pages 1681–1691.

Tomás Jordán, Pamela Figueroa, Rodrigo Araya, and Carolina Gómez. 2016. Constituent Process open to Citizenship (in Spanish). Ministry General Secretariat of the Presidency of Chile https://unaconstitucionparachile.cl/guia_metodologica_proceso_constituyente_abierto_a_la_ciudadania.pdf.

Armand Joulin, Edouard Grave, Piotr Bojanowski, and Tomas Mikolov. 2016. Bag of tricks for efficient text classification. *arXiv preprint arXiv:1607.01759* .

Yoon Kim. 2014. Convolutional neural networks for sentence classification. In *Proceedings of the 2014 Conference on Empirical Methods in Natural Language Processing, EMNLP 2014, October 25-29, 2014, Doha, Qatar, A meeting of SIGDAT, a Special Interest Group of the ACL*. pages 1746–1751.

Matthias Liebeck, Katharina Esau, and Stefan Conrad. 2016. What to Do with an Airport? Mining Arguments in the German Online Participation Project Tempelhofer Feld. In *Proceedings of the Third Workshop on Argument Mining, hosted by the 54th Annual Meeting of the Association for Computational Linguistics, ArgMining@ACL 2016, August 12, Berlin, Germany*.

Tomas Mikolov, Ilya Sutskever, Kai Chen, Gregory S. Corrado, and Jeffrey Dean. 2013. Distributed representations of words and phrases and their compositionality. In *Advances in Neural Information Processing Systems 26: 27th Annual Conference on Neural Information Processing Systems 2013. Proceedings of a meeting held December 5-8, 2013, Lake Tahoe, Nevada, United States.*. pages 3111–3119.

Fabian Pedregosa, Gael Varoquaux, Alexandre Gramfort, Vicent Michel, Bertrand Thirion, Olivier Grisel, Mathieu Blondel, Peter Prettenhofer, Ron Weiss, Vincent Dubourg, Jake Vanderplas, Alexandre Passos, David Cournapeau, Matthieu Brucher, Matthieu Perrot, and Èdouard Duchesnay. 2011. Scikit-learn: Machine learning in Python. *Journal of Machine Learning Research* 12:2825–2830.

Jeffrey Pennington, Richard Socher, and Christopher D. Manning. 2014. GloVe: Global vectors for word representation. In *Proceedings of the 2014 Conference on Empirical Methods in Natural Language Processing, EMNLP 2014, October 25-29, 2014, Doha, Qatar, A meeting of SIGDAT, a Special Interest Group of the ACL*. pages 1532–1543.

Political Constitution of the Republic of Chile. 1980. *Decreto 1150: Texto de la Constitución Política de la República de Chile* (in Spanish). National Library of Chile.

John R. Searle. 2014. *Creando el mundo social: la estructura de la civilización humana*. Grupo Planeta Spain.

Alfred Snider and Maxwell Schnurer. 2002. *Many sides: Debate across the curriculum*. International Debate Education Association: New York.

Swapna Somasundaran and Janyce Wiebe. 2010. Recognizing Stances in Ideological On-line Debates. In *Proceedings of the NAACL HLT 2010 Workshop on Computational Approaches to Analysis and Generation of Emotion in Text*. Association for Computational Linguistics, Stroudsburg, PA, USA, CAAGET '10, pages 116–124. http://dl.acm.org/citation.cfm?id=1860631.1860645.

Raimo Tuomela. 2013. *Social ontology: Collective intentionality and group agents*. Oxford University Press.

Marilyn A. Walker, Pranav Anand, Jean E. Fox Tree, Rob Abbot, and Joseph King. 2012. A Corpus for Research on Deliberation and Debate. In *LREC*. pages 812–817.

Analyzing the Semantic Types of Claims and Premises in an Online Persuasive Forum

Christopher Hidey
Computer Science Department
Columbia University
chidey@cs.columbia.edu

Elena Musi
Data Science Institute
Columbia University
em3202@columbia.edu

Alyssa Hwang
Computer Science Department
Columbia University
a.hwang@columbia.edu

Smaranda Muresan
Data Science Institute
Columbia University
smara@columbia.edu

Kathleen McKeown
Computer Science Department
Columbia University
kathy@cs.columbia.edu

Abstract

Argumentative text has been analyzed both theoretically and computationally in terms of argumentative structure that consists of argument components (e.g., claims, premises) and their argumentative relations (e.g., support, attack). Less emphasis has been placed on analyzing the semantic types of argument components. We propose a two-tiered annotation scheme to label claims and premises and their semantic types in an online persuasive forum, *Change My View*, with the long-term goal of understanding what makes a message persuasive. Premises are annotated with the three types of persuasive modes: *ethos*, *logos*, *pathos*, while claims are labeled as *interpretation*, *evaluation*, *agreement*, or *disagreement*, the latter two designed to account for the dialogical nature of our corpus.

We aim to answer three questions: 1) can humans reliably annotate the semantic types of argument components? 2) are types of premises/claims positioned in recurrent orders? and 3) are certain types of claims and/or premises more likely to appear in persuasive messages than in non-persuasive messages?

1 Introduction

Argumentation is a type of discourse where speakers try to persuade their audience about the reasonableness of a claim by displaying supportive arguments. As underlined in Rhetorics and Argumentation Theory (Perelman and Olbrechts-Tyteca, 1973; van Eemeren and Eemeren, 2009), the persuasiveness of a message lies at the interface between discourse form (i.e., use of hedges, connectives, rhetorical questions) and conceptual form such as the artful use of ethos (credibility and trustworthiness of the speaker), pathos (appeal to audience feelings), and logos (appeal to the rationality of the audience through logical reasoning). Recent work in argumentation mining and detection of persuasion has so far mainly explored the persuasive role played by features related to discourse form (Stab and Gurevych, 2014a; Peldszus and Stede, 2016; Habernal and Gurevych, 2016; Tan et al., 2016; Ghosh et al., 2016). However, due to the lack of suitable training data, the detection of conceptual features is still nascent.

On these grounds, we propose and validate a systematic procedure to identify conceptual aspects of persuasion, presenting a two-stage annotation process on a sample of 78 threads from the sub-reddit *Change My View* (Section 3). *Change My View* constitutes a suitable environment for the study of persuasive argumentation: users award a *Delta point* to the users that managed to changed their views, thus providing a naturally labeled dataset for persuasive arguments. In the first stage, expert annotators are asked to identify claims and premises among the propositions forming the post. In the second stage, using crowdsourcing (Amazon Mechanical Turk) claims and premises are annotated with their semantic types. For premises, the semantic types are based on the Aristotelian modes of persuasion *logos*, *pathos* and *ethos*, or a combination of them. For claims, we have considered two proposition types among those in Freeman's taxonomy (Freeman, 2000) that can work as claims since their truth is assailable, namely *interpretations* and *evaluations (rational/emotional)*.

11

Proceedings of the 4th Workshop on Argument Mining, pages 11–21
Copenhagen, Denmark, September 8, 2017. ©2017 Association for Computational Linguistics

A | CMV: Patriotism is the belief that being born on one side of a line makes you better

...

↑

[I would define patriotism quite simply as supporting one's country, but not *necessarily* disparaging others] CLAIM_DISAGREEMENT

B | ...

[Someone who assists another country that is in worse shape instead of assisting their own can still be a patriot, but also recognize significant need in other nations and decide to assist them as well] PREMISE_LOGOS/PATHOS

↑

A | [This is true]CLAIM_AGREEMENT, but, [I think, supporting the common good is also more important than supporting your country]CLAIM_RATIONAL EVALUATION

↑

B | [Yes]CLAIM_AGREEMENT, but [the two are often one the same]CLAIM_INTERPRETATION, [especially when you live in a country as large as the U.S. most acts which serve the common good generally support your country]PREMISE_LOGOS.

Figure 1: Annotation Example

We have furthermore distinguished propositions expressing *agreement* and *disagreement* because they present an anaphoric function inherent to the dialogic nature of the corpus. An example is given in Figure 1.[1]

We aim to answer three questions: 1) can humans reliably annotate claim and premises and their semantic types? (Section 4) 2) are types of premises/claims positioned in recurrent orders? and 3) are certain types of claims and/or premises more likely to appear in persuasive messages than in non-persuasive messages? (Section 5.2). Our findings show that claims, premises and premise types can be annotated with moderate agreement (Kripendorff's $\alpha > 0.63$), while claim types are more difficult for annotators to reliably label ($\alpha = 0.46$) (Section 4). To answer the second question, we perform an analysis of the correlations between types of argumentative components (premises and claims), as well as their position in the post and discuss our findings in Section 5.1. Our results for the third question show that there are several significant differences between persuasive and non-persuasive comments as to the types of claims and premises (Section 5.2). We present our future work in Section 6. The annotated dataset is available on GitHub to the research community[2].

2 Related Work

There are three areas relevant to the work presented in this paper, which we address in turn.

Persuasion detection and prediction. Recent studies in argument mining and computational social science have focused on persuasion detection and prediction. A bulk of them have focused on the identification of structural and lexical features that happen to be associated with persuasive arguments. Ghosh et al. (2016) have shown that the number of supported/unsupported claims and the structure of arguments directly affect persuasion. Habernal and Gurevych (2016) have experimented with SVM and bidirectional LSTM to predict arguments scored by annotators as convincing mainly using lexical linguistic features (e.g., modal verbs, verb tenses, sentiment scores). Taking advantage of the *Change My View* dataset, (Tan et al., 2016), have investigated whether lexical features and interaction patterns affect persuasion, finding that lexical diversity plays a major role. In a similar vein, other studies have ranked arguments according to their karma scores (Wei et al., 2016), showing that aspects of argumentative language and social interaction are persuasive features. In this paper, we focus on the conceptual aspects of a persuasive message by analyzing the semantic types of claims and premises. A closely related area of research is the detection of situational influencers — participants in a discussion

---

[1]Note that premises are labeled at proposition level and not clause level.

[2]https://github.com/chridey/change-my-view-modes

who have credibility in the group, persist in attempting to convince others, and introduce ideas that others pick up on or support (Rosenthal and Mckeown, 2017; Biran et al., 2012). In particular, Rosenthal and Mckeown (2017) draw their approach from Cialdini's (Cialdini, 2005) idea of "weapons of influence," which include reciprocation (sentiment and agreement components), commitment (claims and agreement), social proof (dialog patterns), liking (sentiment and credibility), authority (credibility), and scarcity (author traits). Our approach zooms into the detection of commitment analyzing not only the presence of claims/arguments, but also their conceptual type. We, moreover, treat credibility as an argument type.

Modes of persuasion: logos, pathos, ethos. At the conceptual level, the distinction between different modes of persuasion dates back to Aristotle's Rhetorics. Aristotle considered that a good argument consists of the contextually appropriate combination of *pathos*, *ethos*, and *logos*. Duthie et al. (2016) have developed a methodology to retrieve *ethos* in political debates. Higgins and Walker (2012) traced back *ethos*, *pathos* and *logos* as strategies of persuasion in social and environmental reports. Their definition of *logos* applies both to premises and claims, while we consider *logos* as referred to arguments only. Habernal and Gurevych (2017) have also included *logos* and *pathos*, but not *ethos*, among the labels for an argumentatively annotated corpus of 990 user generated comments. They obtained moderate agreement for the annotation of *logos*, while low agreement for *pathos*. Our study shows moderate agreement on all types of persuasion modes. On the computational side, the Internet Argument Corpus (IAC) (Walker et al., 2012) — data from the online discussion sites *4forums.com* and *CreateDebate* — includes the distinction between fact and emotion based arguments. Das et al. (2016) looked at the diffusion of information through social media and how author intent affects message propagation. They found that persuasive messages were more likely to be received positively if the emotional or logical components of a message were selected according to the given topic. Lukin et al. (2017) examined how personality traits and emotional or logical arguments affect persuasiveness.

Semantics of argument components. Recently, new interest has arisen in analyzing the semantics of argument components. Becker et al. (2016) have investigated correlations between situation entity types and claims/premises.Park et al. (2015) have proposed a classification of claims in relation to the subjectivity/objectivity of the premises in their support. On a different note, a scalable and empirically validated annotation scheme has been proposed for the analysis of illocutionary structures in argumentative dialogues drawing from *Inference Anchoring Theory* (Budzynska et al., 2014; Budzynska and Reed, 2011), relying on different types of *pragmatic* information. However, distinct taxonomies to account for semantic differences characterizing claims vs. premises and their degrees of persuasiveness has so far not been investigated.

Our study contributes to previous work in proposing a novel and reliable annotation scheme, which combines semantic types for both claims and premises at the propositional level, allowing to observe relevant combinations in persuasive messages.

3 Annotation Process

3.1 Source data

Change My View is a discussion forum on the site reddit.com. The initiator of the discussion will create a title for their post (which contains the major claim of the argument) and then describe the reasons for their belief. Other posters will respond and attempt to change the original poster's view. If they are successful, the original poster will indicate that their view was changed by providing a Δ point. We use the same dataset from the Change My View forum created in previous work (Tan et al., 2016). We extract dialogs from the full dataset where only the original poster and one responder interacted. If the dialogue ends with the original poster providing a Δ, the thread is labeled as positive; if it ends prematurely without a Δ, it is labeled negative. We select 39 positive and 39 negative threads to be annotated.

3.2 Annotation of argumentative components

In the first stage of the annotation process, the goal is to label claims and premises at the proposition level. We recruited 8 students with a background either in Linguistics or in Natural Language Processing to be annotators. Students were asked to read the guidelines and were given an example with gold labels (see Figure 1). During a one-hour long training session they were asked to annotate a pilot example and comparison between their preliminary annotations and the gold labels was discussed. Each student annotated from a minimum of 5 to a maximum of 22 threads depending on their availability.

The guidelines provide an intuitive definition of claims/premises paired with examples. While the definitions are similar to those provided in previous annotation projects (Stab and Gurevych, 2014b), we took as annotation unit the proposition instead of the clause, given that premises are frequently propositions that conflate multiple clauses (see Figure 1).

- **claim**: proposition that expresses the speaker's stance on a certain matter. They can express predictions ('I think that the left wing will win the election"), interpretations ("John probably went home"), evaluations ("Your choice is a bad one") as well as agreement/disagreement with other peoples claims ("I agree"/"I think you are totally wrong"). Complex sentences where speakers at first agree and then disagree with other speakers' opinion (*concessions*) constitute separate claims ("I agree with you that the environmental consequences are bad, but I still think that freedom is more important.").

- **premise**: proposition that expresses a justification provided by the speaker in support of a claim to persuade the audience of the validity of the claim. Like claims, they can express opinions but their function is not that of introducing a new stance, but that of supporting one expressed by another proposition ("John probably went home. I don't see his coat anywhere"; "Look at the polls; I think that the right wing will win the election").

Both claims and premises can be expressed by rhetorical questions, questions that are not meant to require an answer — which is obvious — but to implicitly convey an assertive speech act. Their argumentative role, thus, has to to be decided in context: in the sentence "We should fight for our privacy on the Web. Dont you love that Google knows your favorite brand of shoes?", the rhetorical question functions as an argument in support of the recommendation to fight for privacy.

Completely untagged sections mostly contain greetings, farewells, or otherwise irrelevant text. Thus, occasionally entire paragraphs are left unmarked. Furthermore, we left the title unannotated, assuming that it works as the original poster's major claim, while we are interested in the comments that could persuade the original poster to change his view. When the original poster's text starts with an argument, it is by default to be considered in support of the title.

3.3 Annotation of types of premises and claims

The second stage aims to label the semantic type of claims and premises using crowdsourcing. We used *Amazon Mechanical Turk* (AMT) as our crowdsourcing platform. Using the previous annotations of claim/premises, Turkers were asked to identify the semantic type of premises and claims. The novelty of this study relies in the proposal of a fine-grained, non context-dependent annotation of semantic types of premises and of claims. On the other hand, existing semantic classifications focus either on premises or on claims (section 2). Current Studies have by far tackled types of premises and claims combinations specific to a restricted set of argument schemes (Atkinson and Bench-Capon, 2016; Lawrence and Reed, 2016) mainly for classification purposes.

For each claim, we showed the workers the entire sentence containing the claim. For each premise, we showed the Turkers the entire sentence containing the premise and the sentence containing the claim. Each HIT consisted of 1 premise or 1 claim classification task and the Turkers were paid 5 cents for each HIT.

For claims, the Turkers were asked to choose among four different choices. The distinction between interpretations and evaluations recalls Freeman's (Freeman, 2000) classification of contingent statements. We have decided to treat agreements/disagreements as distinct types of claims since, depending on the semantics of the embedded proposition, they can express sharedness (or not) of interpretations as well as evaluations. The provided definitions are:

- **interpretation**: expresses predictions or explanations of states of affairs ("I think he will win the election." or "He probably went home.")

- **evaluation**: the claim expresses a more or

less positive or negative judgement. Drawing from the distinction made in sentiment analysis and opinion mining, (Liu, 2012) evaluations are sub-classified as:

- **evaluation-rational**: expresses an opinion based on rational reasoning, non-subjective evidence or credible sources ("His political program is very solid." or "He is a very smart student.")
- **evaluation-emotional**: expresses an opinion based on emotional reasons and/or subjective beliefs ("Going to the gym is an unpleasant activity." or "I do not like doing yoga.")

- **agreement** or **disagreement**: expresses that the speaker shares/does not share to a certain degree the beliefs held by another speaker, i.e. "I agree that going to the gym is boring" or "you are right" or "I do not think that he went home." or "You are not logically wrong." or "I do not like your ideas." or "It may be true."

For premises, the Turkers were provided with the following labels:

- **logos**: appeals to the use of reason, such as providing relevant examples and other kinds of factual evidence ("Eating healthy makes you live longer. The oldest man in the US followed a strictly fat-free diet." or "He will probably win the election. He is the favorite according to the polls.")

- **pathos**: aims at putting the audience in a certain frame of mind, appealing to emotions, or more generally touching upon topics in which the audience can somehow identify ("Doctors should stop prescribing antibiotics at a large scale. The spread of antibiotics will be a threat for the next generation." or "You should put comfy furniture into your place. The feeling of being home is unforgettable").

- **ethos**: appeals to the credibility established by personal experience/expertise ("I assure you the consequences of fracking are terrible. I have been living next to a pipeline since I was a child." or "I assure you the consequences of fracking are terrible. I am a chemical engineer.") as well as title/reputation ("I trust his predictions about climate change. He is a Nobel Prize winner." or "I trust his predictions about climate change. They say he is a very sincere person.")

In operational terms, the workers were asked to select *true* for the persuasion mode used and *false* for the ones that were not applicable. They were given the choice to select from 1 to 3 modes for the same premise. If the workers did not select any modes, their HIT was rejected.

4 Annotation Results

The 78 discussion threads comprise 278 turns of dialogue consisting of 2615 propositions in 2148 total sentences. Of these sentences, 786 contain a claim and 1068 contain a premise. Overall at the sentence-level, 36.5% of sentences contain a claim and 49.7% contain a premise. 22% of sentences contain no annotations at all. In terms of claims,[3] 15.8% of sentences contain a rational evaluation, 8.7% contain an interpretation, and 7.3% contain an emotional evaluation, while only 2.5% contain agreement and 2.3% contain disagreement. For premises, 44% contain logos, 29% contain pathos, and only 3% contain ethos.

We computed Inter-Annotator Agreement for claims and premises by requiring 3 of the annotators to annotate an overlapping subset of 2 threads. We compare annotations at the sentence level, similar to previous work (Stab and Gurevych, 2014a), as most sentences contain only 1 proposition, making this approximation reasonable. We compute IAA using Kripendorff's alpha (Krippendorff, 1970), obtaining 0.63 and 0.65, respectively. These scores are considered moderate agreement and are similar to the results on persuasive essays (Stab and Gurevych, 2014a).

We also compute IAA for types of premises, comparing the majority vote of the Turkers to gold labels from our most expert annotator (based on highest average pair-wise IAA). As Kripendorff's alpha is calculated globally and compares each item directly between annotators, it is well-suited for handling the multi-label case here (Ravenscroft et al., 2016). The resulting IAA was 0.73.

Finally, we compute IAA for the types of claims, again comparing the majority vote to gold labels annotated by an expert linguist. The resulting IAA is 0.46, considered low agreement. This

---

[3]We took the majority vote among Turkers to determine the types of claims and premises.

result is in line with those attested in similar experiments (Walker et al., 2012).

In our case, we hypothesize that the nature of the claims provided as unit of annotations may have led to confusion. According to the expert linguist annotator, some of the claims are complex sentences being formed by two propositions liable to two different types of claims. In a sentence such as "Your first paragraph is intriguing, and I definitely agree with it," for instance, the first proposition constitutes an emotional-evaluation, while the second an agreement. The choice of one of the two labels may, thus, give rise to divergent annotations.

4.1 Qualitative analysis: the disagreement space

To investigate the disagreement space in the annotation of types of claims, we present a confusion matrix in Table 1 between the majority vote and the label chosen by each of the 5 Turkers. The major disagreement is between the claim types "interpretation" (C_I) and "evaluation-rational" (C_{ER}), followed by the pairs "evaluation-emotional" (C_{EE})/ "evaluation-rational"(C_{ER}). While the label "disagreement" (C_D) also seems to be controversial, the scarcity of occurrences makes it less relevant for the analysis of the disagreement space. The higher consensus in the labeling of "agreement"(C_A) versus other types of evaluations can be explained looking at linguistic triggers: while "agreement" is signaled by unambiguous linguistic clues (*I agree, you are right, yes*), the degree of rationality/emotions conveyed by a judgment is not always transparent given the semantics of the sentiment expressed, but may call for wider contextual features. Given a sentence such as "I don't think I'm better than the people I'd be denying citizenship" it is clear that what the speaker is expressing is a subjective evaluation, while in the sentence "This is the best argument I have seen" the type of evaluation at stake depends on the criteria at the basis of the judgment.

In order to verify and explain difficulties encountered in deciding whether the claim is C_{ER} or C_I we compared the Turkers annotation with the gold annotations of an expert linguist annotator. The trends in the disagreement space are the same as those noticed among Turkers. The qualitative analysis shows that Turkers tend to misclassify interpretation (C_I) as evaluation-rational (C_{ER}). This is mainly due to a tendency of an-

L \ M	C_A	C_D	C_{EE}	C_{ER}	C_I
C_A	186	8	17	35	19
C_D	6	133	18	53	35
C_{EE}	21	35	424	187	112
C_{ER}	45	56	157	1150	220
C_I	23	45	105	205	459

Table 1: Confusion Matrix for Claims
L: individual labels **M**: majority vote

notating claims as evaluations in the presence of a sentiment word regardless of the overall meaning of the proposition: the sentence "The problem isnt always bad parenting, though that can play a role, the problem is a black and white educational system" was annotated as an evaluation probably due to the axiological adjective *bad*. However, the primary meaning is not that of providing a negative judgment, but that of providing an explanation for a state of affairs (problems encountered at school).

5 Quantitative Analysis

In order to investigate what conceptual features are persuasive, we first observe correlations between types of argumentative components (premises and claims) as well as their position in the post. We then look at how different patterns are distributed in positive and/or negative threads.

5.1 Argumentative Components

We present an analysis of correlations between types of claims and premises, with the aim to check the presence of an ordering effect (research question 2). As we do not have supporting and attacking relations at this stage of the annotation process, we consider two approaches, both at the sentence-level, for analyzing dependencies.

We first report the results of the sequential transitions at the proposition level between types of claims (agreement, disagreement, rational evaluation, emotional evaluation, and interpretation) and premises (pathos, ethos, and logos, and their respective combinations). If the previous proposition is not labeled as claim or premise, we set the previous category to "None." If the sentence is the start of a post, we set the previous category to "BOP" (beginning of post). We also include transitions to the end of the post (EOP). We present results for the annotations from the AMT workers in Figure 2. The heatmap represents the transition matrix, normalized by the row count. The rows represent the label for the previous proposition and the columns represent the label for the current proposition.

For the second approach, we report the counts for the type of premise given the most recent claim type in the post. We assume here that the premise always attaches to the preceding claim, providing an approximation for this type of structure. We chose this heuristic since we observed that users tend first to express their view and then back it up with subsequent arguments to achieve a clear argument structure as advocated by *ChangeMyView* submission rules. However, we acknowledge that premises may be positioned in front of a claim or refer anaphorically to a textually distant claim. We manually evaluated a sample of 100 premises-claims pairs: the correct pairs were identified 75% of the time. If the previous claim occurs either in the title or the previous post, we just indicate the previous claim to be "EOP." This scenario occurs when the original poster writes a premise that depends on the main claim or when a post responds directly to a claim in a preceding post. The heatmap in Figure 3 represents the claim/premise distribution for AMT annotations, with claims as rows and premises as columns, normalized by the counts of premises.

We compute significance for individual cells using the chi-squared test for cells, computing a 2x2 contingency table. All results discussed have $p < 0.001$ after the Bonferroni correction, unless otherwise specified. Considering only claims at the beginning of the post, rational evaluations (23%), agreements (5%), and interpretations (13%) are more likely to appear at the start than in general. On the other end, premises expressing *pathos* are less likely to appear at the end of the post (only 7% of the time), while less surprisingly, unannotated sentences (farewell messages, for example) are more likely to appear at the end (20% of the time). As far as sequences of modes of persuasion, arguments expressing *logos* or *pathos* are more likely to occur consecutively (for logos, 46% following logos and 48% following pathos and for pathos, 31% and 34% respectively) than in the overall distribution (37% *logos* and 24% *pathos*). Finally, *logos* is more likely to follow a rational evaluation (49% of the time) when compared to the overall distribution of *logos* and the same is true for emotional evaluations and pathos (39%).

As for premise/claim pairs, premises classified as *pathos* are in support of rational evaluations 34% of the time that pathos occurs, while *logos* supports rational evaluations 38% of the time ($p < 0.05$) and *ethos* 28% of the time. Similarly, there is a slight preference ($p < 0.05$) for pathos to support evaluation-emotional claims, with 20% of pathos arguments supporting that type, 17% of logos arguments and 17% of ethos supporting it, respectively. Finally, authors demonstrate a preference for *logos* when addressing the claims of an author in the previous post ($p < 0.01$). The qualitative analysis of those cases reveals that when supporting rational evaluations, *pathos* arguments refer to situations that everyone could experience, as underlined by the use of the pronoun *you* in its impersonal use (e.g. "If you don't break up, you are stuck with a person who doesn't value you enough to stay loyal. It's just a logical conclusion that breaking up is the right choice in most if not all situations.").

5.2 Semantic types and persuasive role

To investigate whether certain types of claims/premises correlate with persuasive/non-persuasive messages (research question 3), we conduct a preliminary analysis of the relationship between claims and premises in different contexts, in winning vs. non winning arguments. We re-compute the transition matrix and conditional claim/premise matrix by splitting the dataset according to whether the responding poster received a delta or not. We also only consider the components written by the author of the response, and discard the posts from the original poster in order to understand whether certain patterns are more likely to be persuasive.

We compute statistical significance between the positive and negative label distributions and conditional and transition matrices using Pearson's chi-squared test of independence. As the chi-squared test considers the distribution of the data and does not require equal sample sizes[4], this test is appropriate for significance. We again use the Yates correction for low frequencies. For the AMT annotations, we obtain a p-value of $p < 0.00001$ for all distributions: the unigram labels, the transition matrix, and the claim/premise matrix. For the gold annotations, the p-value of the overall label distri-

---

[4] Positive threads tend to be longer so they have more sentences and thus a higher number of claims and premises

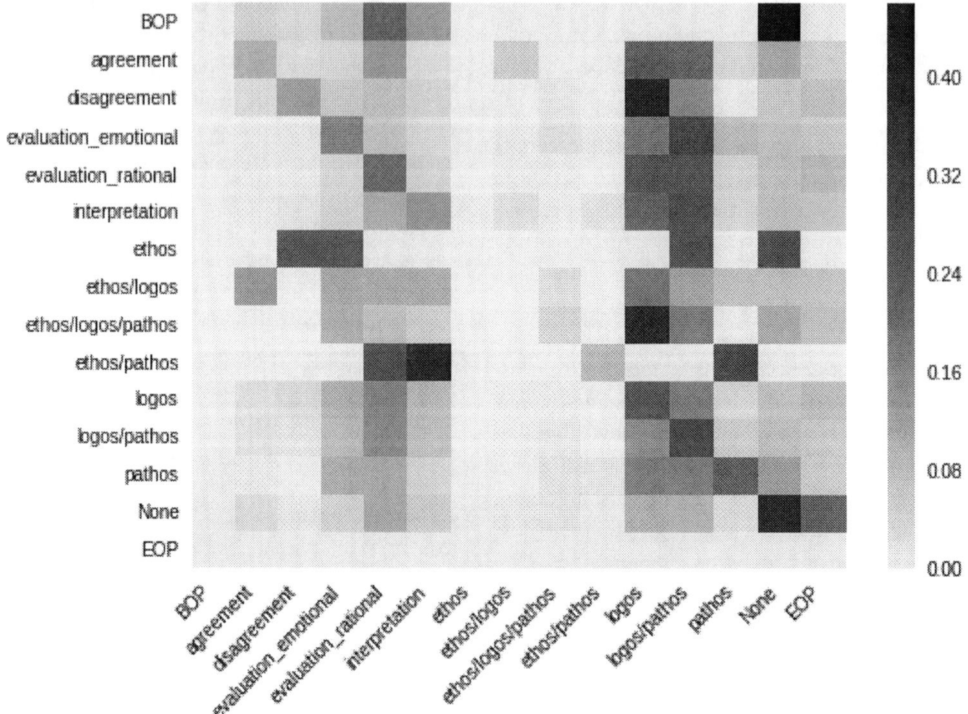

Figure 2: Transition Heatmap

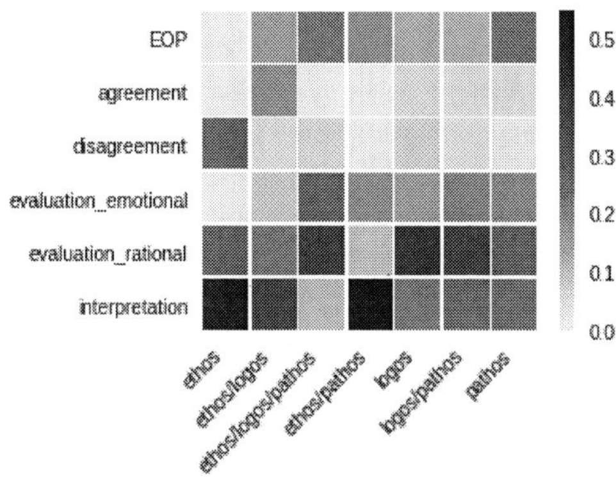

Figure 3: Claim and Premise Heatmap

bution is $p < 0.05$, but for the transition matrix the p-value is $p = 0.59$, likely due to the very low counts for some cells. However, the value for the claim/premise matrix is $p < 0.001$, indicating significant differences even for this small dataset.

Finally, similar to the analysis of the entire dataset, we compute significance for individual cells using the same chi-squared test. We first find that for the unigram distribution rational evaluations are *less* likely to be found in winning arguments with 9% of propositions in positive and 14% in negative ($p < 0.01$). When we consider the joint distribution of premise combinations, we find that *pathos* and *logos* are more likely to occur together in successful threads, with 23% and 17% respectively ($p < 0.01$).

For the transition distribution, compared to positive threads, negative threads show fewer agreements opening up the posts ($p < 0.05$). Agreeing with what was previously said by another speaker before expressing a possibly divergent opinion constitutes a traditional persuasive rhetorical strategy (Anscombre and Ducrot, 1983). In a sentence such as "I do agree that today's moderates are potentially tomorrow's conservatives. However this isn't about being just a bit conservative. It's about ...", the speaker concedes the previous user's point and then expresses a slightly contrasting point of view. In doing so, he exhibits his reasonableness and he avoids face-threatening disagreement. Moreover, positive threads are slightly more likely to show consecutive arguments of the same type (logos/logos; pathos/pathos) ($p < 0.01$), suggesting the hypothesis that conceptual coherence plays a role as persuasive strategy. The reasons provided by the original posters for awarding a Δ point frequently includes positive evaluations about the followed reasoning lines (e.g. "Well thought out response", "Thanks for the brilliant and well thought out answer").

Examining premise/claim patterns qualitatively, it seems that positive threads generally feature more interpretations, especially based on arguments of the *logos* type, at the expense of the number of evaluations. This type of claim/premise pattern is likely to be perceived as less subjective.

Evaluations, even when of the rational type, necessarily contain a subjective component in assessing the criteria to judge something as more or less positive or negative: the judgment "networking is discriminatory" during the hiring process would not, for instance, be shared by someone who considers social skills as a crucial quality for a job candidate. On the other hand, interpretations, when backed up by *logos*, encode states of affairs presented as intersubjective (Nuyts, 2012). For instance, in the premise-claim pair "American patriots have a general mentality against immigration. This is prominent in many ads and political champagnes, namely the slogan 'Creating jobs for americans' ", ads and political campaigns can be accessed by anyone. Since their goal is that of communicating a specific message to the public, the interpretation of their content promises to raise limited disagreement. This difference in degree of (inter)subjectivity is mirrored by the fact that evaluations, differently from interpretations, tend to be introduced by propositional attitude indicators at the first person singular (e.g. "I think", "I find","I point out") that put the speaker in a position of prominence as responsible for the truth of the asserted proposition. Moreover, evaluations are more frequently backed up by *pathos* arguments (e.g. the claim "Enjoying the moment is possible, but doesn't make life have a point" and the matching premise "For once I die, all memories and all point is gone" (pathos).

6   Conclusions and Future Work

In this study we propose an annotation scheme for the identification of persuasive conceptual features. Compared to previous pilot works in the same vein, we distinguish different semantic types of premises and of claims with the long term goal of investigating their persuasive role. We empirically validate the devised procedure through a two-tiered annotation project on a sample of 78 threads from the subreddit *Change My View*.

While the annotation of argumentative components (claims, premises) was carried out by expert annotators, for the annotation of semantic types of premises and claims we relied on crowdsourcing. The annotation of premises and claims achieves moderate agreement, in line with state-of-the-art results. The same applies to the semantic types of premises, showing improvement with respect to previous attempts. The identification of the semantic types of claims appears to be more difficult due to the confusion between interpretations and rational evaluations. We plan to improve the guidelines to account for this difficulty.

In order to understand the persuasive role of the semantic types of claims and premises under study, we observe the recurrent combinations of argumentative components, their preferred position in the post and their distribution in winning and non winning threads.

Going forward, we plan to conduct a broader annotation project including the labeling of support/attack relations to be carried out as part of the identification of premise/claim pairs. We also plan to explore other aspects of the data. We expect that certain topics are more emotional or rational than others and winning arguments are generated accordingly. For example, moral issues may be more effective based on personal/emotional arguments while issues in science may require rational arguments. We also expect that the distribution of labels in the original post determines the effectiveness of a response, i.e. a post consisting mostly of emotional claims and pathos might require a similar response. Finally, we plan to experiment with predictive sequential models on claim and premise types and joint models for overall persuasiveness.

Acknowledgement

This paper is based on work supported by DARPA-DEFT program. The second author has been supported by the Early Post Doc SNFS Grant n. $P2TIP1_165081$ and was mainly responsible for the design of the guidelines (sections 3.2./3.3.), supervision of annotations and the qualitative analysis of the results. The views expressed are those of the authors and do not reflect the official policy or position of the SNFS, Department of Defense or the U.S. Government. We would like to thank the annotators for their work and the anonymous reviewers for their valuable feedback.

References

Jean-Claude Anscombre and Oswald Ducrot. 1983. *L'argumentation dans la langue*. Editions Mardaga.

Katie Atkinson and Trevor JM Bench-Capon. 2016. Argument schemes for reasoning about the actions of others. In *COMMA*. pages 71–82.

Maria Becker, Alexis Palmer, and Anette Frank. 2016. Argumentative texts and clause types. *ACL 2016* page 21.

Or Biran, Sara Rosenthal, Jacob Andreas, Kathleen McKeown, and Owen Rambow. 2012. Detecting influencers in written online conversations. In *Proceedings of the Second Workshop on Language in Social Media*. Association for Computational Linguistics, pages 37–45.

Katarzyna Budzynska, Mathilde Janier, Chris Reed, Patrick Saint-Dizier, Manfred Stede, and Olena Yaskorska. 2014. A model for processing illocutionary structures and argumentation in debates. In *LREC*. pages 917–924.

Katarzyna Budzynska and Chris Reed. 2011. Speech acts of argumentation: Inference anchors and peripheral cues in dialogue. In *Computational Models of Natural Argument*.

Robert B Cialdini. 2005. Influence: The psychology of persuasion collins. *Revised edition (October 7, 2005)*.

Abhimanyu Das, Sreenivas Gollapudi, Emre Kıcıman, and Onur Varol. 2016. Information dissemination in heterogeneous-intent networks. In *Proceedings of the 8th ACM Conference on Web Science*. ACM, pages 259–268.

Rory Duthie, Katarzyna Budzynska, and Chris Reed. 2016. Mining ethos in political debate. In *Proceedings of 6th International Conference on Computational Models of Argument (COMMA 2016). IOS Press, Frontiers in Artificial Intelligence and Applications*.

James B Freeman. 2000. What types of statements are there? *Argumentation* 14(2):135–157.

Debanjan Ghosh, Aquila Khanam, Yubo Han, and Smaranda Muresan. 2016. Coarse-grained argumentation features for scoring persuasive essays. In *Proceedings of the 54th Annual Meeting of the Association for Computational Linguistics*. pages 549–554.

Ivan Habernal and Iryna Gurevych. 2016. Which argument is more convincing? analyzing and predicting convincingness of web arguments using bidirectional lstm. In *Proceedings of the 54th Annual Meeting of the Association for Computational Linguistics (ACL)*.

Ivan Habernal and Iryna Gurevych. 2017. Argumentation mining in user-generated web discourse. *Computational Linguistics* .

Colin Higgins and Robyn Walker. 2012. Ethos, logos, pathos: Strategies of persuasion in social/environmental reports. In *Accounting Forum*. Elsevier, volume 36, pages 194–208.

Klaus Krippendorff. 1970. Estimating the reliability, systematic error and random error of interval data. *Educational and Psychological Measurement* 30(1):61–70.

John Lawrence and Chris Reed. 2016. Argument mining using argumentation scheme structures. In *COMMA*. pages 379–390.

Bing Liu. 2012. Sentiment analysis and opinion mining. *Synthesis lectures on human language technologies* 5(1):1–167.

Stephanie Lukin, Pranav Anand, Marilyn Walker, and Steve Whittaker. 2017. Argument strength is in the eye of the beholder: Audience effects in persuasion .

Jan Nuyts. 2012. Notions of (inter) subjectivity. *English Text Construction* 5(1):53–76.

Joonsuk Park, Cheryl Blake, and Claire Cardie. 2015. Toward machine-assisted participation in erulemaking: An argumentation model of evaluability. In *Proceedings of the 15th International Conference on Artificial Intelligence and Law*. ACM, pages 206–210.

Andreas Peldszus and Manfred Stede. 2016. An annotated corpus of argumentative microtexts. In D. Mohammed and M. Lewinski, editors, *Argumentation and Reasoned Action - Proc. of the 1st European Conference on Argumentation, Lisbon, 2015*, College Publications, London.

Chaim Perelman and Lucie Olbrechts-Tyteca. 1973. *The new rhetoric: A treatise on argumentation*. University of Notre Dame Pess.

James Ravenscroft, Anika Oellrich, Shyamasree Saha, and Maria Liakata. 2016. Multi-label annotation in scientific articles - the multi-label cancer risk assessment corpus. In *Proceedings of the Tenth International Conference on Language Resources and Evaluation LREC 2016, Portorož, Slovenia, May 23-28, 2016.*. http://www.lrec-conf.org/proceedings/lrec2016/summaries/928.html.

Sara Rosenthal and Kathleen Mckeown. 2017. Detecting influencers in multiple online genres. *ACM Transactions on Internet Technology (TOIT)* 17(2):12.

Christian Stab and Iryna Gurevych. 2014a. Annotating argument components and relations in persuasive essays. In *Proceedings of COLING*

2014, the 25th International Conference on Computational Linguistics: Technical Papers. Dublin City University and Association for Computational Linguistics, Dublin, Ireland, pages 1501–1510. http://www.aclweb.org/anthology/C14-1142.

Christian Stab and Iryna Gurevych. 2014b. Identifying argumentative discourse structures in persuasive essays. In *EMNLP*. pages 46–56.

Chenhao Tan, Vlad Niculae, Cristian Danescu-Niculescu-Mizil, and Lillian Lee. 2016. Winning arguments: Interaction dynamics and persuasion strategies in good-faith online discussions. In *Proceedings of the 25th International Conference on World Wide Web*. International World Wide Web Conferences Steering Committee, pages 613–624.

Frans H van Eemeren and Frans Hendrik Eemeren. 2009. *Examining argumentation in context: Fifteen studies on strategic maneuvering*, volume 1. John Benjamins Publishing.

Marilyn A Walker, Jean E Fox Tree, Pranav Anand, Rob Abbott, and Joseph King. 2012. A corpus for research on deliberation and debate. In *LREC*. pages 812–817.

Zhongyu Wei, Yang Liu, and Yi Li. 2016. Is this post persuasive? ranking argumentative comments in the online forum. In *The 54th Annual Meeting of the Association for Computational Linguistics*. page 195.

Annotation of argument structure in Japanese legal documents

Hiroaki Yamada[†]   **Simone Teufel**[‡ †]   **Takenobu Tokunaga**[†]
[†]Tokyo Institute of Technology   [‡]University of Cambridge
yamada.h.ax@m.titech.ac.jp   simone.teufel@cl.cam.ac.uk   take@c.titech.ac.jp

Abstract

We propose a method for the annotation of Japanese civil judgment documents, with the purpose of creating flexible summaries of these. The first step, described in the current paper, concerns content selection, i.e., the question of which material should be extracted initially for the summary. In particular, we utilize the hierarchical argument structure of the judgment documents. Our main contributions are a) the design of an annotation scheme that stresses the connection between legal issues (called *issue topics*) and argument structure, b) an adaptation of rhetorical status to suit the Japanese legal system and c) the definition of a linked argument structure based on legal sub-arguments. In this paper, we report agreement between two annotators on several aspects of the overall task.

1 Introduction

Automatic summarization has become increasingly crucial for dealing with the information overload in many aspects of life. This is no different in the legal arena, where lawyers and other legal practitioners are in danger of being overwhelmed by too many documents that are relevant to their specialized task. The situation is aggravated by the length and complexity of legal documents: for instance, the average sentence length in Japanese legal documents is 93.1 characters, as opposed to 47.5 characters in Japanese news text. One reason for the long sentences is the requirement on judges to define their statement precisely and strictly, which they do by adding additional restrictive clauses to sentences. As a result, it is not possible to read every document returned by a search engine. The final goal of our work is therefore to provide automatic summaries that would enable the legal professions to make fast decisions about which documents they should read in detail.

To this end, we propose an annotation scheme of legal documents based on a combination of two ideas. The first of these ideas is the observation by (Hachey and Grover, 2006) that in the legal domain, content selection of satisfactory quality can be achieved using the argumentative zoning method. The second idea is novel to our work and concerns the connection between legal argumentation and summarization. We propose to identify and annotate each relevant legal issue (called *Issue Topic*), and to provide a linked argumentation structure of sub-arguments related to each Issue Topic separately. This can provide summaries of different levels of granularity, as well as summaries of each Issue Topic in isolation. In the current paper, we describe all aspects of the annotation scheme, including an annotation study between two expert annotators.

2 The structure of judgment documents

Legal texts such as judgment documents have unique characteristics regarding their structure and contents. Japanese judgment documents are written by professional judges, who, after passing the bar examination, are intensively trained to write such judgments. This results in documents with certain unique characteristics, which are reflected in the annotation scheme proposed in this paper. The document type we consider here, the judgment document, is one of the most important types of legal text in the Japanese legal system. Judgment documents provide valuable information for the legal professions to construct or analyze their cases. They are the direct output of court trials. The Japanese Code of Civil Procedure demands that "the court renders its

22

Proceedings of the 4th Workshop on Argument Mining, pages 22–31
Copenhagen, Denmark, September 8, 2017. ©2017 Association for Computational Linguistics

judgment based on the original judgment document" (Japanese Ministry of Justice, 2012a, Article 252). The types of documents we work with in particular are Japanese Civil (as opposed to Criminal) case judgment documents from courts of first instance.

There also exist official human summaries of judgment documents, which we can use to inform our summary design, although they were issued only for a small number of documents.

2.1 Argument structure

The legal system that is in force in a particular country strongly affects the type and structure of legal documents used, which in turn has repercussions for summarization strategies. The first source of information for our summary design is a guideline document for writing judgment documents of civil cases (Judicial Research and Training Institute of Japan, 2006). In 1990, the "new format" was proposed, based on the principle that issue-focused judgment should make the document clearer, more informative and thus more reader-friendly (The Secretariat of Supreme Court of Japan, 1990). Although both the use of the guidelines and of the "new format" is voluntary, in practice we observed a high degree of compliance with the new format of the guidelines in recent Japanese judgment documents. This is for instance evidenced in the common textual structure shared amongst the documents. The "Fact and Reasons" section takes up the biggest portion of the document and is therefore the target of our summarization task. "Facts and Reasons" consists of a claim (typically brought forward by the plaintiff), followed by a description of the case, the facts agreed among the interested parties in advance, the issues to be contested during the trial, and statements from both plaintiff and defendant. The final part is the judicial decision. The entire structure described above is often marked typographically and structurally, e.g. in headlines.

Our second source of information concerns the argument structure of the legal argument. A Japanese Civil Case judgment document forms one big argument, depicted in Fig. 1. This argument structure includes the plaintiff's statements, the defendant's statements, and the judges' statement supporting their arguments. At the top of the

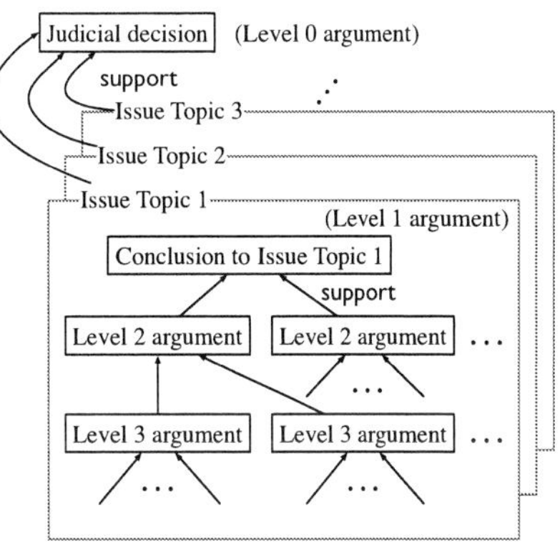

Figure 1: Argument structure of judgment document

structure, there is the root of the argument which states the judicial decision as the final conclusion to the plaintiff's accusation. We call this the level 0 argument.

The level 0 argument breaks down into several sub-arguments, which usually each cover one important topic to be debated. We call this the level 1 argument. Each level 1 argument might itself consist of sub-arguments at lower levels (levels 2, 3, 4, . . .). The relation between levels is of type "support". In this kind of arguments, there are also "attack" relations. These occur, for instance, when a plaintiff argues *in favor of the negated* claim of the defendant, and vice versa. However, because these "attack" relationships follow the logic of the legal argumentation in a regular and systematic way, we decided not to explicitly model them in order to avoid redundancy in our annotation.

Our annotation scheme models this fact by calling level 2 units "FRAMING-main", units at level 3 or lower "FRAMING-sub", and by providing "support" links in the form of FRAMING linking between them. At the bottom of the argument structure, facts provide the lowest level of support, although in this work we do not model argumentation below level 3.

2.2 Issue Topics

The main organizing principle in the structure of the judgment document are the topics of each of the argumentation strands. This structure is a direct outcome of the Japanese judicial system, where most civil cases start with "preparatory proceedings". The goal of this procedure, which is carried out ahead of the trial under participation of all parties, is to define the issues to be tried

(Japanese Ministry of Justice, 2012b). These are called *Issue Topics*. Issue Topics are the main contentious items to be argued about between the interested parties. What could be a possible Issue Topics depends on the case alone; the number of issue topics is therefore unlimited. Examples include "whether the defendant X was negligent in supervising", "the defendant Y's exact actions during the crucial time frame" or "what is the effect of the law Z".

It is our working hypothesis that Issue Topics (which correspond to level 1 topics in our parlance) are extremely important in generating meaningful, coherent and useful summaries. Most legal cases consist of several Issue Topics; note that each Issue Topic is covered by its own argument subtree as depicted in Figure 1. In the best summaries the logical flow is organized in such a way that the final judicial decision can be traced back through each Issue Topic's connections. Minimally, this requires recognizing which sentence refers to which Issue Topic, i.e., linking each Issue Topic with the textual material supporting it. In what followes, we will call this task "Issue Topic linking".

2.3 Rhetorical structure

To exploit the idea that argument structure is a crucial aspect for legal summarization, we take a rhetorical status based approach. This method was originally defined for the summarization of scientific articles by Teufel and Moens (2002), but later studies such as Hachey and Grover (2006) applied the rhetorical status approach to the legal text domain for the context of English law.

Hachey and Grover defined the following seven labels: In English law, the judgment first states the facts and events, corresponding to category "FACT". "PROCEEDINGS" labels sentences which restate the details of previous judgments in lower courts. "BACKGROUND" is the label for quotations or citations of law materials which Law Lords use to discuss precedents and legislation. "FRAMING" is a rhetorical role that captures all aspects of the Law Lord's argumentation for their judgment. "DISPOSAL" is the actual decision of the lord which indicates the agreement or disagreement with a previous ruling[1]. "TEXTUAL" is used in situations where the sentence

---

[1]Since Hachey and Grover's target documents are from the UK House of Lords, trials are always brought forward at Courts of Appeal.

describes the structure of the document, rather than discussing content related to the case.

Hachey and Grover reported an inter-annotator agreement of K=0.83 (N=1955, n=7, k=2; where K is the kappa coefficient, N is the number of sentences, n is the number of categories and k is the number of annotators). Other researchers adopted the rhetorical status approach to their respective legal systems (Farzindar and Lapalme (2004) for the Canadian law and (Saravanan and Ravindran, 2010) for the Indian law). Farzindar and Lapalme's agreement figures are not available, but Saravanan and Ravindran's inter-annotator agreement of K=0.84 (N=16000; n=7, k=2) is remarkably similar to that of Hachey and Grover.

Our approach follows these studies in also using rhetorical structure (which we adapt to the Japanese system), but we combine this analysis with the two other levels of annotation motivated earlier (FRAMING linking and Issue Topic linking). We therefore model argument structure at a more detailed level than the earlier studies, by also considering the lower level hierarchical structure of argumentative support.

Based on the Issue Topic structure given in Figure 1, we propose to build summaries of different granularities, which have been inspired by the human summaries. Figure 2 shows an ideal sample of a structure-aware summary, using material manually extracted from an actual judgment document (our translation). The sample focuses on a specific Issue Topic of the case, namely "whether the execution officer D was negligent or not".

While full Issue Topic and FRAMING linking annotation would allow very sophisticated summaries, our fall-back strategy is to create simpler summaries using only the final conclusion and the main supporting text such as judicial decisions. For these simple summaries, performing only automatic rhetorical status classification is sufficient.

3 Annotation scheme

As discussed above, we use rhetorical status classification, which is a standard procedure in legal text processing. We also introduce two types of linking after rhetorical structure determination. These two types of linking are very different in nature and therefore need to be treated separately. The first kind of linking, Issue Topic linking, establishes a link from every single rhetorical status segment to the Issue Topic which the segment

The plaintiff insists that the court executing officer was negligent in that the officer didn't notice that a person had committed suicide in the real estate when he performed an investigation of the current condition of the real estate, and also insists that the execution court was negligent in that the court failed to prescribe the matter to be examined on the examination order. As a result, the plaintiff won a successful bid for the estate with a higher price than the actual value of the estate given that the plaintiff did not have the information that the property was stigmatized. The plaintiff claims compensation for damage and delay from the defendant.

[Issue Topic]: Whether the execution officer D was negligent or not.
The measures performed by the officer were those that are normally implemented for examination. From the circumstances which the execution officer D perceived, he could not have realized that the estate was stigmatized. The officer cannot be regarded as negligent in that negligence would imply a dereliction of duty of inspection, which, given that there were sufficient checks, did not happen. Concerning the question whether the officer had the duty to check whether the estate was stigmatized, we can observe various matters – in actuality, the person who killed himself happened to be the owner of the estate and the legal representative of the Revolving Credit Mortgage concerned, the house then became vacant and was offered for auction, but we can also observe the following: other persons but the owner himself could have committed suicide in the estate, for instance friends and family; there was a long time frame during which the suicide could have happened; the neighbors might not have answered the officer's questions in a forthcoming manner, even if they were aware of the fact that the estate was stigmatized; there are several factors to affect the value of the estate beyond the fact that the estate was stigmatized, and it is not realistic neither from a time perspective nor an economic perspective to examine all such factors specifically; and the bidders in the auction were in a position to examine the estate personally as the location of the estate was known – taking these relevant matters into consideration, it is a justified statement that the officer didn't have the duty to check in a proactive manner whether the estate was stigmatized. Therefore, the plaintiff's claim is unreasonable since it is hard to say that the officer was negligent.

[Issue Topic]: Whether the examination court was negligent or not.
The plaintiff's claim is unreasonable for the additional reason that it is hard to say that the examination court was negligent.

Given what has been said above, it is not necessary to judge the other points;the plaintiff's claim is unreasonable so the judgment returns to the main text.

Figure 2: Sample summary/text structure

Label	Description
IDENTIFYING	The text unit identifies a discussion topic.
CONCLUSION	The text unit clearly states the conclusion from argumentation or discussion.
FACT	The text unit describes a fact.
BACKGROUND	The text unit gives a direct quotation or reference to law materials (law or precedent) and applies them to the present case.
FRAMING-main	The text unit consists of argumentative material that directly support a CONCLUSION unit.
FRAMING-sub	The text unit consists of argumentative material that indirectly supports a CONCLUSION unit or that directly supports a FRAMING-main unit.
OTHER	The text unit does not satisfy any of the requirements above.

Table 1: Our Rhetorical Annotation Scheme for Japanese Legal judgment documents

tifiers are given to each Issue Topic; *2. Rhetorical Status Classification* – each text unit is classified into a rhetorical status; *3. Issue Topic Linking* – all rhetorical units identified in the previous stage are linked to a Issue Topic; *4. FRAMING Linking* – for those textual units participating in argumentation links between level 2 and level 3 arguments involving FRAMING-main, FRAMING-sub and BACKGROUND, additional links denoting "argumentative support" are annotated.

Earlier studies (Hachey and Grover, 2006; Saravanan and Ravindran, 2010) chose the sentence as the annotation unit and defined exclusive labeling, i.e., only one category can be assigned to each annotation unit. We also use exclusive labeling, but our definition of the smallest annotation unit is a comma-separated text unit. In Japanese, such units typically correspond to linguistic clauses. This decision was necessitated by the complexity and length of the legal language we observe, where parts of a single long sentence can fulfill different rhetorical functions. While annotators are free to label each comma-separated unit in a sentence separately, they are of course also free to label the entire sentence if they wish.

3.1 Issue Topic Identification

Our annotators are instructed to indicate the spans of each Issue Topic in the text, and to assign a

concerns. In contrast, the second kind of linking, which aims to model the "support" relationship between level 2 and level 3 shown in Figure 1, is much more selective: it only applies to those text units between which a direct "support" relationship holds. We will now introduce the following four annotation tasks: *1. Issue Topic Identification* – Issue Topic spans are marked in text, and iden-

unique identifier to each[2]. Annotators are asked to find the span that best ("in the most straightforward way") describes the Issue Topic. We expect this task to be relatively uncontroversial, because the documents are produced in such a way that it should be clear what the Issue Topics are (cf. our discussion in section 2.2).

3.2 Rhetorical Status Classification

Our annotation scheme (Table 1) is an adaptation of Hachey and Grover's scheme; we introduce six labels for rhetorical status and an "OTHER" label. Two of the labels are retained from Hachey and Grover: the submission of fact (FACT) and the citation of law materials (BACKGROUND). DISPOSAL is redefined as CONCLUSION, in order to capture the conclusion of each Issue Topic. IDENTIFYING is a label for text that states the discussion topic. TEXTUAL is dropped in our annotation scheme since this label is not relevant to our summary design.

Our main modification is to split Hachey and Grover's FRAMING category into FRAMING-main and FRAMING-sub, in order to express the hierarchical argumentation structure discussed in section 2.1. Apart from the fact that the split allows us to recover the argument structure, we found that without the split, the argumentative text under FRAMING would cover too much text in our documents. Since our objective is to generate summaries, having too much material in any extract-worthy rhetorical role is undesirable.

We also introduce a slightly unusual annotation procedure where annotators are asked to trace back the legal argument structure of the case. They first search for the general CONCLUSIONs of the case. They then find each Issue Topic's CONCLUSION; next they find the FRAMING-main which is supporting. Finally, they look for the FRAMING-sub elements that support the FRAMING-main. They will then express the "support" relationship as FRAMING links (as described in section 3.4). Therefore, the annotators simultaneously recover the argument structure while making decisions about the rhetorical status.

3.3 Issue Topic Linking

Issue Topic linking concerns the relation between each textual unit and its corresponding Issue Topic. Every unit is assigned to the single Issue Topic ID the annotators recognize it as most related to. But not all textual material concerns specific Issue Topics; some text pieces such as the introduction and the final conclusion are predominantly concerned with the overall trial and judicial decision. We define a special Issue Topic ID of value 0 to cover such cases.

3.4 FRAMING Linking

Units labeled with BACKGROUND and FRAMING-sub can be linked to FRAMING-main, if the annotator perceives that the BACKGROUND or FRAMING-sub material argumentatively supports the statements in FRAMING-main. The semantics of a link is that the origin (BACKGROUND and FRAMING-sub) supports the destination (FRAMING-main).

4 Agreement metrics

Due to the nature of the four annotation tasks we propose here, different agreement metrics are necessary. While rhetorical status classification can be evaluated by Cohen's Kappa (Cohen, 1960), all other tasks require specialized metrics.

4.1 Issue Topic Identification

We perform a comparison of the *textual* material annotated as Issue Topic rather than the exact *location* of the material in the texts, as we only care to know whether annotators agree about the semantic content of the Issue Topics. We count two spans as agreed if more than 60% of their characters agree. The reason why we introduce the 60% overlap rule is that annotators may differ slightly in how they annotate a source span even if the principal meaning is the same. This difference often concerns short and relatively meaningless adverbial modification and such at the beginning or end of meaningful units. We manually confirmed that no false positives occurred by setting this threshold.

However, as annotators may disagree on the *number* of Issue Topic they recognize in a text, we first calculate an agreement ratio for each annotator by equation (1) and average them to give the overall agreement metric as in equation (2), where $a_s(i)$ is the number of spans agreed between annotator i and others and $spans(i)$ is the number of spans annotated by annotator i:

---

[2]We later normalize the identifiers for comparison across annotators.

$$agreement_{\text{ITI}}(i) = \frac{a_s(i)}{spans(i)}, \qquad (1)$$

$$agreement_{\mathrm{ITI}} = \frac{\sum_i agreement_{\mathrm{ITI}}(i)}{|AnnotatorSet|}, \qquad (2)$$

where $i \in AnnotatorSet$.

4.2 Issue Topic Linking

In the case of Issue Topic linking, the destinations of each link are fixed, as each Issue Topic is uniquely identified by its ID. As far as the sources of the links are concerned, their numbers across annotators should be almost the same. They only differ if the annotators marked different units as "OTHER" during rhetorical status classification, as all units except those marked "OTHER" are linked to an Issue Topic by definition. We therefore report an average agreement ratio as in equation (4) over each annotator agreement given by equation (3), where $a_u(i)$ is the number of units agreed between annotator i and others and $units(i)$ is the number of units annotated by annotator i:

$$agreement_{\mathrm{ITL}}(i) = \frac{a_u(i)}{units(i)}, \qquad (3)$$

$$agreement_{\mathrm{ITL}} = \frac{\sum_i agreement_{\mathrm{ITL}}(i)}{|AnnotatorSet|}, \qquad (4)$$

where $i \in AnnotatorSet$.

4.3 FRAMING Linking

FRAMING linking is the most difficult task in our scheme to evaluate. FRAMING links hold between either BACKGROUND or FRAMING text units as the source, and FRAMING-main text units as the destination. The FRAMING linking task therefore consists of three parts, the identification of source spans, the identification of destination spans, and the determination of the most appropriate destination for each source span (linking).

The destinations are not uniquely identified in terms of an ID (as was the case with Issue Topic linking), but are variable, as the annotators mark them explicitly in the text using a span.[3]

First, we measure how well human annotators can distinguish all categories that participate in FRAMING linking (CONCLUSION, FRAMING-main, FRAMING-sub, BACKGROUND and "anything else"). The degree to which this subdivision is successful can be expressed by Kappa.

This number gives an upper bound of performance that limits all further FRAMING linking tasks.

We also measure agreement on *source* spans for FRAMING linking. We define agreement as "sharing more than 80% of the span in characters", and report the number of spans where this is so, over the entire number of spans, as $agreement_{\mathrm{src}}$, defined in equation (5). We only count those spans that are labeled as FRAMING-sub or BACKGROUND and are linked to somewhere[4].

$$agreement_{\mathrm{src}} = \frac{\#\ of\ agreed\ source\ spans\ with\ link}{\#\ of\ source\ spans\ with\ link} \qquad (5)$$

Finally, we measure agreement on *destination* spans that are linked to from source spans. Destination agreement $agreement_{\mathrm{fl}}$ is the number of agreed[5] source spans which also have agreed destination spans, over all agreed source spans:

$$agreement_{\mathrm{fl}} = \frac{\#\ of\ agreed\ links}{\#\ of\ agreed\ source\ spans\ with\ link}. \qquad (6)$$

4.4 Baselines for FRAMING Linking

We implemented strong baselines in order to interpret our results for FRAMING linking. All baseline models output the linking result for each annotator, given as input the respective other annotator's source spans that have a link, and their destination spans. There is no other well-defined way to give any system options to choose from, and without these options, the baseline is unable to operate at all. In our setup, the baseline models simply simulate the last linking step between pre-identified source and destination spans, by one plausible model (namely, the other annotator).

Our three baseline models are called Random, Popularity and Nearest. The Random model chooses one destination span for each source span randomly. The Popularity model operates random by observed distribution of destinations. The distribution is calculated using the other annotator's data. The Nearest model always chooses the closest following destination candidate span available. This is motivated by our observation that in legal arguments, the supporting material often precedes the conclusion, and is typically adjacent or physically close.

---

[3]Note that the *source* spans are always variable, both in FRAMING linking and in Issue Topic linking.

[4]Although logically all such spans should be linked to somewhere, we observed some cases where annotators mistakenly forgot to link.

[5]For the definition of agreement on destination spans, the 80% rule is applied again.

5 Annotation experiment

Given the intrinsic subjectivity of text-interpretative tasks, and the high complexity of this particular annotation task, achieving acceptable agreement on our annotation is crucial for being able to use the annotated material for the supervised machine learning experiments we are planning for automating the annotation. We therefore perform an experiment to measure the reproducibility of our scheme, consisting of the 4 tasks as described above.

5.1 Annotation procedure

Two annotators were used for the experiment, the first author of this paper (who has a bachelor of Laws degree in Japanese Law), and a PhD candidate in a graduate school of Japanese Law. It is necessary to use expert annotators, due to the special legal language used in the documents. Legal domain texts can be hard to understand for lay persons, because terms have technical meanings which differ from the meaning of the terms when used in everyday language. For example, the terms "悪意 (*aku-i*)" and "善意 (*zen-i*)" (which mean "maliciousness" and "benevolentness" respectively in everyday language), have a different meaning in a legal context, where "悪意" means knowing a fact, and "善意" means not knowing a fact.

The annotators used the GUI-based annotation tool Slate (Kaplan et al., 2011). We gave the annotators a guideline document of 8 pages detailing the procedure. In it, we instructed the annotators to read the target document to understand its general structure and flow of discussion roughly and to pay particular attention to Issue Topics, choosing one textual unit for each Issue Topic. They perform the tasks in the following order: (1) Issue Topic Identification, (2) Rhetorical Status Classification, (3) FRAMING linking and (4) Issue Topic linking. As mentioned earlier, tasks (2) and (3) logically should be performed simultaneously since the process which identifies FRAMING-main, FRAMING-sub and BACKGROUND is closely connected to the FRAMING linking task. The annotators were instructed to perform a final check to verify that each Issue Topic has at least one rhetorical status. As Issue Topics tend to have at least one unit for every rhetorical status, this check often detects slips of the attention.

	An. 1	An. 2
Issue Topic spans	24	27
Agreed spans (overlap)		20
$agreement_{\mathrm{ITI}}(i)$ (overlap)	0.833	0.741
$agreement_{\mathrm{ITI}}$ (overlap)		**0.787**

Table 2: Issue Topic Identification Results (in spans)

	Annotator 2							
	IDT	CCL	FRm	FRs	BGD	FCT	OTR	Total
IDT	171	13	4	19	0	0	3	210
CCL	0	299	142	45	0	6	4	496
FRm	0	89	1187	812	12	13	27	2140
FRs	24	15	229	2327	23	108	12	2738
BGD	3	0	11	21	150	37	1	223
FCT	12	12	52	218	0	3197	18	3509
OTR	26	7	27	9	0	99	395	563
Total	236	435	1652	3451	185	3460	460	9879

(Annotator 1 labels the rows.)

Table 3: Confusion Matrix for Rhet. Status (units)

We used Japanese Civil Case judgment documents written in several district courts, which are available publicly from a Japanese Court website (http://www.courts.go.jp/). We annotated 8 Japanese civil case judgment documents, which consist of 9,879 comma-separated units and 201,869 characters in total. The documents are written by various judges from several courts and cover the following themes: "Medical negligence during a health check", "Threatening behavior in connection to money lending", "Use of restraining devices by police", "Fence safety and injury", "Mandatory retirement from private company", "Road safety in a bus travel sub-contract situation", "Railway crossing accident", and "Withdrawal of a company's garbage license by the city".

5.2 Results

5.2.1 Issue Topic Identification

The results for the Issue Topic identification task are given in Table 2. The overall agreement ratio observed is 0.787. An error analysis showed that the two main remaining problems were due to the splitting of an Issue Topic by one annotator and not by the other, and a different interpretation of whether compensation calculations should be annotated or not.

5.2.2 Rhetorical Status agreement

Agreement of rhetorical classification was measured at K=0.70 (N=9879; n=7, k=2; Cohen). Note that the number of units N (entities assessed) is the number of comma- (or sentence-final punc-

	An. 1	An. 2
Annotated units	9336	9446
Agreed units		8169
$agreement_{\text{ITL}}(i)$	0.875	0.865
$agreement_{\text{ITL}}$	**0.870**	

Table 4: Issue Topic Linking Results (in units)

	An. 1	An. 2
# of source spans(FRs or BGD)	544	666
# of source spans with links	527	602
# of agreed source spans with link	378 (67.26%)	
# of agreed links	250	
$agreement_{\text{fl}}$	**0.661**	

Table 5: FRAMING Linking Results

Baseline Model	$agreement_{\text{fl}}$
Random	0.016
Popularity	0.024
Nearest	0.644

Table 6: FRAMING Linking Baselines

tuation) separated text pieces, as opposed to sentences in previous work. Table 3 gives the confusion matrix for the Rhetorical Status Classification task. Although the Kappa value indicates good agreement for rhetorical classification overall, the confusion matrix shows certain systematic assignment errors. In particular, FRAMING-main and FRAMING-sub are relatively often confused, indicating that our current annotation guidelines should be improved in this respect.

5.2.3 Issue Topic Linking agreement

The result for Issue Topic linking is shown in Table 4. At 0.870, the agreement ratio indicates good agreement. The annotators seem to have little trouble in determining which Issue Topic each sentence relates to. This is probably due to the fact that the judgment documents are closely structured around Issue Topics, as per our working hypothesis. Annotators often arrive the same interpretation because the argument is logically structured and the components necessary for interpretation can be found nearby, as the strong performance of the Nearest baseline demonstrates. However, we also noticed an adverse effect concerning Issue Topics. Judges sometimes reorganize the Issue Topics that were previously defined, for instance, by merging smaller Issue Topics, or in the case of dependencies between Issue Topics, by dropping dependent Issue Topics when the Issue Topics they depend on have collapsed during the trial. Such reorganizations can cause disagreement among annotators.

In sum, the detection of Issue Topic level argument structure seems to be overall a well-defined task, judging by the combined results of Issue Topic Identification and Linking.

5.2.4 FRAMING Linking agreement

Agreement of rhetorical status classification of text units involved in FRAMING linking was measured at K=0.69 (N=9879; n=4, k=2) and source agreement is given in Table 5. The baseline results are given in Table 6. The Near-

est baseline model shows a rather high score ($agreement_{\text{fl}}$=0.644) when compared to the human annotators ($agreement_{\text{fl}}$=0.661). The distance between source spans and destination spans clearly influences the FRAMING linking task, showing a strong preference by the judges for a regular argumentation structure. We also observe that the distances involving FRAMING links are shorter than those for Issue Topics.

Trying to explain the relatively low human agreement, we performed an error analysis of the linking errors, classifying the 128 errors made during FRAMING linking. We distinguish destination spans that show character position overlap across annotators, from those that do not. For those that have overlapping spans, we check whether this corresponds to shared content in a meaningful manner. Even for those spans that are not shared in terms of character positions, content could still be shared, as the spans could be paraphrases of each other, so we check this as well. We found that 26 error links had meaningful overlap and 22 error links were reformulations. If we were to consider "reformulation" and "meaningful overlap" links as agreed, the $agreement_{\text{fl}}$ value would rise to 0.788. This is potentially an encouraging result for an upper bound on how much annotators naturally agree on FRAMING linking.

Most errors that we categorized as "different meaning" are caused by non-agreement during the FRAMING-main identification stage. From this result, we conclude that improving the instructions for the identification of FRAMING-main is vital for the second phase of our annotation work. However, an interesting result is that even if annotators disagree on FRAMING-main identification, the non-agreed links still share linking structure. We observe that often the same set of source spans are linked to some destination span, although the destination itself is different across annotators. Our agreement metrics are thus underestimating the degree of shared linkage structure.

6 Related Work

There is little work on the summarization of Japanese judgment documents, Banno et al. (2006) amongst them. They used Support Vector Machines (Joachims, 1999) to extract important sentences for the summarization of Japanese Supreme Court judgments.

Several past studies share our interest in capturing the argumentation with rhetorical schemes.

Mochales and Moens (2011) presented an argumentation detection algorithm using state-of-the-art machine learning techniques. They annotated documents from the European Court of Human Rights (ECHR) and the Araucaria corpus for argumentation detection, achieving inter-annotator agreement of K=0.75 in Cohen's Kappa (ECHR). On a genre other than legal text, Faulkner (2014) annotated student essays using three tags ("for", "against" and "neither"), reaching inter-annotator agreement of K=0.70 (Cohen). As far as the rhetorical status classification part of our scheme is concerned, the closest approach to ours is Al Khatib et al. (2016), but they do not employ any explicit links, and they work on a different genre (news editorials).

A task related to our linking steps is the determination of relations between argument components. Stab and Gurevych (2014) annotated argumentative relations (support and attack) in essays; they reported inter-annotator agreement of K=0.81 (Fleiss) for both support and attack. Hua and Wang (2017) proposed an annotation scheme for labeling sentence-level supporting arguments relations with four types (STUDY, FACTUAL, OPINION, REASONING). Their results for argument type classification are as follows: K=0.61 for STUDY, K=0.75 for FACTUAL, K=0.71 for OPINION, and K=0.29 for REASONING.

However, these two relation-based studies discover only one aspect of argument structure, whereas our combination of linking tasks and a rhetorical status classification task means that we address the global hierarchical argument structure of a text.

There has also been some recent work on agreement metrics for argument relations. As far as agreement on detection of argumentative components is concerned, Kirschner et al. (2015) point out that measures such as kappa and F1 score may cause some inappropriate penalty for slight differences of annotation between annotators, and proposed a graph-based metric based on pair-wise comparison of predefined argument components. This particular metric, while addressing some of the problems of kappa and F1, is not directly applicable to our annotation where annotators can freely chose the beginnings and ends of spans. Duthie et al. (2007) introduce CASS, a further, very recent adaptation of the metric by Kirschner et al. that can deal with disagreement in segmentation. However, the only available implementation is based on the AIF format.

7 Discussion and future work

It is hard to evaluate a newly defined, complex task involving argumentation and judgment. The task we presented here captures much of the information contained in legal judgment documents, but due to its inherent complexity, many different aspects have to be considered to see the entire picture. Our annotation experiment showed particularly good agreement for the rhetorical status labeling task, suggesting that our adaptation to the Japanese legal system was successful. The agreement on Issue Topic Identification and linking was also high. In contrast, the FRAMING linking, which annotators disagreed on to a higher degree than in the other tasks, suffered from the difficulty of identifying destination spans in particular. We can improve the agreement of the FRAMING linking task by refining our guidelines. Moreover, in order to achieve our final goal of building a flexible legal summarizer, we plan to analyze the relationship between human generated summaries and annotated documents on rhetorical status and links.

The next stage of our work is to increase the amount of annotation material for the automatic annotation of judgment documents with the proposed scheme. We will automate the annotation for the rhetorical status classification task with supervised machine learning and extend the automation step by step to linking tasks, based on the result of the rhetorical status classification.

References

Khalid Al Khatib, Henning Wachsmuth, Johannes Kiesel, Matthias Hagen, and Benno Stein. 2016. A news editorial corpus for mining argumentation strategies. In *Proceedings of COLING 2016, the 26th International Conference on Computational Linguistics: Technical Papers*, pages 3433–3443, Osaka, Japan. The COLING 2016 Organizing Committee.

Shinji Banno, Shigeki Mtsubara, and Masatoshi Yoshikawa. 2006. Identification of Important parts in judgments based on Machine Learning (機械学習に基づく判決文の重要箇所特定). In *Proceedings of the 12th Annual Meeting of the Association for Natural Language Processing*, pages 1075–1078. the Association for Natural Language Processing.

Jacob Cohen. 1960. A Coefficient of Agreement for Nominal Scales. *Educational and Psychological Measurement*, 20(1):37–46.

Rory Duthie, John Lawrence, Katarzyna Budzynska, and Chris Reed. 2007. The CASS Technique for Evaluating the Performance of Argument Mining. In *Proceedings of the 3rd Workshop on Argument Mining*, pages 40–49, Berlin, Germany. Association for Computational Linguistics.

Atefeh Farzindar and Guy Lapalme. 2004. LetSum, an automatic Legal Text Summarizing system. *Jurix*, pages 11–18.

Adam Faulkner. 2014. Automated Classification of Argument Stance in Student Essays: A Linguistically Motivated Approach with an Application for Supporting Argument Summarization. *All Graduate Works by Year: Dissertations, Theses, and Capstone Projects*.

Ben Hachey and Claire Grover. 2006. Extractive summarisation of legal texts. *Artificial Intelligence and Law*, 14(4):305–345.

Xinyu Hua and Lu Wang. 2017. Understanding and detecting supporting arguments of diverse types. In *Proceedings of the 55th Annual Meeting of the Association for Computational Linguistics (Volume 2: Short Papers)*, Vancouver, Canada. Association for Computational Linguistics.

Japanese Ministry of Justice. 2012a. Japanese code of civil procedure (article 252).

Japanese Ministry of Justice. 2012b. Japanese Code of Civil Procedure Subsection 2 Preparatory Proceedings.

Thorsten Joachims. 1999. Making large scale SVM learning practical. In *Advances in kernel methods: support vector learning*.

Judicial Research and Training Institute of Japan. 2006. *The guide to write civil judgements* (民事判決起案の手引), 10th edition. Housou-kai (法曹会).

Dain Kaplan, Ryu Iida, Kikuko Nishina, and Takenobu Tokunaga. 2011. Slate A Tool for Creating and Maintaining Annotated Corpora. *Jlcl*, 26(Section 2):91–103.

Christian Kirschner, Judith Eckle-Kohler, and Iryna Gurevych. 2015. Linking the Thoughts: Analysis of Argumentation Structures in Scientific Publications. pages 1–11.

Raquel Mochales and Marie Francine Moens. 2011. Argumentation mining. *Artificial Intelligence and Law*, 19(1):1–22.

M. Saravanan and B. Ravindran. 2010. Identification of Rhetorical Roles for Segmentation and Summarization of a Legal Judgment. *Artificial Intelligence and Law*, 18(1):45–76.

Christian Stab and Iryna Gurevych. 2014. Annotating argument components and relations in persuasive essays. In *Proceedings of COLING 2014, the 25th International Conference on Computational Linguistics*, pages 1501–1510.

Simone Teufel and Marc Moens. 2002. Summarizing scientific articles: Experiments with relevance and rhetorical status. *Computational Linguistics*, 28(4):409–445.

The Secretariat of Supreme Court of Japan. 1990. *The new format of Civil judgements : The group suggestion from the improving civil judgments committee of Tokyo High/District Court and the improving civil judgments committee of Osaka High/District Court* (民事判決書の新しい様式について：東京高等・地方裁判所民事判決書改善委員会, 大阪高等・地方裁判所民事判決書改善委員会の共同提言). Housou-kai (法曹会).

Improving Claim Stance Classification with Lexical Knowledge Expansion and Context Utilization

Roy Bar-Haim
IBM Research - Haifa
Mount Carmel
Haifa, 3498825, Israel
roybar@il.ibm.com

Lilach Edelstein
IBM Research - Haifa
Mount Carmel
Haifa, 3498825, Israel
lilache@il.ibm.com

Charles Jochim
IBM Research - Ireland
Damastown Industrial Estate
Dublin 15, Ireland
charlesj@ie.ibm.com

Noam Slonim
IBM Research - Haifa
Mount Carmel
Haifa, 3498825, Israel
noams@il.ibm.com

Abstract

Stance classification is a core component in on-demand argument construction pipelines. Previous work on *claim stance classification* relied on background knowledge such as manually-composed sentiment lexicons. We show that both accuracy and coverage can be significantly improved through automatic expansion of the initial lexicon. We also developed a set of contextual features that further improves the state-of-the-art for this task.

1 Introduction

Debating technologies aim to help humans debate and make better decisions. A core capability for these technologies is the on-demand construction of pro and con arguments for a given controversial topic. Most previous work was aimed at detecting topic-dependent argument components, such as claims and evidence (Levy et al., 2014; Rinott et al., 2015). Recently, Bar-Haim et al. (2017) introduced the related task of *claim stance classification*. For example, given the topic

(1) ***The monarchy** should be abolished.*$\ominus$

and the following two claims

(2) ***Social traditions or hierarchies** are essential for social order.* $\oplus$ $\Leftrightarrow$

(3) *People feel greater dignity when **choosing their head of state**.* $\oplus$ $\nLeftrightarrow$

the goal is to classify (2) as *Con* and (3) as *Pro* with respect to (1).

Bar-Haim et al. proposed a model that breaks this task into several sub-tasks: (a) Identify the sentiment targets of the topic and the claim (b) Determine the sentiment of the topic and the claim towards their sentiment targets, and (c) Determine the relation between the targets. Target A is *consistent/contrastive* with target B if the stance towards A implies the same/opposite stance towards B, respectively.

In (1)–(3), targets are marked in bold, positive/negative sentiment is indicated as $\oplus$/$\ominus$ and consistent/contrastive relation is marked as $\Leftrightarrow$/$\nLeftrightarrow$. For instance, (3) has positive sentiment towards its target, *choosing their head of state*, which implies negative sentiment towards *the monarchy*, since the targets are contrastive. The topic's sentiment towards *the monarchy* is also negative, hence it is a *Pro* claim.

On-demand argument generation is inherently an open-domain task, so one cannot learn topic-specific features for stance classification from the training data. Furthermore, claims are short sentences, and the number of claims in the training data is relatively small as compared to common sentiment analysis and stance classification benchmarks. Consequently, external knowledge such as sentiment lexicons is crucial for this task. However, the coverage of manually-constructed sentiment lexicons is often incomplete. As reported by Bar-Haim et al., the sentiment lexicon they used was able to match sentiment terms in fewer than 80% of the claims. Moreover, manually composed sentiment lexicons lack the notion of (numeric) sentiment strength.

A more general limitation of sentiment-based approaches is that some claims express stance but do not convey explicit sentiment. As an example,

Proceedings of the 4th Workshop on Argument Mining, pages 32–38
Copenhagen, Denmark, September 8, 2017. ©2017 Association for Computational Linguistics

consider the following *Pro* claim for (1):

(4) *The people, not the members of one family, should be sovereign.*

In this work we present several improvements to the system of Bar-Haim et al. (2017) (henceforth, the *baseline system*), which address the above limitations. First, we present a method for automatic expansion of a given sentiment lexicon, which leads to a substantial performance increase. Second, while the baseline system only considers the claim itself, we developed a set of contextual features that further boosts the performance of the system. In particular, these contextual features allow classification of claims with no explicit sentiment. Overall, we outperformed the best published results for this task by a large margin.

2 Baseline System

We first give a high-level description of the Bar-Haim et al. system, which we build upon in this work. Given a topic t and a claim c, let x_t and x_c be their sentiment targets, respectively, and let $s_t, s_c \in [-1, 1]$ be the sentiment of the topic and the claim towards their respective targets. Positive/negative values indicate positive/negative sentiment. Let $\mathcal{R}(x_c, x_t) \in [-1, 1]$ denote the relation between the claim target and the topic target. Positive/negative values indicate consistent/contrastive targets (as defined in the previous section). The absolute value of both scores indicates confidence. The stance of c towards t is predicted as:

$$Stance(c, t) = s_c \times \mathcal{R}(x_c, x_t) \times s_t \qquad (1)$$

Positive/negative prediction indicates *Pro/Con* stance. As before, the absolute value indicates confidence. Having an effective confidence measure is important for on-demand argument construction, where we typically want to present to the user only high-confidence predictions, or rank them higher in the output.

Bar-Haim et al. assumed that the topic target x_t and sentiment s_t are given as input, and developed three classifiers for predicting x_c, s_c and $\mathcal{R}(x_c, x_t)$. The system predicts the stance of the claim c towards the given topic target x_t (e.g., *the monarchy*) as $s_c \times \mathcal{R}(x_c, x_t)$. The result is multiplied by the given topic target sentiment s_t to obtain $Stance(c, t)$.[1]

---

[1] For example, a claim in favor of *the monarchy* is *Pro* for *"The monarchy should be preserved"*, and *Con* for *"The monarchy should be abolished"* with s_t=+1/-1, respectively.

Most relevant to our work is the sentiment classifier, which predicts the sentiment s_c towards the target x_c. It is based on matching sentiment terms from a lexicon, detecting polarity flips by sentiment shifters, and aggregating sentiment scores for matched terms, which decay based on their distance from the target.

The claim stance classification dataset introduced by Bar-Haim et al. includes 2,394 claims, manually found in Wikipedia articles for 55 topics, their stance (*Pro/Con*), and fine-grained annotations for targets (x_t, x_c), sentiments (s_t, s_c) and target relations $(\mathcal{R}(x_c, x_t))$.

In this dataset, 94.4% of the claims were found to be compatible with the above modeling, out of which 20% of the claims have contrastive targets. Since identifying contrastive targets with high precision is hard, the implemented relation classifier only predicts $\mathcal{R}(x_c, x_t) \in [0, 1]$, (i.e., always predicts *consistent*). Even so, multiplying by the classifier's confidence improves the accuracy of top predictions, since it ranks claims with consistent targets higher; this reduces stance classification errors caused by contrastive targets.

3 Lexicon Expansion

To obtain a wide-coverage sentiment lexicon that also includes weak sentiment, we took the following approach. Given a seed lexicon, we trained a classifier to predict the sentiment polarity for unseen words. We trained the classifier over the words in the lexicon, where the feature vector was the word embedding and the label was its polarity.

We started with the Opinion Lexicon (Hu and Liu, 2004), used in the baseline system, as a seed sentiment lexicon containing 6,789 words. For word embeddings, we trained a skip-gram model (Mikolov et al., 2013) over Wikipedia, using `word2vec`. With the 200-dimensional word embedding feature vectors and labels from the lexicon, we trained a linear SVM classifier (LIBLINEAR, Fan et al., 2008). Following Rothe et al. (2016), we only trained on high-frequency words (4,861 words with frequency > 300).

We checked the classifier's accuracy with a leave-one-out experiment over the original lexicon. For each word in the lexicon, which also had a word embedding (6,438 words), we trained our classifier on the remaining frequent words and tested the prediction of the held-out word. The resulting accuracy was 90.5%.

After removing single character terms and terms containing non-alphabetic characters, we predicted sentiment for the remaining 938,559 terms with word embeddings. The predicted SVM scores are roughly in $[-3, 3]$, and we adapted max-min scaling to return sentiment scores in $[-1, 1]$ (the sentiment scores in the seed lexicon are either 1 or -1).

To obtain a more compact lexicon, we applied a filtering step using WordNet relations (Miller, 1995; Fellbaum, 1998). For each term in the expanded lexicon, we looked up all its synsets. Then, for each of those synsets we collected all terms in the synset along with the terms that are derivationally related, hypernyms, or antonyms. Next, we looked up each of the terms from this collection in the seed lexicon and counted the number of positive and negative matches (the polarity of the antonyms was reversed). If the term had no matches, or the majority count did not agree with the SVM prediction, the term was discarded. This filter drastically reduced the expanded lexicon size to only 28,670 terms (including the seed lexicon), while achieving similar performance on the stance classification task.

4 Contextual Features

Following the assumption that neighboring texts tend to agree on sentiment, we enhanced the system to use the claim's context.

We trained a linear SVM classifier, which includes the baseline system (with the expanded lexicon) as a feature, together with a set of contextual features, described below. Similar to the baseline system, the classifier aims to predict the stance towards the topic target x_t, and the result is multiplied by the given s_t to obtain $Stance(c, t)$.[2]

We employed the following features.

Header Features: Each article in Wikipedia is divided into titled sections, subsections and sub-subsections. We assume the sentiment is shared by the section header and the claims presented in the section. For example, a claim under the *"Criticism"* section is usually of negative sentiment, while the header *"Advantages"* would govern positive claims. We considered the headers of the claim's enclosing section, subsection and sub-subsection. The sentiment of each header was taken as a feature. In addition, we performed

a Fisher Exact Test (Agresti, 1992) on the training data and composed two short lists of prevalent header words that were found to be the most significantly associated with positive (or negative) claims in their sections. The difference between the number of positive and negative words appearing in the claim's enclosing headers was taken as an additional feature.[3]

Claim Sentence: In some cases, the claim's enclosing sentence contains helpful cues for the claim polarity (e.g., in: *"Unfortunately, it's clear that <claim>"*). Therefore, the sentiment score of the entire sentence also served as a feature.[4]

Neighboring Sentences: We computed the average sentiment score of sentences preceding and following the claim sentence in the same paragraph. Specifically, we considered the maximal set of consecutive sentences that do not contain contrastive discourse markers and terms indicating controversy (listed in Table 1, row 2). If the claim sentence itself contained certain terms indicating contrast or controversy (Table 1, row 1), the context was ignored and the feature value was set to zero.

Neighboring Claims: Neighboring claims tend to agree on sentiment : in article sections that include more than one claim in our training data, 88% of the claims shared the majority polarity. Thus, we clustered the claims so that each pair in the same paragraph shared a cluster unless a term indicating potential polarity flip was found before the two claims or between them. The polarity flip indicators considered between/before the claims are listed in Table 1, rows 2/3, respectively. For example, consider the following claim pairs:

(5) <u>While</u> **adoption can provide stable families to children in need**, it is also suggested that **adoption in the immediate aftermath of a trauma might not be the best option**.

(6) **Democracy is far from perfect.** <u>However,</u> **it's the best form of government created so far**.

In both cases, the underlined discourse marker indicates a polarity shift between the claims (shown in **bold**), so the claims are not clustered together. For each claim, we summed the sentiment scores

---

[2] Accordingly, the training labels were $\frac{Stance(c,t)}{s_t}$.

[3] The positive words are *support, benefit, overview, pro, growth, reform,* and the negative words are *criticism, anti, failure, abuse, dissent, corrupt, opposite, disadvantage*.

[4] Since the whole sentence is likely to have the same target x_c as the claim itself, we multiplied this feature by the consistent/contrastive relation score $\mathcal{R}(x_c, x_t)$.

#	Context	Terms
1	Claim Sentence	though, although, even if, dispute, but, while, challenge, criticize, incorrect, wrong, however
2	Surrounding Sentences/ Between Claims	dispute, disagree, although, though, nevertheless, otherwise, but, nonetheless, notwithstanding, in contrast, after all, opponent[s] claim, however, on the other hand, on the contrary, contend
3	Before Claims	though, although, even if, dispute, but, while

Table 1: Contrast and controversy indicators considered for each context type by the *neighboring sentences* feature (rows 1+2), and the *neighboring claims* feature (rows 2+3).

5 Evaluation

We followed the experimental setup of Bar-Haim et al., including the train/test split of the dataset and the evaluation measures, and predicted the majority class in the train set with a constant, very low confidence when the classifier's output was zero. The training set contained 25 topics (1,039 claims), and the test set contained 30 topics (1,355 claims).

The evaluation explored the trade-off between *accuracy* (fraction of correct stance predictions) and *coverage* (fraction of claims for which we make a non-zero prediction). This tradeoff was controlled by setting a minimum confidence threshold for making a prediction. Given a coverage level β, Accuracy@β is defined as the maximal accuracy such that the corresponding coverage is at least β, found by exhaustive search over the threshold values. Coverage and accuracy for each threshold are macro-averaged over the tested topics.

The results are summarized in Table 2. Rows (1-2) quote the two best-performing configurations reported by Bar-Haim et al. The first is the baseline configuration used in this work, which performed best on lower coverage rates. The second is a combination of the baseline system and an SVM with unigram features, which was the best performer on higher coverage rates. Row 3 is our rerun of the baseline system. The results are close to the EACL '17 results (row 1) but not identical. This is due to some changes in low-level tools used by the system, such as the wikifier.[5]

The configurations in rows 4-6 are the contributions of this work. Row 4 reports the results for the baseline system with the expanded lexicon (Section 3). Like the baseline system, this configuration only considers the claim itself. The results show substantial improvements over the baseline (row 3), as well as the best previously reported results (rows 1-2). The expanded lexicon increased the (macro-averaged) coverage of the system from 78.2% to 98.1%.

The next two configurations use increasingly richer contexts, in addition to using the expanded lexicon. Row 5 shows the results for the classifier described in Section 4, using all the contextual features except for the *neighboring claims* feature. We refer to this feature set as *local contextual features*. The results show that these features achieve further improvement.

Last, row 6 shows the results for adding the *neighboring claims* feature, which achieves the best results. This configuration requires additional knowledge about other claims in the proximity of the given claim. While in this experiment the labeled data provides perfect knowledge about neighboring claims, in actual implementations of argument construction pipelines this information is obtained from the imperfect output of a claim detection module.

Overall, our results represent significant advancement of the state-of-the-art for this task, both for lower coverage rates (top predictions) and over the whole dataset (Accuracy@1.0).

6 Related Work

Stance classification has been applied to several different means of argumentation, for example congressional debates (Thomas et al., 2006; Yessenalina et al., 2010) or online discussions (Somasundaran and Wiebe, 2009; Walker et al., 2012b; Hasan and Ng, 2013). Some previous

over all other claims in its cluster. Note that this feature requires additional information about other claims for the topic.

---

[5]As explained by Bar-Haim et al. (2017), the baseline results (rows 1,3) for each coverage level$\geq$ 0.8 are the same, since they all add the default majority class predictions.

#	Configuration	Accuracy@Coverage									
		0.1	0.2	0.3	0.4	0.5	0.6	0.7	0.8	0.9	1.0
1	Baseline (EACL'17)	0.849	0.847	0.836	0.793	0.767	0.740	0.704	0.632	0.632	0.632
2	Baselne+SVM (EACL'17)	0.784	0.758	0.749	0.743	0.730	0.711	0.682	0.671	0.658	0.645
3	Baseline (Rerun)	0.846	0.841	0.823	0.787	0.771	0.742	0.706	0.633	0.633	0.633
4	+Lexicon Expansion	0.899	0.867	0.844	0.803	0.765	0.749	0.731	0.705	0.697	0.677
5	+Local Contextual Features	0.935	0.892	0.866	0.833	0.805	0.773	0.749	0.729	0.704	0.690
6	+Neighboring Claims	0.954	0.935	0.882	0.856	0.811	0.776	0.764	0.734	0.708	0.691

Table 2: Stance classification results. Majority baseline Accuracy@1.0=51.9%

work has improved stance classification by using the conversation structure (e.g., discussion reply links) (Walker et al., 2012a; Sridhar et al., 2015) or by applying classification to groups of arguments linked by citations or agreement/disagreement (Burfoot et al., 2011; Sridhar et al., 2014). However, many features used in previous works were not available for our task. Instead, we leveraged other context information present in Wikipedia articles, and assume sentiment agreement across neighboring text fragments.

A number of approaches in the literature can generate sentiment lexicons (Hatzivassiloglou and McKeown, 1997; Turney and Littman, 2003), many of which rely on graph-based approaches over WordNet (Hu and Liu, 2004; Esuli and Sebastiani, 2006; Blair-Goldensohn et al., 2008) or over a graph of distributionally similar n-grams (Velikovich et al., 2010). Our approach (Section 3) differs in that we leverage larger existing sentiment lexicons, instead of relying on small seed sets. Moreover, we opt for classifying word embeddings instead of graph-based approaches, which are sensitive to parameter settings.

More similar recent work includes Amir et al. (2015), who also used manually-created sentiment lexicons (annotated with discrete sentiment levels) and word embeddings to train linear regression models that aim to predict the polarity and intensity of new terms. Out of the tested methods, *Support Vector Regression* was found to perform best. However, they did not filter the resulting lexicon.

7 Conclusion

We addressed two of the main limitations of previous work on claim stance classification: insufficient coverage of manually-composed sentiment lexicons, and ignoring the claim's context. We presented a lexicon expansion method and a set of effective contextual features, which together significantly advance the state-of-the-art. A remain-

ing challenge is accurate prediction of contrastive targets, which seems crucial for further substantial improvement over the whole dataset.

Acknowledgments

We would like to thank Francesco Dinuzzo for his contribution to the initial stages of this work. We also thank Francesca Bonin for her helpful feedback on this work.

References

Alan Agresti. 1992. A survey of exact inference for contingency tables. *Statistical science* pages 131–153.

Silvio Amir, Ramón Astudillo, Wang Ling, Bruno Martins, Mario J. Silva, and Isabel Trancoso. 2015. Inesc-id: A regression model for large scale twitter sentiment lexicon induction. In *Proceedings of the 9th International Workshop on Semantic Evaluation (SemEval 2015)*. Association for Computational Linguistics, Denver, Colorado, pages 613–618. http://www.aclweb.org/anthology/S15-2102.

Roy Bar-Haim, Indrajit Bhattacharya, Francesco Dinuzzo, Amrita Saha, and Noam Slonim. 2017. Stance classification of context-dependent claims. In *Proceedings of the 15th Conference of the European Chapter of the Association for Computational Linguistics: Volume 1, Long Papers*. Association for Computational Linguistics, Valencia, Spain, pages 251–261. http://www.aclweb.org/anthology/E17-1024.

Sasha Blair-Goldensohn, Tyler Neylon, Kerry Hannan, George A. Reis, Ryan Mcdonald, and Jeff Reynar. 2008. Building a sentiment summarizer for local service reviews. In *NLP in the Information Explosion Era*.

Clinton Burfoot, Steven Bird, and Timothy Baldwin. 2011. Collective classification of congressional floor-debate transcripts. In *Proceedings of the 49th Annual Meeting of the Association for Computational Linguistics: Human Language Technologies*. Association for Computational Linguistics, Portland, Oregon, USA, pages 1506–1515. http://www.aclweb.org/anthology/P11-1151.

Andrea Esuli and Fabrizio Sebastiani. 2006. SENTI-WORDNET: A publicly available lexical resource for opinion mining. In *Proceedings of the 5th Conference on Language Resources and Evaluation (LREC '06)*. pages 417–422.

Rong-En Fan, Kai-Wei Chang, Cho-Jui Hsieh, Xiang-Rui Wang, and Chih-Jen Lin. 2008. LIBLINEAR: A library for large linear classification. *Journal of Machine Learning Research* 9:1871–1874.

Christiane Fellbaum, editor. 1998. *WordNet: An Electronic Lexical Database*. The MIT Press, Cambridge, MA.

Kazi Saidul Hasan and Vincent Ng. 2013. Stance classification of ideological debates: Data, models, features, and constraints. In *Proceedings of the Sixth International Joint Conference on Natural Language Processing*. Asian Federation of Natural Language Processing, Nagoya, Japan, pages 1348–1356. http://www.aclweb.org/anthology/I13-1191.

Vasileios Hatzivassiloglou and Kathleen R. McKeown. 1997. Predicting the semantic orientation of adjectives. In *Proceedings of the 35th Annual Meeting of the Association for Computational Linguistics*. Association for Computational Linguistics, Madrid, Spain, pages 174–181. https://doi.org/10.3115/976909.979640.

Minqing Hu and Bing Liu. 2004. Mining and summarizing customer reviews. In *Proceedings of the Tenth ACM SIGKDD International Conference on Knowledge Discovery and Data Mining*. ACM, New York, NY, USA, KDD '04, pages 168–177. https://doi.org/10.1145/1014052.1014073.

Ran Levy, Yonatan Bilu, Daniel Hershcovich, Ehud Aharoni, and Noam Slonim. 2014. Context dependent claim detection. In *Proceedings of COLING 2014, the 25th International Conference on Computational Linguistics: Technical Papers*. Dublin City University and Association for Computational Linguistics, Dublin, Ireland, pages 1489–1500. http://www.aclweb.org/anthology/C14-1141.

Tomas Mikolov, Ilya Sutskever, Kai Chen, Greg Corrado, and Jeffrey Dean. 2013. Distributed representations of words and phrases and their compositionality. In *Proceedings of the 26th International Conference on Neural Information Processing Systems*. Curran Associates Inc., USA, NIPS'13, pages 3111–3119. http://dl.acm.org/citation.cfm?id=2999792.2999959.

George A. Miller. 1995. Wordnet: A lexical database for english. *Commun. ACM* 38(11):39–41. https://doi.org/10.1145/219717.219748.

Ruty Rinott, Lena Dankin, Carlos Alzate Perez, Mitesh M. Khapra, Ehud Aharoni, and Noam Slonim. 2015. Show me your evidence - an automatic method for context dependent evidence detection. In *Proceedings of the 2015 Conference on Empirical Methods in Natural Language Processing*. Association for Computational Linguistics, Lisbon, Portugal, pages 440–450. http://aclweb.org/anthology/D15-1050.

Sascha Rothe, Sebastian Ebert, and Hinrich Schütze. 2016. Ultradense word embeddings by orthogonal transformation. In *Proceedings of the 2016 Conference of the North American Chapter of the Association for Computational Linguistics: Human Language Technologies*. Association for Computational Linguistics, San Diego, California, pages 767–777. http://www.aclweb.org/anthology/N16-1091.

Swapna Somasundaran and Janyce Wiebe. 2009. Recognizing stances in online debates. In *Proceedings of the Joint Conference of the 47th Annual Meeting of the ACL and the 4th International Joint Conference on Natural Language Processing of the AFNLP*. Association for Computational Linguistics, Suntec, Singapore, pages 226–234. http://www.aclweb.org/anthology/P/P09/P09-1026.

Dhanya Sridhar, James Foulds, Bert Huang, Lise Getoor, and Marilyn Walker. 2015. Joint models of disagreement and stance in online debate. In *Proceedings of the 53rd Annual Meeting of the Association for Computational Linguistics and the 7th International Joint Conference on Natural Language Processing (Volume 1: Long Papers)*. Association for Computational Linguistics, Beijing, China, pages 116–125. http://www.aclweb.org/anthology/P15-1012.

Dhanya Sridhar, Lise Getoor, and Marilyn Walker. 2014. Collective stance classification of posts in online debate forums. In *Proceedings of the Joint Workshop on Social Dynamics and Personal Attributes in Social Media*. Association for Computational Linguistics, Baltimore, Maryland, pages 109–117. http://www.aclweb.org/anthology/W14-2715.

Matt Thomas, Bo Pang, and Lillian Lee. 2006. Get out the vote: Determining support or opposition from congressional floor-debate transcripts. In *Proceedings of the 2006 Conference on Empirical Methods in Natural Language Processing*. Association for Computational Linguistics, Sydney, Australia, pages 327–335. http://www.aclweb.org/anthology/W/W06/W06-1639.

Peter D. Turney and Michael L. Littman. 2003. Measuring praise and criticism: Inference of semantic orientation from association. *ACM Trans. Inf. Syst.* 21(4):315–346. https://doi.org/10.1145/944012.944013.

Leonid Velikovich, Sasha Blair-Goldensohn, Kerry Hannan, and Ryan McDonald. 2010. The viability of web-derived polarity lexicons. In

Human Language Technologies: The 2010 Annual Conference of the North American Chapter of the Association for Computational Linguistics. Association for Computational Linguistics, Los Angeles, California, pages 777–785. http://www.aclweb.org/anthology/N10-1119.

Marilyn Walker, Pranav Anand, Rob Abbott, and Ricky Grant. 2012a. Stance classification using dialogic properties of persuasion. In *Proceedings of the 2012 Conference of the North American Chapter of the Association for Computational Linguistics: Human Language Technologies*. Association for Computational Linguistics, Montréal, Canada, pages 592–596. http://www.aclweb.org/anthology/N12-1072.

Marilyn A. Walker, Pranav Anand, Rob Abbott, Jean E. Fox Tree, Craig Martell, and Joseph King. 2012b. That is your evidence?: Classifying stance in online political debate. *Decis. Support Syst.* 53(4):719–729. https://doi.org/10.1016/j.dss.2012.05.032.

Ainur Yessenalina, Yisong Yue, and Claire Cardie. 2010. Multi-level structured models for document-level sentiment classification. In *Proceedings of the 2010 Conference on Empirical Methods in Natural Language Processing*. Association for Computational Linguistics, Cambridge, MA, pages 1046–1056. http://www.aclweb.org/anthology/D10-1102.

Mining Argumentative Structure from Natural Language text using Automatically Generated Premise-Conclusion Topic Models

John Lawrence and **Chris Reed**
Centre for Argument Technology,
University of Dundee, UK

Abstract

This paper presents a method of extracting argumentative structure from natural language text. The approach presented is based on the way in which we understand an argument being made, not just from the words said, but from existing contextual knowledge and understanding of the broader issues. We leverage high-precision, low-recall techniques in order to automatically build a large corpus of inferential statements related to the text's topic. These statements are then used to produce a matrix representing the inferential relationship between different aspects of the topic. From this matrix, we are able to determine connectedness and directionality of inference between statements in the original text. By following this approach, we obtain results that compare favourably to those of other similar techniques to classify premise-conclusion pairs (with results 22 points above baseline), but without the requirement of large volumes of annotated, domain specific data.

1 Introduction

The continuing growth in the volume of data which we produce has driven efforts to unlock the wealth of information this data contains. Automatic techniques such as Opinion Mining and Sentiment Analysis (Liu, 2010) allow us to determine the views expressed in a piece of textual data, for example, whether a product review is positive or negative. Existing techniques struggle, however, to identify more complex structural relationships between concepts.

Argument Mining is the automatic identification of the argumentative structure contained within a piece of natural language text. By automatically identifying this structure and its associated premises and conclusions, we are able to tell not just *what* views are being expressed, but also *why* those particular views are held. Argument mining has recently been enjoying rapid growth, propelled by three drivers: first, the academic and commercial success of opinion mining and sentiment analysis techniques upon which argument mining builds; second, a strong commercial appetite for such technologies from companies such as IBM; and third, the development of infrastructure and tools for (Bex et al., 2013), and theoretical understanding of (Budzynska et al., 2014), argument structure in both monologue and dialogue.

The intuition underlying the work presented here is that there are rich and predictable thematic and lexical commonalities present in the expression of human reasoning, and that these commonalities can be identified in helping to extract the structure of reasoning. For example, in debates concerning abortion, arguments are carefully marshalled on both sides, with religious themes more typically appearing on one side, and feminist philosophy themes more typically on the other. For a debate on the construction of a new road, we may find environmental issues on one side and economic concerns on the other. If such generalisations are possible at a coarse scale, perhaps they are similarly possible at a more fine-grained scale.

These themes are represented in terms of both the topics discussed and the language used to express them: an anti-abortion stance is likely to cover, not just feminist philosophy themes in general, but to use specific terminology more frequently, perhaps mentioning 'choice' or 'freedom' more than views expressed on the other side. When humans hear such a debate, they understand the structure of the arguments being made not only based on the content of the argument itself, but

Proceedings of the 4th Workshop on Argument Mining, pages 39–48
Copenhagen, Denmark, September 8, 2017. ©2017 Association for Computational Linguistics

on a broad general knowledge of the topic and the way in which such arguments are commonly presented.

The argument mining technique which we present in this paper takes the commonly occurring terms in the original text and then uses these terms to gather data from the web on the same topic. This large volume of additional data can be considered as contextual knowledge, and is processed to find pairs of text spans which have an inferential relationship. We then use these pairs to create premise-conclusion topic models, reflecting the ways in which one topic or phraseology is used to support another.

Previous work (Lawrence and Reed, 2015) has shown that discourse indicators such as *because* and *therefore* are very reliable predictors of argument structure. Unfortunately they are also rather rare, occurring with fewer than 10% of argumentative inference steps. With a high-precision/low-recall technique such as is provided by these indicators, it becomes possible to process large amounts of text to extract a dataset in which we can have high confidence. This dataset can be used to capture topical regularities in the argument structure which can then be exploited in analysing text which does not benefit from the presence of indicators.

2 Related Work

The majority of the work carried out to date in the field of argument mining, has used either a supervised learning approach (e.g. (Palau and Moens, 2009; Feng and Hirst, 2011; Stab and Gurevych, 2014)), or a linguistic rule-based approach ((Villalba and Saint-Dizier, 2012; Pallotta and Delmonte, 2011; Wyner et al., 2012)), to determine argumentative function. In both cases these efforts are limited by a lack of consistently annotated argument data. Whilst resources such as the Internet Argument Corpus (IAC) (Walker et al., 2012) and AIFdb (Lawrence et al., 2012), offer rapidly growing volumes of high quality argument analyses, they do not provide the large volumes of data required to train a robust classifier, particularly when considered in the context of a specific topic or domain.

Attempts have been made to mitigate this constraint by the automatic creation of argument corpora, however, the datasets produced are limited to very specific types of data. For example, in (Houngbo and Mercer, 2014), a straightforward feature of co-referring text using the word "this" is used to build a self-annotating corpus extracted from a large biomedical research paper dataset. This is achieved by collecting pairs of sequential sentences where the second sentence begins with "This method...", "This result...", or "This conclusion...", and then categorising the first sentence in each pair respectively as Method, Result or Conclusion sentences.

Similarly, in (Habernal and Gurevych, 2015), unsupervised features are developed for argument component identification which exploit clustering of unlabelled argumentative data from online debate portals. Al-Khatib et al. (2016) likewise leverage online debate portals, applying distant supervision to automatically create a large annotated corpus with argumentative and non-argumentative text segments from several domains.

Our approach to expanding the data available on the topic under discussion relies on the high precision identification of inferential relationships shown by the presence of discourse indicators. Discourse indicators are explicitly stated linguistic expressions of the relationship between statements (Webber et al., 2011), and, when present, can provide a clear indication of argumentative structure. For example, if we take the sentence "Britain should disarm because it would set a good example for other countries", then this can be split into two separate propositions "Britain should disarm" and "it [disarming] would set a good example for other countries". The presence of the word "because" between these two propositions clearly tells us that the second is a reason for the first.

Discourse indicators have been previously used as a component of argument mining techniques, for example in (Stab and Gurevych, 2014) indicators are used as a feature in multiclass classification of argument components, with each clause classified as a major claim, claim, premise or non-argumentative. Similar indicators are used in (Wyner et al., 2012), along with domain terminology (e.g. camera names and properties) to highlight potential argumentative sections of online product reviews. In (Eckle-Kohler et al., 2015) a German language corpus is annotated with arguments according to the common claim-premise model of argumentation and the connection between these annotated connections and the presence of discourse indicators (or discourse markers as they are referred to here) is investigated. The results presented show that discourse markers are again important features for the discrimination of claims and premises in German as well as English language texts.

There are many different ways in which indicators can appear, and a wide range of relations which they can suggest (Knott, 1996). For automatic corpus construction, the ability to identify all of these connections is not relevant and we are able to concentrate solely on those indicators offering a very high chance of describing an inferential relationship.

Using discourse indicators to build such a corpus is supported by the work done in identifying implicit discourse relations, for example (Lin et al., 2009; Park and Cardie, 2012), where a range of relations labelled in the Penn Discourse Tree-Bank (Prasad et al., 2008), but not explicitly indicated, were identified using features from those relations where an explicit indicator did occur. These implicit relations were identified with accuracies of between 70-80% in one-vs-others tests, clearly suggesting that studying cases where indicators are present can give a strong indication of a relationship in those cases where they are omitted.

The relationship between the topics being expressed in a piece of text and the argumentative structure which it contains have been previously explored in (Lawrence et al., 2014), where a Latent Dirichlet Allocation (LDA) topic model is used to determine the topical similarity of consecutive propositions in a piece of text. The intuition is that if a proposition is similar to its predecessor then there exists some argumentative link between them, whereas if there is low similarity between a proposition and its predecessor, the author is going back to address a previously made point and, in this case, the proposition is compared to all those preceding it to determine whether they should be connected. Using this method a precision of 0.72, and recall of 0.77 are recorded when comparing the resulting structure to a manual analysis, however it should be noted that what is being identified here is merely that an inference relationship exists between two propositions, and no indication is given as to the direction of this inference.

3   Experimental Data

The data used in this paper is taken from a transcript of the BBC Radio 4 program *Moral*
Maze[1]. Specifically, we look at the episode from July 4th 2012[2] on the morality of the banking system. Manual argumentative analysis was performed on the transcript, using the OVA+ (Online Visualisation of Argument) analysis tool (Janier et al., 2014) to create a series of argument maps capturing the structure using the Argument Interchange Format (AIF) (Chesñevar et al., 2006). A corpus containing the full manual analysis of the transcript can be found online at `http://corpora.aifdb.org/bankingsystem`. The corpus comprises 5,768 words, split across 327 propositions, with 128 inferential connections (premise/conclusion relations) between them.

Identifying the argumentative structure contained within a piece of text can be viewed as a two-step process: Firstly, identifying the individual units of discourse which the text contains (commonly referred to as 'Argumentative Discourse Units' or ADUs (Peldszus and Stede, 2013)); and then, determining the ways in which these propositions are connected.

Figure 1 shows the AIF compliant representation of a fragment of the Moral Maze dialogue. In this figure, the blue boxes represent individual ADUs, while the arrows show connections, and the diamonds detail the nature of these connections. In this case, the conclusion "I know bankers who behave absolutely splendidly" is supported by the individual premises "who are major benefactors", "who spend their Christmases manning soup kitchens", and "Think about Bill Gates and all the wonderful things that his money is doing".

We can see from this example that the broad concept of charitable works is being used to support the idea that bankers are good people. The knowledge that these premises are both thematically related and support the character of a group of people, whilst clear to a human analyst, is not explicitly indicated in the original text.

For our purposes, we are aiming to identify inferential connections between pairs of ADUs. Whilst a complete argument mining pipeline would require the automation of this segmentation, this is outside the scope of this paper, and the focus of much additional research within the argument mining field (Lawrence et al., 2014; Mad-

---

[1] `http://www.bbc.co.uk/programmes/b006qk11`

[2] `http://www.bbc.co.uk/programmes/b01kbj37`

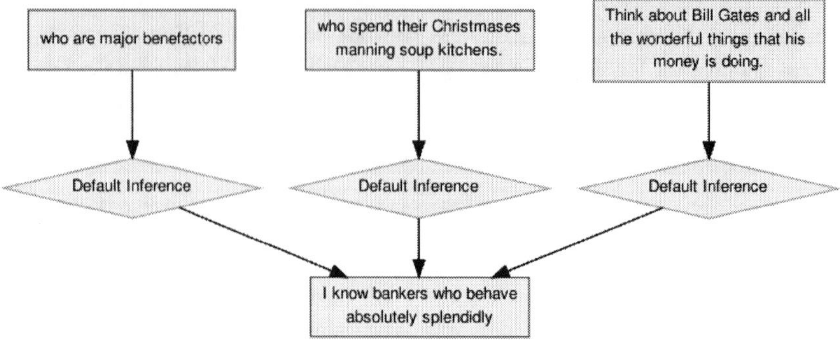

Figure 1: Fragment of Manually Analysed Argument Structure from the BBC Radio 4 program *Moral Maze*

nani et al., 2012; Saint-Dizier, 2012). As such, we use the same segmentation carried out for the manual analysis, and split the possible ADU pairs into those which are connected by an inferential relationship, and those which are not.

4 Implementation

An overview of the methodology used can be seen in Figure 2. Starting with raw, natural language text, manual segmentation is performed to split the text into ADUs. From here these segments are examined in order to find those unigrams and bigrams which occur most frequently throughout the text, giving an indication of the overall theme of the text which we are working with.

The next step is then to build a corpus of related documents by searching the web for those unigram and bigram terms identified as being indicative of the theme. From this extended corpus, we then extract sentences which contain an inferential relationship by searching for those discourse indicators which we have found to have the highest precision. This search results in a large collection of pairs of text fragments where one of the pair is a premise supporting the other.

Using these fragments as documents, we then generate a Latent Dirichlet Allocation (LDA) (Blei et al., 2003) topic model, and from this create a matrix showing the probability of support between each of the identified topics. By matching pairs of ADUs from the original text against the probabilities in this matrix, we are then able to determine the probability that there is an inferential relationship between them, and by thresholding these values, we can then categorise ADU pairs as being 'inferential' or 'non-inferential'.

An alternative approach would be to use the premise/conclusion dataset as training data for a supervised machine learning approach. This is limited by the fact that we only obtain positive examples, and, whilst techniques such as PU-learning (Learning from Positive and Unlabelled examples) (Liu et al., 2003) provide a way of dealing with only positively labelled data, we do not have sufficient quantities of unlabelled examples for these techniques to be applied. In future work, the ability to identify arbitrary ADUs in text could be used to extract large volumes of unlabelled examples, and such approaches may then become more suitable.

4.1 Obtaining Premise/Conclusion Pairs

The first step in the pipeline described above is to determine the overall theme of the text being analysed. This was performed by looking for those unigrams and bigrams which occur most frequently throughout the text. With the text previously segmented into ADUs, we calculated the number of unique ADUs in which each unigram or bigram appeared. This list is then sorted and filtered to remove common stop words. The resulting lists of terms can be seen in Table 1 and Table 2.

Having identified keywords describing the topic, a corpus of related documents was created by searching the web for combinations of these terms. The top ten terms of each kind were combined into search queries by taking all possible combinations of two and three unigrams as well as each bigram both on its own and paired with each unigram. Using these queries, the first 200 Google search results for each were compiled. After filtering the list of related documents to remove

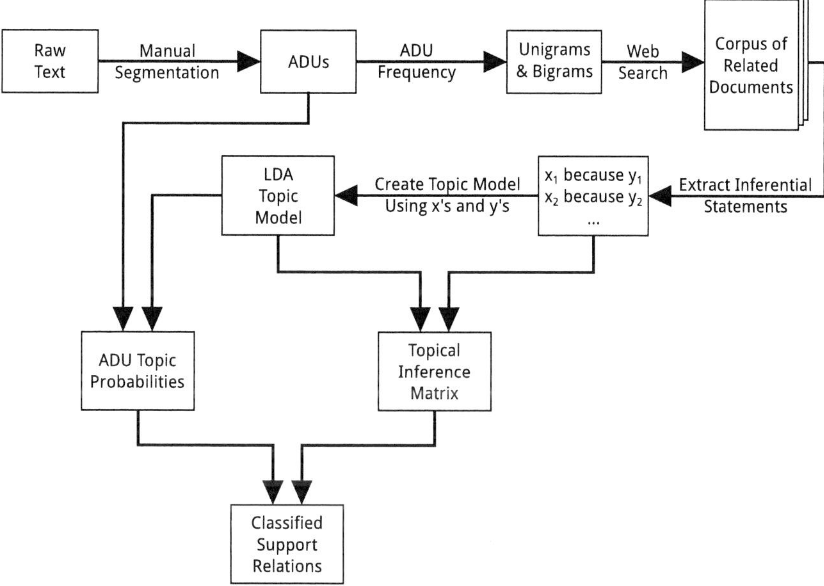

Figure 2: Overview of the Implementation Methodology for Creating Extended Corpus, Creating a Topical Inference Matrix and Classifying Support Relations

Unigram	Count
investment	39
banking	35
banks	28
money	27
problem	16
capitalism	13
culture	12
behaviour	12
rules	12
ethical	10

Table 1: Top ten unigrams by number of ADUs in which they appear

Bigram	Count
investment banks	18
investment banking	12
common good	5
immoral behaviour	3
free market	3
banking industry	3
wealth creation	3
redeemed capitalism	2
moral code	2
dutch bankers	2

Table 2: Top ten bigrams by number of ADUs in which they appear

duplicates, a total of 6,981 pages remained.

Although the pages identified in the previous step are high ranking search results for the terms identified, such pages commonly contain material unrelated to the topic, for example, advertisements and summaries of other articles. In order to extract those sections of the documents most likely to contain the body of an article, the Python *Beautiful Soup* library[3] was used to parse the HTML and extract consecutive paragraphs of text.

These paragraphs were then split into sentences, using the NLTK[4] tokeniser, and each of the resulting sentences searched for the presence of a discourse indicator. Previous work using discourse indicators to identify argumentative structure (Lawrence and Reed, 2015) has shown that, although not common enough to give a full representation of the structure, when present, discourse indicators give a very clear indication of the argumentative connection between two spans of text. As our aim is to extract only those sentences most likely to contain an inferential relationship, we first looked more closely at the relative performance of different indicators. Based on analysis of a separate *Moral Maze* episode, we identified those indicators showing the highest precision (the

---

[3]http://www.crummy.com/software/BeautifulSoup/
[4]http://www.nltk.org/

Indicator	Precision	Recall
therefore	0.95	0.0004
because	0.91	0.0031
consequently	0.82	0.0001
hence	0.76	0.0001
accordingly	0.74	0.0002
so	0.73	0.0005
after	0.69	0.0011
since	0.65	0.0008
then	0.58	0.0013
for	0.57	0.0006

Table 3: Top ten discourse indicators sorted by precision

precision and recall for the top ten indicators can be seen in Table 3). These results show that, when present, "therefore" and "because" give the highest indication of inference with a significant drop in accuracy for the remaining indicators. As such, we limited our generated corpus to only those sentences containing one of these two words.

Where the number of words either before or after the matching indicator was less than 5, the sentence was discarded. After carrying out this process, a total of 7,162 inferential sentences were identified (6,288 containing "because" and 874 containing "therefore"), giving a dataset of premise conclusion pairs, either *premise **therefore** conclusion* or *conclusion **because** premise*.

Whilst we do not have 100% precision for either of the discourse indicators used, the impact of this is mitigated by the way in which the resulting pairs are subsequently used. The use of the topic models described in the next section means that we neither need *all* of the inferential relations contained within our search results, or for *every* premise conclusion pair to be correctly labelled as such. The models which we produce may have a small amount of noise generated by false-positives, but these either comprise topics which are not then matched to elements from the original text, or add a small number of lower importance terms to a valid topic.

4.2 Creating the Topical Inference Matrix

To extract the topical nature of the premise conclusion pairs previously identified, a Latent Dirichlet allocation (LDA) topic model was created using the Python gensim library[5]. To produce this

---

[5] https://radimrehurek.com/gensim/

topic model, the sentences were first split where the indicator occurred, giving two documents for each sentence (one representing a premise, and the other, the conclusion). For our experiments, the model was created with forty topics using 20 passes over the supplied corpus.

From the probability distributions for each pair of conclusion (C) and premise (P), a topical inference matrix (T) was created, where the i,jth entry in the matrix corresponds to the product of probabilities that the premise has topic i and the conclusion topic j. For example, in the simplest case, if there is a probability of 1.0 that the premise has topic m and the conclusion topic n, then the matrix will contain 1.0 at m,n and zero for all other possible pairings. So, given topic distributions θ^C for the conclusion, and θ^P for the premise, T is defined thus:

$$t_{i,j} = \theta_i^P * \theta_j^C \tag{1}$$

To investigate the validity of our assumption that there would be a noticeable pattern in the relationships between topic and inference, we first created a combined topical inference matrix for each of the *because* relations identified, by summing all of the matrices resulting from these relations. We then looked at the entropy of this matrix calculated as the sum of the differences between each value in the matrix and the mean of all values. For the *because* matrix, the mean score was 3.67 and the total difference was 2275.58, giving an average difference of 1.42 for each item in the matrix from the mean value (with no relationship between topic and inference, this difference would be $\sim$0).

A corresponding matrix was then produced for the *therefore* relations, and the distance between the *because* and *therefore* matrices calculated. This calculation was performed by first scaling the values in each matrix to a value between zero and one, and then calculating the distance between the resulting matrices:

$$d(A, B) = \sqrt{\sum_{i=1}^{n} \sum_{j=1}^{n} (a_{i,j} - b_{i,j})^2} \tag{2}$$

For identical matrices, this distance would be zero, for a pair of 40×40 matrices where all entries have maximal difference, the distance would be 40, and for a pair of 40×40 matrices where all entries have an average difference of 0.5 (indicating no correlation between the two), the distance would be 28.29. The distance between the *because* and *therefore* matrices was calculated as 18.32, suggesting a positive correlation between the two. We are not aware of any other technique that can be used to quantify the significance between such datasets: our analysis indicates merely that there is indeed some pattern beyond random chance linking the two concepts.

Finally, the *because* and *therefore* matrices were summed to give an overall topical inference matrix.

5 Experiments

In order to test our original hypotheses that the thematic commonalities present in the expression of human reasoning can be identified and used to help determine the structure of that reasoning, a number of experiments were carried out to explore the effectiveness of using this data to determine both the direction of inference between two ADUs that are known to have an inferential relationship, and the connectedness of pairs of arbitrary ADUs.

5.1 Using the Topical Inference Matrix to determine directionality

The manual analysis of our original text contained 128 premise conclusion pairs. As an initial experiment, we investigated how well the produced topical inference matrix could determine the direction of the inference between these pairs. This was achieved by creating a test set containing each pair (a,b) and its reverse (b,a).

Two alternative methods were tested to classify these pairs as being 'inferential' or 'non-inferential'. In each case, the topic probabilities for the ADUs were first inferred from the LDA model and a score determined as to whether there was an inferential relationship. For the first method, (MaxTopic), the score was calculated by taking the highest probability topic for each ADU and using these to look up the corresponding value in the overall topical inference matrix:

$$S_{MaxTopic} = t_{max(\theta^P),max(\theta^C)} \qquad (3)$$

For the second method, (TopicDist), the values in the matrix were multiplied by the corresponding probabilities for each item in the pair and then summed to give an overall score.

$$S_{TopicDist} = \sum_{i=1}^{n} \sum_{j=1}^{n} t_{i,j} * \theta_i^P * \theta_j^C \qquad (4)$$

For each of these two methods, the resulting scores were then compared against the mean of all values in the matrix (mean = 3.15), over which a pair would be classified as being 'inferential', and below which, 'non-inferential'.

Method	Precision	Recall	F_1-score
Random Baseline	0.5	0.5	0.5
MaxTopic	0.51	0.82	0.63
TopicDist	**0.57**	**0.83**	**0.67**

Table 4: Results for the MaxTopic and TopicDist methods to determine directionality of inferential connections compared to the random baseline

The results for directionality can be seen in Table 4. The results show an improvement over the random baseline for both methods, however the improvement in precision is low when just looking at the highest scoring topic. One reason for this is that a reasonable percentage of pairs (twenty-five out of one hundred and twenty-six) have the same highest scoring topic for both items (i.e. a conclusion is being supported by a premise that is closely related). When these same topic pairs are removed, the precision increases to 0.56, comparable to the results for the weighted topic distribution. The results for using the weighted topic distribution are better, and suggest that even in cases where the main topic is similar, there is enough of a difference in the secondary topics to determine the directionality of the pair.

5.2 Using the Topical Inference Matrix to determine connectedness

The second experiment performed looked at whether the produced topical inference matrix could determine inferential connections between arbitrary pairs of ADUs. For this task, a dataset was created containing the known 126 premise conclusion pairs and an equal number of random, unconnected ADUs. The same two methods of classifying these pairs as being 'inferential' or 'non-inferential' were used as in the first experiment, and the results can be seen in Table 5.

The results show that the precision is increased for classifying pairs as being connected over the previous results for directionality.

Method	Precision	Recall	F_1-score
Random Baseline	0.5	0.5	0.5
MaxTopic	0.58	0.79	0.67
TopicDist	**0.60**	**0.82**	**0.69**

Table 5: Results for the MaxTopic and TopicDist methods to determine connectedness of ADU pairs

5.3 Thresholding Topical Values

The experiments presented so far have looked at the likelihood that one topic supports another in terms of its score relative to all other scores in the matrix. However, it is possible that for some topics the scores will generally be higher. For example, if a large number of propositions have a high probability of corresponding to topic n, then all the values in column n of the matrix will be disproportionately high. To overcome any problems caused by this kind of topical skew, we took each column of the matrix and divided each value by the sum of values in that column. This resulting scaled matrix was then used to perform the same experiments as previously. The results for both experiments combined are shown in Table 6.

Method	Precision	Recall	F_1-score
Directionality			
Random Baseline	0.5	0.5	0.5
MaxTopic	0.61	0.77	0.68
TopicDist	**0.65**	**0.78**	**0.71**
Connectedness			
Random Baseline	0.5	0.5	0.5
MaxTopic	0.59	0.75	0.66
TopicDist	**0.64**	**0.83**	**0.72**

Table 6: Results for the MaxTopic and TopicDist methods to determine connectedness and directionality using a thresholded inference matrix

In all cases, we can see that the precision is slightly improved, though (with the exception of the TopicDist results for connectedness) this is at the expense of recall.

6 Discussion

The results we have presented show in all cases that there is some correlation identified between the topics that a pair of ADUs have, and the nature of their potential inferential relationship. By looking at the topics of each item in the pair, we have been able to determine both connectivity and directionality of inference. Overall, the results are better for identifying connectedness than directionality, predominantly resulting from higher

similarity in topics for which the ADUs are connected (in a significant percentage of cases the maximum probability topic was the same).

Currently, the identification of relationships is limited to inferential relationships, and one area of development would be to extend this by examining those discourse indicators which show a conflict relationship. Additionally, no account is taken of the polarity or sentiment of the ADUs. Where we have a conclusion, 'C', and a premise, 'P', then there would be a high topical similarity between P and 'not P', and as such, an inference relationship would be assigned between them. This problem could be overcome by applying sentiment classification to the ADUs as a preliminary step, and where there is negation of one item in the pair, replacing an inference relationship with conflict. Expanding the scope of this technique to give a fuller indication of relations will be carried out in future work.

Although we focus on identifying patterns of inference within a single debate, there is nothing intrinsic to the approach that makes it a better fit for this domain than any other. The automatic determination of the domain being discussed requires only the original text, and from this we are able to build a dataset specific to that domain which, due to the reliability of discourse indicators, contains domain specific pairs that we can say with high confidence have an inferential relationship.

7 Conclusion

This work has demonstrated how by automatically creating large, high-confidence datasets of inferential pairs related to a specific topic, we can closely mirror one of the ways in which humans understand the complex interactions between the individual propositions expressed in a debate.

The approach presented is effective in tackling the challenging high-level pragmatic task of identifying both connectedness and directionality between argumentative discourse units, with results 22 points above baseline.

This outcome represents strong performance for this level of task (cf., for example, (Feng and Hirst, 2011; Peldszus, 2014)), giving results comparable to those of (Palau and Moens, 2009), where each Argument sentence was classified as either premise or conclusion with F_1-scores of 0.68 for classification as premise and 0.74 for conclusion. Furthermore, where existing approaches are often constrained in their generality by a lack of appropriately annotated, domain-specific, data, the same requirement does not apply in this case.

The results show a clear link between the words used to express an argument and its underlying structure, and strongly support the intuition that understanding the structure of an argument requires not only consideration of the text itself, but contextual knowledge and understanding of the broader issues. We see this work as a key component in a larger ensemble approach (Lawrence and Reed, 2015), mirroring the complex process followed by a human annotator whereby general domain knowledge, understanding of linguistic cues and familiarity with common patterns of reasoning are combined to understand the arguments being made.

Acknowledgements

This work was funded in part by EPSRC in the UK under grant EP/N014871/1.

References

Khalid Al-Khatib, Henning Wachsmuth, Hagen Matthias Stein, Jonas Köhler, and Benno Stein. 2016. Cross-domain mining of argumentative text through distant supervision. In *Proceedings of NAACL-HLT*. pages 1395–1404.

Floris Bex, John Lawrence, Mark Snaith, and Chris Reed. 2013. Implementing the argument web. *Communications of the ACM* 56(10):66–73.

David M. Blei, Aandrew Y. Ng, and Michael I. Jordan. 2003. Latent dirichlet allocation. *The Journal of Machine Learning Research* 3:993–1022.

Katarzyna Budzynska, Mathilde Janier, Chris Reed, Patrick Saint-Dizier, Manfred Stede, and Olena Yaskorska. 2014. A model for processing illocutionary structures and argumentation in debates. In *Proceedings of the 9th edition of the Language Resources and Evaluation Conference (LREC)*. pages 917–924.

Carlos Chesñevar, Sanjay Modgil, Iyad Rahwan, Chris Reed, Guillermo Simari, Matthew South, Gerard Vreeswijk, Steven Willmott, et al. 2006. Towards an argument interchange format. *The Knowledge Engineering Review* 21(04):293–316.

Judith Eckle-Kohler, Roland Kluge, and Iryna Gurevych. 2015. On the role of discourse markers for discriminating claims and premises in argumentative discourse. In *Proceedings of the 2015 Conference on Empirical Methods in Natural Language Processing (EMNLP)*. pages 2236–2242.

Vanessa Wei Feng and Graeme Hirst. 2011. Classifying arguments by scheme. In *Proceedings of the 49th Annual Meeting of the Association for Computational Linguistics: Human Language Technologies-Volume 1*. Association for Computational Linguistics, pages 987–996.

Ivan Habernal and Iryna Gurevych. 2015. Exploiting debate portals for semi-supervised argumentation mining in user-generated web discourse. In *Proceedings of the 2015 conference on Empirical Methods in Natural Language Processing (EMNLP)*. pages 2127–2137.

Hospice Houngbo and Robert Mercer. 2014. An automated method to build a corpus of rhetorically-classified sentences in biomedical texts. In *Proceedings of the First Workshop on Argumentation Mining*. Association for Computational Linguistics, Baltimore, Maryland, pages 19–23.

Mathilde Janier, John Lawrence, and Chris Reed. 2014. OVA+: An argument analysis interface. In S. Parsons, N. Oren, C. Reed, and F. Cerutti, editors, *Proceedings of the Fifth International Conference on Computational Models of Argument (COMMA 2014)*. IOS Press, Pitlochry, pages 463–464.

Alistair Knott. 1996. *A data-driven methodology for motivating a set of coherence relations*. Ph.D. thesis, Department of Artificial Intelligence, University of Edinburgh.

John Lawrence, Floris Bex, Chris Reed, and Mark Snaith. 2012. AIFdb: Infrastructure for the argument web. In *Proceedings of the Fourth International Conference on Computational Models of Argument (COMMA 2012)*. pages 515–516.

John Lawrence and Chris Reed. 2015. Combining argument mining techniques. In *Proceedings of the 2nd Workshop on Argumentation Mining*. Association for Computational Linguistics, Denver, CO, pages 127–136.

John Lawrence, Chris Reed, Colin Allen, Simon McAlister, and Andrew Ravenscroft. 2014. Mining arguments from 19th century philosophical texts using topic based modelling. In *Proceedings of the First Workshop on Argumentation Mining*. Association for Computational Linguistics, Baltimore, Maryland, pages 79–87.

Ziheng Lin, Min-Yen Kan, and Hwee Tou Ng. 2009. Recognizing implicit discourse relations in the penn discourse treebank. In *Proceedings of the 2009 Conference on Empirical Methods in Natural Language Processing: Volume 1-Volume 1*. Association for Computational Linguistics, pages 343–351.

Bing Liu. 2010. Sentiment analysis and subjectivity. *Handbook of natural language processing* 2:627–666.

Bing Liu, Yang Dai, Xiaoli Li, Wee Sun Lee, and Philip S Yu. 2003. Building text classifiers using positive and unlabeled examples. In *Proceedings of the Third IEEE International Conference on Data Mining (ICDM-03)*. IEEE, pages 179–186.

Nitin Madnani, Michael Heilman, Joel Tetreault, and Martin Chodorow. 2012. Identifying high-level organizational elements in argumentative discourse. In *Proceedings of the 2012 Conference of the North American Chapter of the Association for Computational Linguistics: Human Language Technologies*. Association for Computational Linguistics, pages 20–28.

Raquel M. Palau and Marie-Francine Moens. 2009. Argumentation mining: the detection, classification and structure of arguments in text. In *Proceedings of the 12th international conference on artificial intelligence and law*. ACM, pages 98–107.

Vincenzo Pallotta and Rodolfo Delmonte. 2011. Automatic argumentative analysis for interaction mining. *Argument & Computation* 2(2-3):77–106.

Joonsuk Park and Claire Cardie. 2012. Improving implicit discourse relation recognition through feature set optimization. In *Proceedings of the 13th Annual Meeting of the Special Interest Group on Discourse and Dialogue*. Association for Computational Linguistics, pages 108–112.

Andreas Peldszus. 2014. Towards segment-based recognition of argumentation structure in short texts. In *Proceedings of the First Workshop on Argumentation Mining*. Association for Computational Linguistics, Baltimore, Maryland, pages 88–97.

Andreas Peldszus and Manfred Stede. 2013. From argument diagrams to argumentation mining in texts: a survey. *International Journal of Cognitive Informatics and Natural Intelligence (IJCINI)* 7(1):1–31.

Rashmi Prasad, Nikhil Dinesh, Alan Lee, Eleni Miltsakaki, Livio Robaldo, Aravind K Joshi, and Bonnie L Webber. 2008. The penn discourse treebank 2.0. In *Proceedings of the 6th Language Resources and Evaluation Conference (LREC-2008)*.

Patrick Saint-Dizier. 2012. Processing natural language arguments with the <TextCoop> platform. *Argument & Computation* 3(1):49–82.

Christian Stab and Iryna Gurevych. 2014. Identifying argumentative discourse structures in persuasive essays. In *Proceedings of the 2014 Conference on Empirical Methods in Natural Language Processing (EMNLP)*. Association for Computational Linguistics, Doha, Qatar, pages 46–56.

Maria Paz G. Villalba and Patrick Saint-Dizier. 2012. Some facets of argument mining for opinion analysis. In *Proceedings of the Fourth International Conference on Computational Models of Argument (COMMA 2012)*. pages 23–34.

Marilyn A Walker, Jean E Fox Tree, Pranav Anand, Rob Abbott, and Joseph King. 2012. A corpus for research on deliberation and debate. In *Proceedings of the 8th edition of the Language Resources and Evaluation Conference (LREC)*. pages 812–817.

Bonnie Webber, Markus Egg, and Valia Kordoni. 2011. Discourse structure and language technology. *Natural Language Engineering* 18(4):437–490.

Adam. Wyner, Jodi. Schneider, Katie. Atkinson, and Trevor. Bench-Capon. 2012. Semi-automated argumentative analysis of online product reviews. In *Proceedings of the Fourth International Conference on Computational Models of Argument (COMMA 2012)*. pages 43–50.

Building an Argument Search Engine for the Web

Henning Wachsmuth   Martin Potthast   Khalid Al-Khatib   Yamen Ajjour
Jana Puschmann Jiani Qu Jonas Dorsch Viorel Morari Janek Bevendorff Benno Stein
Webis Group, Faculty of Media, Bauhaus-Universität Weimar, Germany
`<firstname>.<lastname>@uni-weimar.de`

Abstract

Computational argumentation is expected to play a critical role in the future of web search. To make this happen, many search-related questions must be revisited, such as how people query for arguments, how to mine arguments from the web, or how to rank them. In this paper, we develop an argument search framework for studying these and further questions. The framework allows for the composition of approaches to acquiring, mining, assessing, indexing, querying, retrieving, ranking, and presenting arguments while relying on standard infrastructure and interfaces. Based on the framework, we build a prototype search engine, called *args*, that relies on an initial, freely accessible index of nearly 300k arguments crawled from reliable web resources. The framework and the argument search engine are intended as an environment for collaborative research on computational argumentation and its practical evaluation.

1 Introduction

Web search has arrived at a high level of maturity, fulfilling many information needs on the first try. Today, leading search engines even answer factual queries directly, lifting the answers from relevant web pages (Pasca, 2011). However, as soon as there is not one single correct answer but many controversial opinions, getting an overview often takes long, since search engines offer little support. This is aggravated by what is now called fake news and alternative facts, requiring an assessment of the credibility of facts and their sources (Samadi et al., 2016). Computational argumentation is essential to improve the search experience in these regards.

The delivery of arguments for a given issue is seen as one of the main applications of computa-

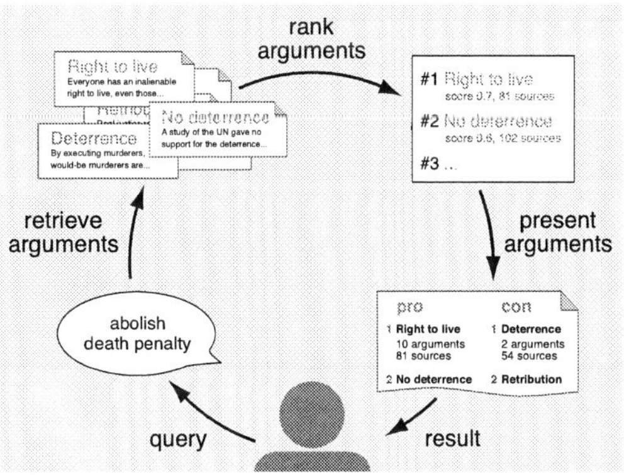

Figure 1: High-level view of the envisioned process of argument search from the user's perspective.

tional argumentation (Rinott et al., 2015). Also, it plays an important role in others, such as automated decision making (Bench-Capon et al., 2009) and opinion summarization (Wang and Ling, 2016). Bex et al. (2013) presented a first search interface for a collection of argument resources, while recent work has tackled subtasks of argument search, such as mining arguments from web text (Habernal and Gurevych, 2015) and assessing their relevance (Wachsmuth et al., 2017b). Still, the actual search for arguments on the web remains largely unexplored (Section 2 summarizes the related work).

Figure 1 illustrates how an argument search process could look like. Several research questions arise in light of this process, starting from what information needs users have regarding arguments and how they query for them, over how to find arguments on the web, which of them to retrieve, and how to rank them, to how to present the arguments and how to interact with them.

This paper introduces a generic framework that we develop to study the mentioned and several further research questions related to argument search on the web. The framework pertains to the two

49

Proceedings of the 4th Workshop on Argument Mining, pages 49–59
Copenhagen, Denmark, September 8, 2017. ©2017 Association for Computational Linguistics

main tasks of search engines, *indexing* and *retrieval* (Croft et al., 2009). The former covers the acquisition of candidate documents, the mining and assessment of arguments, and the actual indexing. The latter begins with the formulation of a search query, which triggers the retrieval and ranking of arguments, and it ends with the presentation of search results. The outlined steps are illustrated in Figure 2 and will be detailed in Section 3.

To achieve a wide proliferation and to foster collaborative research in the community, our framework implementation relies on standard technology. The argument model used represents the common ground of existing models, yet, in an extensible manner. Initially, we crawled and indexed a total of 291,440 arguments from five diverse online debate portals, exploiting the portals' structure to avoid mining errors and manual annotation while unifying the arguments based on the model (Section 4).

Given the framework and index, we created a prototype argument search engine, called *args*, that ranks arguments for any free text query (Section 5). *args* realizes the first argument search that runs on actual web content, but further research on argument mining, assessment, and similar is required to scale the index to large web crawls and to adapt the ranking to the specific properties of arguments. Our framework allows for doing so step by step, thereby providing a shared platform for shaping the future of web search and for evaluating approaches from computational argumentation in practice.

Altogether, the contributions of this paper are:[1]

1. *An argument search framework.* We present an extensible framework for applying and evaluating research on argument search.

2. *An argument search index.* We provide an index of 291,440 arguments, to our knowledge the largest argument resource available so far.

3. *A prototype argument search engine.* We develop a search engine for arguments, the first that allows retrieving arguments from the web.

2   Related Work

Teufel (1999) was one of the first to point out the importance of argumentation in retrieval contexts, modeling so called argumentative zones of scientific articles. Further pioneer research was conducted by Rahwan et al. (2007), who foresaw a *world wide argument web* with structured argument

ontologies and tools for creating and analyzing arguments — the semantic web approach to argumentation. Meanwhile, key parts of the approach have surfaced: the argument interchange format (AIF), a large collection of human-annotated corpora, and tool support, together called *AIFdb* (Bex et al., 2013). Part of AIFdb is a query interface to *browse arguments in the corpora* based on words they contain.[2] In contrast, we face a "real" *search for arguments*, i.e., the retrieval of arguments from the web that fulfill information needs. AIFdb and our framework serve complementary purposes; an integration of the two at some point appears promising.

Web search is the main subject of research in information retrieval, centered around the ranking of web pages that are relevant to a user's information need (Manning et al., 2008). While the scale of the web comes with diverse computational and infrastructural challenges (Brin and Page, 1998), in this paper we restrict our view to the standard architecture needed for the indexing process and the retrieval process of web search (Croft et al., 2009). Unlike standard search engines, though, we index and retrieve arguments, not web pages. The challenges of argument search resemble those IBM's debating technologies address (Rinott et al., 2015). Unlike IBM, we build an open research environment, not a commercial application.

For indexing, a common argument representation is needed. Argumentation theory proposes a number of major models: Toulmin (1958) focuses on fine-grained roles of an argument's units, Walton et al. (2008) capture the inference scheme that an argument uses, and Freeman (2011) investigates how units support or attack other units or arguments. Some computational approaches adopt one of them (Peldszus and Stede, 2015; Habernal and Gurevych, 2015). Others present simpler, application-oriented models that, for instance, distinguish claims and evidence only (Rinott et al., 2015). From an abstract viewpoint, all models share that they consider a single argument as a conclusion (in terms of a claim) together with a set of premises (reasons). Similar to the AIF mentioned above, we thus rely on this basic premise-conclusion model. AIF focuses on inference schemes, whereas we allow for flexible model extensions, as detailed in Section 3. Still, AIF and our model largely remain compatible.

To fully exploit the scale of the web, the arguments to be indexed will have to be mined by a

---

¹The framework, index, and search engine can be accessed at: `http://www.arguana.com/software.html`

²AIFdb query interface: `http://www.aifdb.org`

50

crawler. A few argument mining approaches deal with online resources. Among these, Boltužić and Šnajder (2014) as well as Park and Cardie (2014) search for supporting information in online discussions, and Swanson et al. (2015) mine arguments on specific issues from such discussions. Habernal and Gurevych (2015) study how well mining works across genres of argumentative web text, and Al-Khatib et al. (2016) use distant supervision to derive training data for mining from a debate portal. No approach, however, seems robust enough, yet, to obtain arguments reliably from the web. Therefore, we decided not to mine at all for our initial index. Instead, we follow the distant supervision idea to obtain arguments automatically.

The data we compile is almost an order of magnitude larger than the aforementioned AIFdb corpus collection currently, and similar in size to the Internet Argument Corpus (Walker et al., 2012). While the latter captures dialogical structure in debates, our data has actual argument structure, making it the biggest argument resource we are aware of.

The core task in the retrieval process is to rank the arguments that are relevant to a query. As surveyed by Wachsmuth et al. (2017a), several quality dimensions can be considered for arguments, from their logical cogency via their rhetorical effectiveness, to their dialectical reasonableness. So far, our prototype search engine makes use of a standard ranking scheme only (Robertson and Zaragoza, 2009), but recent research hints at future extensions: In (Wachsmuth et al., 2017b), we adapt the PageRank method (Page et al., 1999) to derive an objective relevance score for arguments from their relations, ranking arguments on this basis. Boltužić and Šnajder (2015) cluster arguments to find the most prominent ones, and Braunstain et al. (2016) model argumentative properties of texts to better rank posts in community question answering. Others build upon logical frameworks in order to find accepted arguments (Cabrio and Villata, 2012) or credible claims (Samadi et al., 2016).

In addition to such structural approaches, some works target intrinsic properties of arguments. For instance, Feng and Hirst (2011) classify the inference scheme of arguments based on the model of Walton et al. (2008). Persing and Ng (2015) score the argument strength of persuasive essays, and Habernal and Gurevych (2016) predict which of a pair of arguments is more convincing. Such approaches may be important for ranking.

Concept	Description
Argument	
ID	Unique argument ID.
Conclusion	Text span defining the conclusion.
Premises	$k \geq 0$ text spans defining the premises.
Stances	$k \geq 0$ labels, defining each premise's stance.
Argument context	
Discussion	Text of the web page the argument occurs in.
URL	Source URL of the text.
C'Position	Start + end index of the conclusion in the text.
P'Positions	$k \geq 0$ start + end indices, once per premise.
Previous ID	ID of preceding argument in the text if any.
Next ID	ID of subsequent argument in the text if any.
Model extensions (exemplary)	
P'Roles	$k \geq 0$ labels, defining each premise's role.
Scheme	Label defining the argument's scheme.
Scores	$m \geq 0$ values from $[0, 1]$, defining scores.

Table 1: Concepts in our model of an argument and its context as well as examples of model extensions.

3 A Framework for Argument Search

We now introduce the framework that we propose for conducting research related to argument search on the web. It relies on a common argument model and on a standard indexing and retrieval process.

3.1 A Common Argument Model

The basic items to be retrieved by the envisaged kind of search engines are arguments, which hence need to be indexed in a uniform way. We propose a general, yet extensible model to which all arguments can be mapped. The model consists of two parts, overviewed in Table 1, and detailed below.

Argument Each argument has an *ID* and is composed of two kinds of units: a *conclusion* (the argument's claim) and $k \geq 0$ *premises* (reasons). Both the conclusion and the premises may be implicit but not all units. Each premise has a *stance* towards the conclusion (pro or con).[3]

Argument Context We represent an argument's context by the full text of the web page it occurs on (called *discussion* here) along with the page's *URL*.[4] To locate the argument, we model the character indices of conclusions and premises (*C'Position, P'Positions*) and we link to the preceding and subsequent argument in the text (*Previous ID, Next ID*).

---

[3] We specify stance only for premises, because a conclusion's stance depends on the issue the argument is used for. For instance, the "right to live" conclusion from Figure 1 supports "abolish death penalty" but it attacks "reintroduce death penalty." For these issues, it takes the role of a premise.

[4] By including the full text, the context of an argument can directly be considered during retrieval. An index, however, would store only a reference to avoid redundancy.

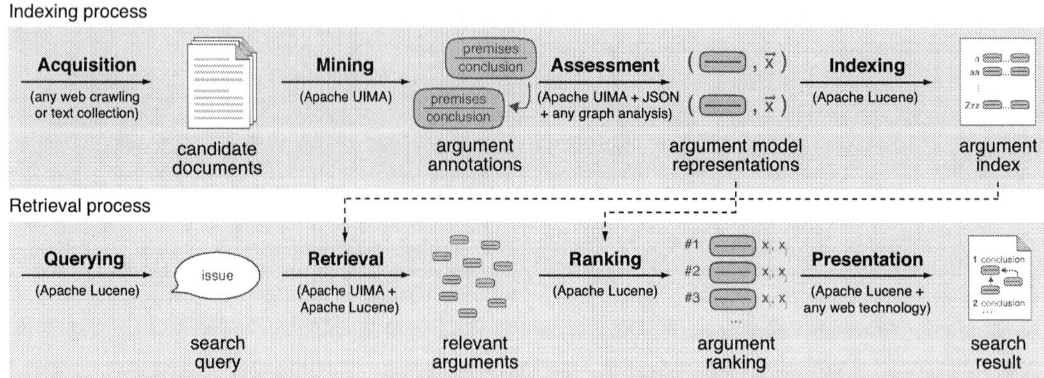

Figure 2: Illustration of the main steps and results of the indexing process and the retrieval process of our argument search engine framework. In parentheses: Technology presupposed in our implementation.

This model represents the common ground of the major existing models (see Section 2), hence abstracting from concepts specific to these models. However, as Table 1 exemplifies, we allow for model extensions to integrate most of them, such as the roles of Toulmin (1958) or the schemes of Walton et al. (2008). Similarly, it is possible to add the various scores that can be computed for an argument, such as different quality ratings (Wachsmuth et al., 2017a). This way, they can still be employed in the assessment and ranking of arguments.

A current limitation of our model pertains to the support or attack between *arguments* (as opposed to *argument units*), investigated by Freeman (2011) among others. While these cannot be represented perfectly in the given model, a solution is to additionally index relations between arguments. We leave such an extension to future work.

3.2 The Indexing Process

Figure 2 concretizes the two standard processes of web search (Croft et al., 2009) for the specific tasks in argument search. The indexing process consists of the *acquisition* of documents, the *mining* and *assessment* of arguments, and the actual *indexing*.

Acquisition The first task is the acquisition of candidate documents, from which the arguments to be indexed are taken. Web search engines employ crawlers to continuously acquire new web pages and to update pages crawled before. The output of this step will usually be HTML-like files or some preprocessed intermediate format. In principle, any text collection in a parsable format may be used.

Mining Having the candidate documents, argument mining is needed to obtain arguments. Sev-

eral approaches to this task exist as well as to subtasks thereof, such as argument unit segmentation (Ajjour et al., 2017). These approaches require different text analyses as preprocessing. We thus rely on Apache UIMA for this step, which allows for a flexible composition of natural language processing algorithms. UIMA organizes algorithms in a (possibly parallelized) pipeline that iteratively processes each document and adds annotations such as tokens, sentences, or argument units. It is a de facto standard for natural language processing (Ferrucci and Lally, 2004), and it also forms the basis of other text analysis frameworks, such as DKPro (Eckart de Castilho and Gurevych, 2014).

UIMA will allow other researchers to contribute, simply by supplying UIMA implementations of approaches to any subtasks, as long as their output conforms to the set of annotations needed to instantiate our argument model. By collecting implementations for more and more subtasks over time, we aim to build a shared argument mining library.

Assessment State-of-the-art retrieval does not only match web pages with queries, but it also uses meta-properties pre-computed for each page, e.g., the probability of a page being spam, a rating of its reputation, or a query-independent relevance score. For arguments, different structural and intrinsic quality criteria may be assessed, too, as summarized in Section 2. Often, such assessments can be computed from individual arguments, again using UIMA. But some may require an analysis of the graph induced by *all* arguments, such as the PageRank adaptation for arguments we presented (Wachsmuth et al., 2017b). This is why we separate the assessment from the preceding mining step. At the end, the argument annotations as well as the computed scores are returned in a serializable format (JSON) representing our extended argument model to be fed to the indexer.

Indexing Finally, we create an index of all arguments from their representations, resorting to Apache Lucene due to its wide proliferation. While Lucene automatically indexes all fields of its input (i.e., all concepts of our argument model), the conclusion, the premises, and the discussion will naturally be the most relevant. In this regard, Lucene supplies proven defaults but also allows for a fine-grained adjustment of what is indexed and how.

3.3 The Retrieval Process

The lower part of Figure 2 illustrates the retrieval process of our search framework. When a user *queries* for a controversial issue or similar, relevant arguments are *retrieved*, *ranked*, and *presented*.

Querying We assume any free text query as input. The standard way to process such a query is to interpret it as a set of words or phrases. This is readily supported by Lucene, although some challenges remain, such as how to segment a query correctly into phrases (Hagen et al., 2012). In the context of argument search, the standard way seems perfectly adequate for simple topic queries (e.g., "life-long imprisonment"). However, how people query for arguments exactly and what information needs they have in mind is still largely unexplored. Especially, we expect that many queries will indicate a stance already (e.g., "death penalty is bad" or "abolish death penalty"), ask for a comparison (e.g., "death penalty vs. life-long imprisonment"), or both ("imprisonment better than death penalty").

As a result, queries may need to be preprocessed, for instance, to identify a required stance inversion. Our framework provides interfaces to extend Lucene's query analysis capabilities in this regard. Aside from query interpretation, user profiling may play a role in this step, in order to allow for personalized ranking, but this is left to future work.

Retrieval For a clear separation of concerns, we conceptually decouple argument retrieval from argument ranking. We see the former as the determination of those arguments from the index that are generally relevant to the query. On one hand, this pertains to the problems of term matching known from classic retrieval, including spelling correction, synonym detection, and further (Manning et al., 2008). On the other hand, argument-specific re-

trieval challenges arise. For instance, what index fields to consider may be influenceed by a query (e.g., "*conclusions* on death penalty"). Our framework uses Lucene for such configurations. Also, we see as part of this step the stance classification of retrieved arguments towards a queried topic (and a possibly given stance), which was in the focus of recent research (Bar-Haim et al., 2017). To analyze arguments, UIMA is employed again.

Ranking The heart of every search engine is its ranker for the retrieved items (here: the arguments). Lucene comes with a number of standard ranking functions for web search and allows for integrating alternative ones. Although a few approaches exist that rank arguments for a given issue or claim (see Section 2), it is still unclear how to determine the most relevant arguments for a given query. Depending on the query and possibly the user, ranking may exploit the content of an argument's conulsion and premises, the argument's context, meta-properties assessed during indexing (see above), or any other metadata. Therefore, this step's input is the full model representations of the retrieved arguments. Its output is a ranking score for each of them.

The provision of a means to apply and evaluate argument ranking functions in practice is one main goal of our framework. An integration of empirical evaluation methods will follow in future work. While we published first benchmark rankings lately (Wachsmuth et al., 2017b), datasets of notable size for this purpose are missing so far.

Presentation Given the argument model representations together with the ranking scores, the last step is to present the arguments to the user along with adequate means of interaction. As exemplified in Figure 1 and 2, both textual and visual presentations may be considered. The underlying snippets of textual representations can be generated with default methods or extensions of Lucene. We do not presuppose any particular web technology for the user interface. Our own approach focusing on the ranking and contrasting of pro and con arguments is detailed in Section 5.

4 An Initial Argument Search Index

The framework from Section 3 serves as a platform for research towards argument search on the web. This section describes an initial data basis that we crawled for carrying out such research. To obtain this data basis, we unified diverse web arguments based on our common argument model.

4.1 Crawling of Online Debate Portals

Being the core task in computational argumentation, argument mining is one of the main analyses meant to be deployed within our framework. As outlined in Section 2, however, current approaches are not yet reliable enough to mine arguments from the web. Following related work (Habernal and Gurevych, 2015; Al-Khatib et al., 2016), we thus automatically derive arguments from the structure given in online debate portals instead.

In particular, we crawled all debates found on five of the largest portals: (1) *idebate.org*, (2) *debatepedia.org*, (3) *debatewise.org*, (4) *debate.org*, and (5) *forandagainst.com*. Except for the second, which was superseded by idebate.org some years ago, these portals have a living community. While the exact concepts differ, all five portals organize pro and con arguments for a given issue on a single debate page. Most covered issues are either of ongoing societal relevance (e.g., "abortion") or of high temporary interest (e.g., "Trump vs. Clinton"). The stance is generally explicit.[5]

The first three portals aim to provide comprehensive overviews of the best arguments for each issue. These arguments are largely well-written, have detailed reasons, and are often supported by references. In contrast, the remaining two portals let users discuss controversies. While on debate.org any two users can participate in a traditional debate, forandagainst.com lets users share own arguments and support or attack those of others.

Although all five portals are moderated to some extent, especially the latter two vary in terms of argument quality. Sometimes users vote rather than argue ("I'm FOR it!"), post insults, or just spam. In addition, not all portals exhibit a consistent structure. For instance, issues on debate.org are partly specified as claims ("Abortion should be legal"), partly as questions ("Should Socialism be preferred to Capitalism?"), and partly as controversial issues ("Womens' rights"). This reflects the web's noisy nature which argument search engines will have to cope with. We therefore index all five portals, taking their characteristics into account.[6]

---

[5] Other portals were not considered for different reasons. For instance, *createdebate.com* does not represent stance in a pro/con manner, but it names the favored side instead. Hence, an *automatic* conversion into instances of our argument model from Section 3 is not straightforward.

[6] Although not a claim, an issue suffices as a conclusion given that the stance of a premise is known. In contrast, the interpretation of a question as a conclusion may be unclear (e.g., "Why is Confucianism not a better policy?").

4.2 Indexing of Reliable Web Arguments

Given all crawled debates, we analyzed the web page structure of each underlying portal in order to identify how to reliably map the comprised arguments to our common argument model for indexing. An overview of all performed mappings is given in Table 2. For brevity, we only detail the mapping for debatewise.org.[7]

In the majority of debates on debatewise.org, the *debate title* is a claim, such as "Same-sex marriage should be legal". *Yes points* and *no points* are listed that support and attack the claim respectively. For each point, we created one argument where the title is the conclusion and the point is a single premise with either pro stance (for yes points) or con stance (no points). In addition, each point comes with a *yes because* and a *no because*. For a yes point, yes because gives reasons why it holds; for a no point, why it does not hold (in case of no because, vice versa). We created one argument with yes because as the premise and one with no because as the premise, both with the respective point as conclusion. We set the premise stance accordingly.

We abstained from having multiple premises for the arguments derived from any of the portals. Though some reasons are very long and, in fact, often concatenate two or more premises, an automatic segmentation would not be free of errors, which we sought to avoid for the first index. Nevertheless, the premises can still be split once a sufficiently reliable segmentation approach is at hand.

As a result of the mapping, we obtained a set of 376,129 candidate arguments for indexing. To reduce noise that we observed in a manual analysis of samples, we then conducted four cleansing steps: (1) Removal of 368 candidates (from debatepedia.org) whose premise stance could not be mapped automatically to pro or con (e.g., "Clinton" for the issue "Clinton is better than Trump"). (2) Removal of 46,169 candidates whose conclusion is a question, as these do not always constitute proper arguments. (3) Removal of 9930 candidates where either the conclusion or the premise was empty, in order to avoid implicit units in the first index. (4) Removal of 28,222 candidates that were stored multiple times due to the existence of 2852 duplicate debates on debate.org.

Table 3 lists the number of arguments finally indexed from each debate portal, along with the

---

[7] Besides the actual argument, we also stored all context information reflected in our model, such as the debate's URL.

# Debate Portal	Concept	Mapping to our Common Argument Model	
1 idebate.org	Debate title	Conclusion	of each argument where a pro/con claim is the premise.
	Point for	Pro premise	of one argument where the debate title is the conclusion.
		Conclusion	of the argument where the associated point is the premise.
		Conclusion	of the argument where the associated counterpoint is the premise.
	Point against	Con premise	of one argument where the debate title is the conclusion.
		Conclusion	of the argument where the associated point is the premise.
		Conclusion	of the argument where the associated counterpoint is the premise.
	Point	Pro premise	of the argument where the associated point for/against is the conclusion.
	Counterpoint	Con premise	of the argument where the associated point for/against is the conclusion.
2 debatepedia.org	Debate title	Conclusion	of each argument where a pro/con claim is the premise.
	Pro claim	Pro premise	of one argument where the debate title is the conclusion.
		Conclusion	of the argument where the associated premises are the premise.
	Con claim	Con premise	of one argument where the title is the conclusion.
		Conclusion	of the argument where the associated premises are the premise.
	Premises	Pro premise	of the argument where the associated pro/con claim is the conclusion.
3 debatewise.org	Debate title	Conclusion	of each argument where a pro/con claim is the premise.
	Yes point	Pro premise	of one argument where the debate title is the conclusion.
		Conclusion	of the argument where the associated yes because is the premise.
		Conclusion	of an argument where the associated no because is the premise.
	No point	Con premise	of one argument where the debate title is the conclusion.
		Conclusion	of an argument where the associated yes because is the premise.
		Conclusion	of an argument where the associated no because is the premise.
	Yes because	Pro/Con prem.	of the argument where the associated yes/no point is the conclusion.
	No because	Pro/Con prem.	of the argument where the associated no/yes point is the conclusion.
4 debate.org	Debate title	Conclusion	of each argument of a debate.
	Pro argument	Pro premise	of one argument where the debate title is the conclusion.
	Con argument	Con premise	of one argument where the debate title is the conclusion.
5 forandagainst.com	Claim	Conclusion	of each argument of a debate.
	For	Pro premise	of one argument where the claim is the conclusion.
	Against	Con premise	of one argument where the claim is the conclusion.

Table 2: The concepts given in each debate portal and the mapping we performed to derive arguments.

# Debate Portal	Argument Units	Arguments	Debates
1 idebate.org	16 084	15 384	698
2 debatepedia.org	34 536	33 684	751
3 debatewise.org	39 576	33 950	2 252
4 debate.org	210 340	182 198	28 045
5 forandagainst.com	29 255	26 224	3 038
$\sum$ Complete index	329 791	291 440	34 784

Table 3: Argument units, arguments, and debates from each portal stored in our initial search index.

number of different argument units composed in the arguments and the number of debates they are taken from. On average, the indexed conclusions and premises have a length of 7.4 and 202.9 words respectively. With a total of 291,440 arguments, to the best of our knowledge, our index forms the largest argument resource available so far.

Naturally, not all indexed arguments have the quality of those from manually annotated corpora. Particularly, we observed that some texts contain phrases specific to the respective debate portal that seemed hard filter out automatically with general rules (e.g., "if we both forfeit every round"). Still, as far as we could assess, the vast majority matches the concept of an argument, which lets our index appear suitable for a first argument search engine.

5 args — The Argument Search Engine

As a proof of concept, we implemented the prototype argument search engine *args* utilizing our framework and the argument index. This section outlines the main features of *args* and reports on some first insights obtained from its usage.[8]

5.1 Content-based Argument Search

The debate portal arguments in our index were collected by a focused crawler and stored directly in the JSON format for indexing. As per our framework, the prototype implements the retrieval process steps of argument search outlined in Section 3 and shown in the lower part of Figure 2.

Querying At server side, our search engine exposes an API, allowing for free text queries to be submitted via HTTP. As on traditional search engines, the entered terms are interpreted as an *AND*

---

[8]*args* is available at http://www.arguana.com/args. Notice that the prototype is under ongoing development and periodically updated. As a consequence, some of the features described here may change over time.

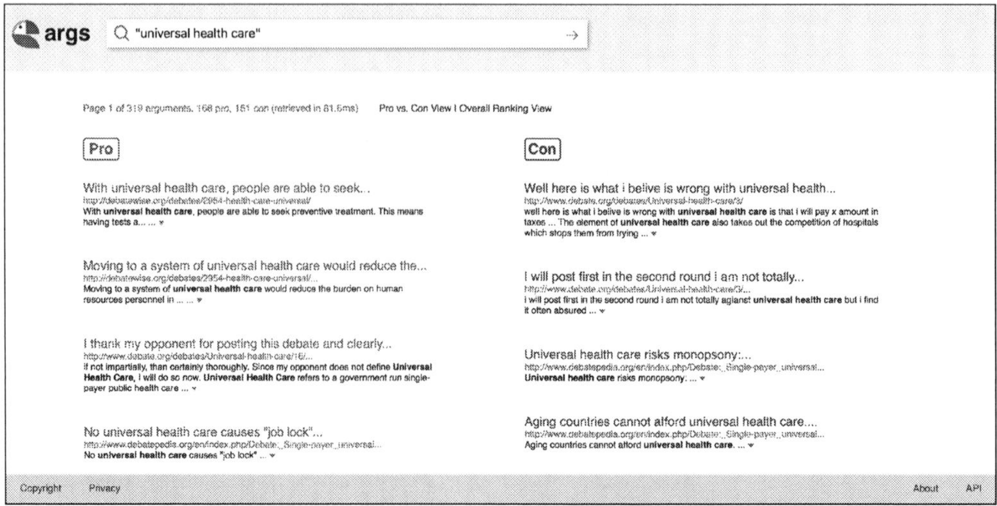

Figure 3: The user interface of the prototype argument search engine *args*, showing the *Pro vs. Con View*.

query, but more search operators are implemented, such as quotes for a *phrase query*. Unlike traditional search engines, stop words are not ignored, since they may be subtle indicators in argumentation (e.g., "arguments *for* feminism").

Retrieval Currently, our prototype retrieves arguments with exact matches of the query terms or phrases. The matching is performed based on conclusions only, making the relevance of the returned arguments to the query very likely. As detailed below, we explored different weightings of the indexed fields though. We derive an argument's stance so far from the stance of its premises stored in our index, which serves as a good heuristic as long as the given query consists of a topic only.

Ranking Before working on rankings based on the specific characteristics of arguments, we seek to assess the benefit and limitations of standard ranking functions for arguments. We rely on *Okapi BM25* here, a sophisticated version of TF-IDF that has proven strong in content-based information retrieval (Croft et al., 2009). In particular, we compute ranking scores for all retrieved arguments with *BM25F*. This variant of BM25 allows a weighting of fields, here of conclusions, premises, and discussions (Robertson and Zaragoza, 2009).

Presentation As a client, we offer the user interface in Figure 3. Right now, search results are presented in two ways: By default, the *Pro vs. Con View* is activated, displaying pro and con arguments separately, opposing each other. In contrast, the *Overall Ranking View* shows an integrated ranking of all arguments, irrespective of stance, making their actual ranks explicit. Views could be chosen automatically depending on the query and user, but this is left to future work. The snippet of a result is created from the argument's premises. A click on the attached arrow reveals the full argument.

5.2 First Insights into Argument Search

Given the prototype, we carried out a quantitative analysis of the arguments it retrieves for controversial issues. The goal was *not* to evaluate the rankings of arguments or their use for downstream applications, since the prototype does not perform an argument-specific ranking yet (see above). Rather, we aimed to assess the coverage of our index and the importance of its different fields. To obtain objective insights we did not compile queries manually nor did we extract them from the debate portals, but referred to an unbiased third party: Wikipedia. In particular, we interpreted all 1082 different controversial issues, which are listed on Wikipedia, as query terms (access date June 2, 2017).[9] Some of these issues are general, such as "nuclear energy" or "drones", others more specific, such as "Park51" or "Zinedine Zidane".

For each issue, we posed a phrase query (e.g., "zinedine zidane"), an AND query (e.g., "zinedine" *and* "zidane"), and an OR query (e.g., "zinedine" *or* "zidane"). Arguments were retrieved using three weightings of BM25F that differ in the fields taken into account: (1) the conclusion field only, (2) the

---

[9]Issue list: `https://en.wikipedia.org/wiki/Wikipedia:List_of_controversial_issues`

	Conclusions		Arguments		Contexts	
Query Type	≥ 1	$\tilde{x}$	≥ 1	$\tilde{x}$	≥ 1	$\tilde{x}$
Phrase query	41.6%	24	77.6%	40	77.9%	269
AND query	45.1%	27	88.2%	53	90.0%	498
OR query	84.6%	237	98.0%	1249	98.1%	8800

Table 4: Percentage of the controversial issues on Wikipedia, for which at least one argument is retrieved by our prototype (≥ 1) as well as the median number of arguments retrieved then ($\tilde{x}$); once for each query type based on the *conclusions* only, the full *arguments*, and the full argument *contexts*.

full arguments (i.e., conclusions and premises), and (3) the full contexts (discussions). For all combinations of query type and fields, we computed the proportion of queries, for which arguments were retrieved, and the median number of arguments retrieved then. Table 4 lists the results.

With respect to the different fields, we see that the conclusions, although being short, match with 41.6%–84.6% of all queries, depending on the type of query. Based on the full argument, even phrase queries achieve 77.6%. These numbers indicate that the coverage of our index is already very high for common controversial issues. Moreover, a comparison of the median number of arguments there (40) to those retrieved based on the full context (269) suggests that many other possibly relevant arguments are indexed that do not mention the query terms themselves. While the numbers naturally increase from phrase queries over AND queries to OR queries, our manual inspection confirmed the intuition that especially lower-ranked results of OR queries often lack relevance (which is why our prototype focuses on the other types).

In terms of the weighting of fields, it seems like the highest importance should be given to the conclusion, whereas the discussion should only receive a small weight, but this is up to further evaluation. In general, we observed a tendency towards ranking short arguments higher, implicitly caused by BM25F. Even though, in cases of doubt, short arguments are preferable, we expect that the most relevant arguments need some space to lay out their reasoning. However, to investigate such hypotheses, ranking functions are required that go beyond the words in an argument and its context.

6 Conclusion and Outlook

Few applications exist that exploit the full potential of computational argumentation so far. This paper has introduced a generic argument search framework that is meant to serve as a shared platform for bringing research on computational argumentation to practice. Based on a large index of arguments crawled from the web, we have implemented a prototype search engine to demonstrate the capabilities of our framework. Both the index and the prototype can be freely accessed online.

Currently, however, the index covers only semi-structured arguments from specific debate portals, whereas the prototype is restricted to standard retrieval. While the framework, index, and prototype are under ongoing development, much research on argument mining, argument ranking, and other tasks still has to be done, in order to provide relevant arguments in future search engines.

Laying a solid foundation for research is crucial, since the biggest challenges of argument search transcend basic keyword retrieval. They include advanced retrieval problems, such as learning to rank, user modeling, and search result personalization — all problems with intricate ethical issues attached. Much more than traditional information systems, argument search may affect the convictions of its users. A search engine can be built to do so either blindly, by exposing users to its ranking results as is, or intentionally, by tailoring results to its users. Neither of the two options is harmless:

Training a one-fits-all ranking function on the argumentative portion of the web and on joint user behaviors will inevitably incorporate bias from both the web texts and the dominating user group, affecting the search results seen by the entire user base. On the other hand, tailoring results to individual users would induce a form of confirmation bias: Presuming that the best arguments of either side will be ranked high, should a user with a left-wing predisposition see the left-wing argument on first rank, or the right-wing one? In other words, should a search engine "argue" like the devil's advocate or not? This decision is of utmost importance; it will not only affect how users perceive the quality of the results, but it may also change the stance of the users on the issues they query for. And this, finally, raises the question as to what are actually the *best* arguments: only those that reasonably conclude from acceptable premises — or also those that may be fallacious, yet, persuasive?

Computational argumentation needs to deal with these topics. We believe that this should be done in a collaborative, application-oriented environment.

References

Yamen Ajjour, Wei-Fan Chen, Johannes Kiesel, Henning Wachsmuth, and Benno Stein. 2017. Unit Segmentation of Argumentative Texts. In *Proceedings of the Fourth Workshop on Argument Mining*. Association for Computational Linguistics.

Khalid Al-Khatib, Henning Wachsmuth, Matthias Hagen, Jonas Köhler, and Benno Stein. 2016. Cross-Domain Mining of Argumentative Text through Distant Supervision. In *Proceedings of the 2016 Conference of the North American Chapter of the Association for Computational Linguistics: Human Language Technologies*. Association for Computational Linguistics, pages 1395–1404. https://doi.org/10.18653/v1/N16-1165.

Roy Bar-Haim, Indrajit Bhattacharya, Francesco Dinuzzo, Amrita Saha, and Noam Slonim. 2017. Stance Classification of Context-Dependent Claims. In *Proceedings of the 15th Conference of the European Chapter of the Association for Computational Linguistics: Volume 1, Long Papers*. Association for Computational Linguistics, pages 251–261. http://aclweb.org/anthology/E17-1024.

Trevor Bench-Capon, Katie Atkinson, and Peter McBurney. 2009. Altruism and Agents: An Argumentation Based Approach to Designing Agent Decision Mechanisms. In *Proceedings of The 8th International Conference on Autonomous Agents and Multiagent Systems - Volume 2, AAMAS 2009*. pages 1073–1080. http://dl.acm.org/citation.cfm?id=1558109.1558163.

Floris Bex, John Lawrence, Mark Snaith, and Chris Reed. 2013. Implementing the Argument Web. *Communications of the ACM* 56(10):66–73.

Filip Boltužić and Jan Šnajder. 2014. Back up your Stance: Recognizing Arguments in Online Discussions. In *Proceedings of the First Workshop on Argumentation Mining*. Association for Computational Linguistics, pages 49–58. https://doi.org/10.3115/v1/W14-2107.

Filip Boltužić and Jan Šnajder. 2015. Identifying Prominent Arguments in Online Debates Using Semantic Textual Similarity. In *Proceedings of the 2nd Workshop on Argumentation Mining*. Association for Computational Linguistics, pages 110–115. https://doi.org/10.3115/v1/W15-0514.

Liora Braunstain, Oren Kurland, David Carmel, Idan Szpektor, and Anna Shtok. 2016. Supporting Human Answers for Advice-Seeking Questions in CQA Sites. In *Proceedings of the 38th European Conference on IR Research*. pages 129–141. https://doi.org/10.1007/978-3-319-30671-1_10.

Sergey Brin and Lawrence Page. 1998. The Anatomy of a Large-scale Hypertextual Web Search Engine. In *Proceedings of the Seventh International Conference on World Wide Web*. pages 107–117. http://dl.acm.org/citation.cfm?id=297805.297827.

Elena Cabrio and Serena Villata. 2012. Combining Textual Entailment and Argumentation Theory for Supporting Online Debates Interactions. In *Proceedings of the 50th Annual Meeting of the Association for Computational Linguistics (Volume 2: Short Papers)*. Association for Computational Linguistics, pages 208–212. http://aclweb.org/anthology/P12-2041.

Bruce Croft, Donald Metzler, and Trevor Strohman. 2009. *Search Engines: Information Retrieval in Practice*. Addison-Wesley, USA, 1st edition.

Richard Eckart de Castilho and Iryna Gurevych. 2014. A Broad-Coverage Collection of Portable NLP Components for Building Shareable Analysis Pipelines. In *Proceedings of the Workshop on Open Infrastructures and Analysis Frameworks for HLT*. Association for Computational Linguistics and Dublin City University, pages 1–11. http://www.aclweb.org/anthology/W14-5201.

Vanessa Wei Feng and Graeme Hirst. 2011. Classifying Arguments by Scheme. In *Proceedings of the 49th Annual Meeting of the Association for Computational Linguistics: Human Language Technologies*. Association for Computational Linguistics, pages 987–996. http://aclweb.org/anthology/P11-1099.

David Ferrucci and Adam Lally. 2004. UIMA: An Architectural Approach to Unstructured Information Processing in the Corporate Research Environment. *Natural Language Engineering* 10(3–4):327–348.

James B. Freeman. 2011. *Argument Structure: Representation and Theory*. Springer.

Ivan Habernal and Iryna Gurevych. 2015. Exploiting Debate Portals for Semi-Supervised Argumentation Mining in User-Generated Web Discourse. In *Proceedings of the 2015 Conference on Empirical Methods in Natural Language Processing*. Association for Computational Linguistics, pages 2127–2137. https://doi.org/10.18653/v1/D15-1255.

Ivan Habernal and Iryna Gurevych. 2016. Which Argument is More Convincing? Analyzing and Predicting Convincingness of Web Arguments using Bidirectional LSTM. In *Proceedings of the 54th Annual Meeting of the Association for Computational Linguistics (Volume 1: Long Papers)*. Association for Computational Linguistics, pages 1589–1599. https://doi.org/10.18653/v1/P16-1150.

Matthias Hagen, Martin Potthast, Anna Beyer, and Benno Stein. 2012. Towards Optimum Query Segmentation: In Doubt Without. In *21st ACM International Conference on Information and Knowledge Management*. pages 1015–1024. https://doi.org/10.1145/2396761.2398398.

Christopher D. Manning, Prabhakar Raghavan, and Hinrich Schütze. 2008. *Introduction to Information Retrieval*. Cambridge University Press, New York, NY, USA.

Lawrence Page, Sergey Brin, Rajeev Motwani, and Terry Winograd. 1999. The PageRank Citation Ranking: Bringing Order to the Web. Technical Report 1999-66, Stanford InfoLab. Previous number = SIDL-WP-1999-0120. http://ilpubs.stanford.edu:8090/422/.

Joonsuk Park and Claire Cardie. 2014. Identifying Appropriate Support for Propositions in Online User Comments. In *Proceedings of the First Workshop on Argumentation Mining*. Association for Computational Linguistics, pages 29–38. https://doi.org/10.3115/v1/W14-2105.

Marius Pasca. 2011. Web-based Open-Domain Information Extraction. In *Proceedings of the 20th ACM International Conference on Information and Knowledge Management*. pages 2605–2606. https://doi.org/10.1145/1963192.1963319.

Andreas Peldszus and Manfred Stede. 2015. Joint Prediction in MST-style Discourse Parsing for Argumentation Mining. In *Proceedings of the 2015 Conference on Empirical Methods in Natural Language Processing*. Association for Computational Linguistics, pages 938–948. https://doi.org/10.18653/v1/D15-1110.

Isaac Persing and Vincent Ng. 2015. Modeling Argument Strength in Student Essays. In *Proceedings of the 53rd Annual Meeting of the Association for Computational Linguistics and the 7th International Joint Conference on Natural Language Processing (Volume 1: Long Papers)*. Association for Computational Linguistics, pages 543–552. https://doi.org/10.3115/v1/P15-1053.

Iyad Rahwan, Fouad Zablith, and Chris Reed. 2007. Laying the Foundations for a World Wide Argument Web. *Artificial Intelligence* 171(10):897–921.

Ruty Rinott, Lena Dankin, Carlos Alzate Perez, M. Mitesh Khapra, Ehud Aharoni, and Noam Slonim. 2015. Show Me Your Evidence — An Automatic Method for Context Dependent Evidence Detection. In *Proceedings of the 2015 Conference on Empirical Methods in Natural Language Processing*. Association for Computational Linguistics, pages 440–450. https://doi.org/10.18653/v1/D15-1050.

Stephen Robertson and Hugo Zaragoza. 2009. The Probabilistic Relevance Framework: BM25 and Beyond. *Foundations and Trends in Information Retrieval* 3(4):333–389.

Mehdi Samadi, Partha Pratim Talukdar, Manuela M. Veloso, and Manuel Blum. 2016. ClaimEval: Integrated and Flexible Framework for Claim Evaluation Using Credibility of Sources. In *Proceedings of the Thirtieth AAAI Conference on Artificial Intelligence*. pages 222–228.

Reid Swanson, Brian Ecker, and Marilyn Walker. 2015. Argument Mining: Extracting Arguments from Online Dialogue. In *Proceedings of the 16th Annual Meeting of the Special Interest Group on Discourse and Dialogue*. Association for Computational Linguistics, pages 217–226. https://doi.org/10.18653/v1/W15-4631.

Simone Teufel. 1999. *Argumentative Zoning: Information Extraction from Scientific Text*. Ph.D. thesis, University of Edinburgh.

Stephen E. Toulmin. 1958. *The Uses of Argument*. Cambridge University Press.

Henning Wachsmuth, Nona Naderi, Yufang Hou, Yonatan Bilu, Vinodkumar Prabhakaran, Alberdingk Tim Thijm, Graeme Hirst, and Benno Stein. 2017a. Computational Argumentation Quality Assessment in Natural Language. In *Proceedings of the 15th Conference of the European Chapter of the Association for Computational Linguistics: Volume 1, Long Papers*. Association for Computational Linguistics, pages 176–187. http://aclweb.org/anthology/E17-1017.

Henning Wachsmuth, Benno Stein, and Yamen Ajjour. 2017b. "PageRank" for Argument Relevance. In *Proceedings of the 15th Conference of the European Chapter of the Association for Computational Linguistics: Volume 1, Long Papers*. Association for Computational Linguistics, pages 1117–1127. http://aclweb.org/anthology/E17-1105.

Marilyn Walker, Jean Fox Tree, Pranav Anand, Rob Abbott, and Joseph King. 2012. A Corpus for Research on Deliberation and Debate. In *Proceedings of the Eighth International Conference on Language Resources and Evaluation (LREC-2012)*. European Language Resources Association (ELRA), pages 812–817. http://www.lrec-conf.org/proceedings/lrec2012/pdf/1078_Paper.pdf.

Douglas Walton, Christopher Reed, and Fabrizio Macagno. 2008. *Argumentation Schemes*. Cambridge University Press.

Lu Wang and Wang Ling. 2016. Neural Network-Based Abstract Generation for Opinions and Arguments. In *Proceedings of the 2016 Conference of the North American Chapter of the Association for Computational Linguistics: Human Language Technologies*. Association for Computational Linguistics, pages 47–57. https://doi.org/10.18653/v1/N16-1007.

Argument Relation Classification Using a Joint Inference Model

Yufang Hou and **Charles Jochim**
IBM Research – Ireland
{yhou|charlesj}@ie.ibm.com

Abstract

In this paper, we address the problem of argument relation classification where argument units are from different texts. We design a joint inference method for the task by modeling *argument relation classification* and *stance classification* jointly. We show that our joint model improves the results over several strong baselines.

1 Introduction

What is a good counterargument or support argument for a given argument? Despite recent advances in computational argumentation, such as argument unit (e.g., claims, premises) mining (Habernal and Gurevych, 2015), argumentative relation (e.g., support, attack) prediction between argument units from the same text (Stab and Gurevych, 2014; Nguyen and Litman, 2016), as well as assessing argument strength of essays (Persing and Ng, 2015) or predicting convincingness of Web arguments (Habernal and Gurevych, 2016), this question is still an unsolved problem.

In this work we focus on the problem of argument relation classification where argument units are from different texts, i.e., given a set of arguments related to the same topic, we aim to predict relations (e.g., *agree* or *disagree*) between any two arguments. We are aware of argumentative relations between premises and the conclusion within a structured argument. Instead, here we are interested in modeling relations among atomic argument units in dialogic argumentation. This task is important for argumentation in debates (Zhang et al., 2016), stance classification (Sridhar et al., 2015), or persuasion analysis (Tan et al., 2016), among others.

There are various different views on the meaning of "support" and "attack" in argumenta-

tion theory (Cayrol and Lagasquie-Schiex, 2005, 2013). In this paper, we use "agree" and "disagree" to represent relations between two arguments which bear a stance regarding the same topic. Specifically, if a_1 agrees with a_2 regarding the topic t then a_1 and a_2 are conflict-free. And if a_1 disagrees with a_2 then they are not conflict-free.

There is a close relationship between *argument relation classification* and *stance classification*. First, argument relation classification can benefit from knowing the stance information of arguments. Specifically, if two arguments hold different stances with regard to the same topic, then they likely disagree with each other. Likewise, two arguments that hold the same stance regarding the same topic tend to agree with each other. Secondly, stance classification can benefit from modeling relations between arguments. For instance, we would expect two arguments that disagree with each other to hold different stances.

There has been a large amount of work focusing on stance classification in on-line debate forums by integrating disagreement information between posts connected with reply links (Somasundaran and Wiebe, 2009; Murakami and Raymond, 2010; Sridhar et al., 2015). However, disagreement information is mainly used as an auxiliary variable and is not explicitly evaluated. Our goal in this paper is to examine argument relation classification in dialogic argumentation. Our task is more challenging because unlike most previous work on disagreement classification, which can explore meta information (e.g., reply links between posts are strong indicators of disagreement), we are only provided with text information (see examples in Table 1).

In this paper, we model *argument relation classification* and *stance classification* jointly. We evaluate our model on a dataset extracted from De-

60

Proceedings of the 4th Workshop on Argument Mining, pages 60–66
Copenhagen, Denmark, September 8, 2017. ©2017 Association for Computational Linguistics

Debate Topic: *Are genetically modified foods (GM foods) beneficial?*		
Sub Topic: *Consumer safety*		
Arg (1)	Pro	Foods with poisonous allergens can be modified to reduce risks.
Arg (2)	Pro	GM crops can be fortified with vitamins and vaccines.
Arg (3)	Con	There are many instances of GM foods proving dangerous.
Sub Topic: *socio-economic impacts*		
Arg (4)	Pro	GM crops are made disease-resistant, which increases yields.
Arg (5)	Con	GM agriculture threatens the viability of traditional farming communities.
Arg (6)	Pro	GM crops generate greater wealth for farming communities.

Table 1: Examples of Debatepedia structure: arguments are organized into different sub-topics, each argument holds a stance regarding the topic.

batepedia[1]. We show that the joint model performs better than several strong baselines for *argument relation classification*. To our knowledge, this is the first work applying joint inference on argument relation classification on dialogic argumentation.

2 Related Work

Argument unit mining. Recent achievements in argument unit mining on different genres has provided us with high quality input for argument relation mining. Teufel (1999) proposed an Argumentative Zoning model for scientific text. Levy et al. (2014) and Rinott et al. (2015) extracted claims and evidences from Wikipedia respectively. Habernal and Gurevych (2015) focused on mining argument components from user-generated Web content. Lippi and Torroni (2016) extracted claims from political debates by utilizing speech features.

Argumentative relation classification. Most existing work on argumentative relation focuses on classifying relations between argument units of monologic argumentation, from a single text. One line of research (Stab and Gurevych, 2014; Persing and Ng, 2016; Nguyen and Litman, 2016) extracted argument units and predicted relations (i.e., support, attack, none) between argument units in persuasive student essays. Peldszus and Stede (2015) identified the argument structure of short texts in a bilingual corpus. In contrast, in our work the argument units are from different texts. Therefore, we do not have discourse connectives (e.g., "on the contrary" or "however") which usually are strong indicators for argument relations.

Cabrio and Villata (2012) used a textual entailment system to predict argument relations between argument pairs which are extracted from Debatepedia. An argument pair could be an argument coupled with the subtopic, or an argument coupled

with another argument of the opposite stance.

Recently, Menini and Tonelli (2016) predicted agreement/disagreement relations between argument pairs of dialogic argumentation in the political domain. The authors also create a large agreement/disagreement dataset by extracting arguments from the same sub-topic of Debatepedia. However, they only consider argument pairs that share a topic keyword. We do not have such constraints (see Arg (1) and Arg (2) in Table 1). In addition, they use SVM while we do joint inference.

Stance classification. There has been an increasing interest on modeling stance in debates (e.g., congressional debates or online political forums) (Thomas et al., 2006; Somasundaran and Wiebe, 2009; Murakami and Raymond, 2010; Walker et al., 2012; Gottipati et al., 2013; Hasan and Ng, 2014). As discussed in Section 1, there is a close relationship between stance classification and argument relation classification. For instance, Sridhar et al. (2015) showed that stance classification in online debate forums can benefit from modeling disagreement of the reply links (e.g., you could assume an argument is attacking the preceding argument). In our work, we focus on modeling argument relations.

Joint inference and Markov logic networks. Markov logic networks (MLNs) (Domingos and Lowd, 2009) are a statistical relational learning framework that combine *first order logic* and *Markov networks*. They have been successfully applied to various NLP tasks such as semantic role labeling (Meza-Ruiz and Riedel, 2009), information extraction (Poon and Domingos, 2010), coreference resolution (Poon and Domingos, 2008) and bridging resolution (Hou et al., 2013). In this paper, we apply MLNs to model *argument relation classification* and *stance classification* jointly.

---

[1]http://www.debatepedia.org/

	Hidden predicates
$p1$	$relation(a_1, a_2, r)$
$p2$	$stance(a_1, t, s)$

	Formulas
$f1$	$\forall a_1, a_2 \in A : relation(a_1, a_2, r) \rightarrow relation(a_2, a_1, r)$
$f2$	$\forall a_1, a_2, a_3 \in A : relation(a_1, a_2, \text{``}agree\text{''}) \wedge relation(a_2, a_3, \text{``}agree\text{''}) \rightarrow relation(a_1, a_3, \text{``}agree\text{''})$
$f3$	$\forall a_1, a_2, a_3 \in A : relation(a_1, a_2, \text{``}agree\text{''}) \wedge relation(a_2, a_3, \text{``}disagree\text{''}) \rightarrow relation(a_1, a_3, \text{``}disagree\text{''})$
$f4$	$\forall a_1, a_2, a_3 \in A : relation(a_1, a_2, \text{``}disagree\text{''}) \wedge relation(a_2, a_3, \text{``}disagree\text{''}) \rightarrow relation(a_1, a_3, \text{``}agree\text{''})$
$f5$	$\forall a_1, a_2 \in A : stance(a_1, t, s_1) \wedge stance(a_2, t, s_2) \wedge s_1 \neq s_2 \rightarrow relation(a_1, a_2, \text{``}disagree\text{''})$
$f6$	$\forall a_1, a_2 \in A : stance(a_1, t, s_1) \wedge stance(a_2, t, s_2) \wedge s_1 = s_2 \rightarrow relation(a_1, a_2, \text{``}agree\text{''})$
$f7$	$\forall a_1, a_2 \in A : stance(a_1, t, s_1) \wedge relation(a_1, a_2, \text{``}disagree\text{''}) \wedge s_1 \neq s_2 \rightarrow stance(a_2, t, s_2)$
$f8$	$\forall a_1, a_2 \in A : stance(a_1, t, s_1) \wedge relation(a_1, a_2, \text{``}agree\text{''}) \rightarrow stance(a_2, t, s_1)$
$f9$	$\forall a_1, a_2 \in A : localRelPrediction(a_1, a_2, r) \rightarrow relation(a_1, a_2, r)$
$f10$	$\forall a_1 \in A : localStancePrediction(a_1, t, s) \rightarrow stance(a_1, t, s)$

Table 2: Hidden predicates and formulas used for argument relation classification. a_1, a_2 represent arguments in the topic t. $r \in \{agree, disagree\}$, $s \in \{pro, con\}$.

3 Method

As stated in the introduction, our goal is *argument relation classification* as opposed to stance classification. Therefore, given a topic t and a set of arguments A which belongs to t, instead of finding the position (i.e., *pro* or *con*) a_i ($a_i \in A$) takes with respect to t, we want to predict the relation (i.e., *agree* or *disagree*) between a_i and a_j.

The approach we propose tries to make the best use of the topics and arguments by classifying the stances of arguments and the relations between arguments jointly, using Markov logic networks (MLNs).

More specifically, given a topic t and its argument set A we would like to find the stance s_i for each argument a_i and the relation r_{ij} between argument a_i and a_j ($a_i, a_j \in A$) jointly. Let r_{ij} be a relation assignment for an argument pair $a_i, a_j \in A$, R_A be a relation classification result for all arguments in A, R_A^n be the set of all relation classification results for A. Let s_a be a stance prediction for an argument $a \in A$, S_A be a stance prediction result for arguments in A, S_A^n be the set of all possible stance prediction results for A. Our joint inference for *argument relation classification* and *stance classification* can be represented as a log-linear model:

$$P(R_A, S_A | A; w) =$$

$$\frac{\exp(w \cdot \Phi(A, R_A, S_A))}{\sum_{R_A{'} \in R_A^n, S_A{'} \in S_A^n} \exp(w \cdot \Phi(A, R_A{'}, S_A{'}))}$$

where w is the model's weight vector, $\Phi(A, R_A, S_A)$ is a "global" feature vector which takes the entire relation and stance assignments for all arguments in A into account. We define $\Phi(A, R_A, S_A)$ as:

$$\Phi(A, R_A, S_A) = \sum_{l \in F_r} \sum_{a_i, a_j \in A} \Phi_l(a_i, a_j, r_{ij})$$
$$+ \sum_{k \in F_s} \sum_{a \in A} \Phi_k(a, s_a)$$
$$+ \sum_{g \in F_g} \sum_{a_i, a_j \in A} \Phi_g(r_{ij}, s_{a_i}, s_{a_j})$$

where $\Phi_l(a_i, a_j, r_{ij})$ and $\Phi_k(a, s_a)$ are local feature functions for *argument relation classification* and *stance classification*, respectively. The former looks at two arguments a_i and a_j, the latter at the argument a and the stance s_a. The global feature function $\Phi_g(r_{ij}, s_{a_i}, s_{a_j})$ looks at the relation and stance assignments for a_i and a_j at the same time (see $f5 - f8$ in Table 2).

This log-linear model can be represented using Markov logic networks (MLNs). Table 2 shows formulas for modeling the problem in MLNs. $p1$ and $p2$ are hidden predicates that we predict, i.e., predicting the relation (i.e., *agree* or *disagree*) between a_1 and a_2, and deciding the stance (i.e., *pro* or *con*) of a_1. $f1$ models the symmetry of argument relation. $f2$ models the transitivity of the agree relation. $f3$ and $f4$ model agree/disagree relations among three arguments. $f5 - f8$ model mutual relation between the two hidden predicates, i.e., arguments holding the same/different stance are likely to agree/disagree with each other. $f9$ and $f10$ integrate predictions from the local classifier for argument relation classification and stance classification respectively.

4 Experiments

4.1 Dataset

Debatepedia is an encyclopedia of arguments collected from different sources on debate topics.

Each debate topic is organized hierarchically. It contains background of the topic and usually a number of subtopics, with *pro* and *con* arguments for or against each subtopic (see Table 1 for an example). An argument typically includes a claim and a few supporting evidences.

	Training	Dev	Testing
topics	607	25	25
subtopics	2512	173	176
arguments	15700	968	1037
— pro	7920	472	534
— con	7780	496	503
arg pairs from same subtopics			
agree arg pairs	28271	1713	1828
disagree arg pairs	30759	1893	2078

Table 3: Training, development and testing data.

We create a corpus by extracting all subtopics and their arguments from Debatepedia. We pair all arguments from the same subtopic and label every argument pair as "agree" (for arguments holding the same stance) or "disagree" (for arguments holding the opposite stance). In total we collect data from 657 topics. We reserve 25 topics as the development set and 25 topics as the test set, using the remaining 607 topics for the training set. Table 3 gives an overview of the whole corpus.[2]

4.2 Experimental Setup

Local argument relation classification (*local-Rel*). We employ logistic regression to train a local argument relation classification model using agree and disagree pairs from the training set. Our local classifier replicates, to the extent possible, the state-of-the-art local stance classifier from Walker et al. (2012) used by Sridhar et al. (2015) as well as the disagreement classifier from Menini and Tonelli (2016). We include features of unigrams, all word pairs of the concatenation of two arguments, the overall sentiment of each argument from Stanford CoreNLP (Socher et al., 2013; Manning et al., 2014), the content overlap of two arguments, as well as the number of negations in each argument using a list of negation cues (e.g., not, no, neither) from Councill et al. (2010). We also include three types of dependency features (Anand et al., 2011) which consist of triples from the dependency parse of the argument. Specifically, a basic dependency feature (rel_i, t_j, t_k) encodes the syntactic relation rel_i between words t_j and t_k. One variant is to replace the head word of

the relation rel_i with its part-of-speech tag. The other variant is replacing tokens in a triple with their polarities (i.e., $+$ or $-$) using MPQA dictionary of opinion words (Wilson et al., 2005).

localStanceToRel. We again employ logistic regression to train a local stance classification model (*localStance*) using the same features as in *localRel*. We construct the training instances by pairing a topic t and all its pro/con arguments in the training set[3]. During testing, we predict two arguments agree/disagree to each other if they have the same/differences stances regarding the topic.

LSTM+attention. We adapt the attention-based LSTM model used for textual entailment in Rocktäschel et al. (2016). We use GloVe vectors (Pennington et al., 2014) with 100 dimensions trained on Wikipedia and Gigaword as word embeddings. To avoid over-fitting, we apply dropout before and after the LSTM layer with the probability of 0.1. We train the model with 60 epochs using cross-entropy loss. We use Adam for optimization with the learning rate of 0.01.

EDIT. We reimplement the approach for argument relation classification from Cabrio and Villata (2012). Specifically, we train the textual entailment system EDIT[4] on our training set using the same configuration used in Cabrio and Villata (2012). We then apply the trained model on the testing dataset.

Joint model. For our approach described in Section 3, we use the output of the two local classifiers (*localRel* and *localStance*) as the input for formulas $f9$ and $f10$ in Table 2.[5] The weights of the formulas are learned on the dev dataset. We use *thebeast*[6] to learn weights for the formulas and to perform inference. *thebeast* employs cutting plane inference (Riedel, 2008) to improve the accuracy and efficiency of MAP inference for Markov logic.

4.3 Results and Discussion

Table 4 shows the results of different approaches on *argument relation classification*. *EDIT* performs the worst among four local classifiers with an accuracy of 0.50. We think this is mainly due to the difference between the corpora, i.e., we don't

---

[3]Although *localRel* and *localStance* use the same features, we notice that logistic regression can pick up informative features for each task based on different training set (i.e., arg1-arg2 v.s. topic-arg).

[4]http://edits.fbk.eu/

[5]Another option is to predict *localRel* and *localStance* using MLNs. We leave this for future research.

[6]http://code.google.com/p/thebeast

	localRel			localStanceToRel			LSTM+attention			EDIT			joint		
	R	P	F	R	P	F	R	P	F	R	P	F	R	P	F
agree	52.6	61.1	56.6	71.6	58.5	64.4	55.5	56.1	56.0	76.1	47.9	58.8	63.6	63.1	63.3
disagree	70.5	62.8	66.5	55.4	68.9	61.4	62.4	61.4	61.9	27.1	56.3	36.6	67.3	67.7	67.5
Acc.	62.1			63.0			59.1			**50.0**			**65.5**		
Macro F.	61.8			63.6			58.9			**51.8**			**65.4**		

Table 4: Experimental results of argument relation classification on the testing dataset. Bold indicates statistically significant differences over the baselines using randomization test ($p < 0.01$).

pair an argument with its topic in our argument relation classification dataset.

Additionally, the results of *LSTM+attention* are worse than *localRel* and *localStanceToRel*. We suspect this is because the amount of our training data is only 1/10 of the SNLI corpus used in Rocktäschel et al. (2016). Also our dataset has a richer lexical variability.

In general, the local model *localRel* is better at predicting *disagree* than *agree*. The approach *localStanceToRel* flips this by predicting more argument pairs as *agree*. Overall, there is a small improvement in accuracy from *localRel* to *localStanceToRel*. Our joint model combines the strengths of the two local classifiers and performs significantly better than both of them in terms of accuracy and macro-average F-score (randomization test, $p < 0.01$).

5 Conclusions

We propose a joint inference model for argument relation classification on dialogic argumentation. The model utilizes the mutual support relations between *argument relation classification* and *stance classification*. We show that our joint model significantly outperforms other local models.

References

Pranav Anand, Marilyn Walker, Rob Abbott, Jean E. Fox Tree, Robeson Bowmani, and Michael Minor. 2011. Cats rule and dogs drool!: Classifying stance in online debate. In *Proceedings of the 2nd Workshop on Computational Approaches to Subjectivity and Sentiment Analysis,* Portland, Oregon, 24 June 2011, pages 1–9.

Elena Cabrio and Serena Villata. 2012. Combining textual entailment and argumentation theory for supporting online debates interactions. In *Proceedings of the 50th Annual Meeting of the Association for Computational Linguistics,* Jeju Island, Korea, 8–14 July 2012, pages 208–212.

Claudette Cayrol and Marie-Christine Lagasquie-Schiex. 2005. On the acceptability of arguments in bipolar argumentation frameworks. In Lluís Godo, editor, *Symbolic and Quantitative Approaches to Reasoning with Uncertainty: 8th European Conference*, pages 378–389. Springer Berlin Heidelberg.

Claudette Cayrol and Marie-Christine Lagasquie-Schiex. 2013. Bipolarity in argumentation graphs: Towards a better understanding. *International Journal of Approximate Reasoning*, 54:876–899.

Isaac Councill, Ryan McDonald, and Leonid Velikovich. 2010. What's great and what's not: learning to classify the scope of negation for improved sentiment analysis. In *Proceedings of the Workshop on Negation and Speculation in Natural Language Processing,* Uppsala, Sweden, 10 July 2010, pages 51–59.

Pedro Domingos and Daniel Lowd. 2009. *Markov Logic: An Interface Layer for Artificial Intelligence.* Morgan Claypool Publishers.

Swapna Gottipati, Minghui Qiu, Yanchuan Sim, Jing Jiang, and Noah A. Smith. 2013. Learning topics and positions from Debatepedia. In *Proceedings of the 2013 Conference on Empirical Methods in Natural Language Processing,* Seattle, Wash., 18–21 October 2013, pages 1858–1868.

Ivan Habernal and Iryna Gurevych. 2015. Exploiting debate portals for semi-supervised argumentation mining in user-generated web discourse. In *Proceedings of the 2015 Conference on Empirical Methods in Natural Language Processing,* Lisbon, Portugal, 17–21 September 2015, pages 2127–2137.

Ivan Habernal and Iryna Gurevych. 2016. Which argument is more convincing? analyzing and predicting convincingness of web arguments using bidirectional lstm. In *Proceedings of the 54th Annual Meeting of the Association for Computational Linguistics,* Berlin, Germany, 7–12 August 2016, pages 1589–1599.

Kazi Saidul Hasan and Vincent Ng. 2014. Why are you taking this stance? identifying and classifying reasons in ideological debates. In *Proceedings of the 2014 Conference on Empirical Methods in Natural Language Processing,* Doha, Qatar, 25–29 October 2014, pages 751–762.

Yufang Hou, Katja Markert, and Michael Strube. 2013. Global inference for bridging anaphora resolution. In *Proceedings of the 2013 Conference of the North*

American Chapter of the Association for Computational Linguistics: Human Language Technologies, Atlanta, Georgia, 9–14 June 2013, pages 907–917.

Ran Levy, Yonatan Bilu, Daniel Hershcovich, Ehud Aharoni, and Noam Slonim. 2014. Context dependent claim detection. In *Proceedings of the 25th International Conference on Computational Linguistics,* Dublin, Ireland, 23–29 August 2014, pages 1489–1500.

Marco Lippi and Paolo Torroni. 2016. Argument mining from speech: Detecting claims in political debates. In *Proceedings of the 30th Conference on the Advancement of Artificial Intelligence,* Phoenix, Arizona, USA, 12–17 February 2016, pages 2979–2985.

Christopher Manning, Mihai Surdeanu, John Bauer, Jenny Finkel, Steven Bethard, and David McClosky. 2014. The stanford corenlp natural language processing toolkit. In *Proceedings of the ACL 2014 System Demonstrations,* Baltimore, USA, 22–27 June 2014, pages 55–50.

Stefano Menini and Sara Tonelli. 2016. Agreement and disagreement: Comparison of points of view in the political domain. In *Proceedings of the 26th International Conference on Computational Linguistics,* Osaka, Japan, 11–16 December 2016, pages 2461–2470.

Ivan Meza-Ruiz and Sebastian Riedel. 2009. Jointly identifying predicates, arguments and senses using Markov logic. In *Proceedings of Human Language Technologies 2009: The Conference of the North American Chapter of the Association for Computational Linguistics,* Boulder, Col., 31 May – 5 June 2009, pages 155–163.

Akiko Murakami and Rudy Raymond. 2010. Support or oppose? classifying positions in online debates from reply activities and opinion expressions. In *Proceedings of the 23rd International Conference on Computational Linguistics,* Beijing, China, 23–27 August 2010, pages 869–875.

Huy Nguyen and Diane Litman. 2016. Context-aware argumentative relation mining. In *Proceedings of the 54th Annual Meeting of the Association for Computational Linguistics,* Berlin, Germany, 7–12 August 2016, pages 1127–1137.

Andreas Peldszus and Manfred Stede. 2015. Joint prediction in MST-style discourse parsing for argumentation mining. In *Proceedings of the 2015 Conference on Empirical Methods in Natural Language Processing,* Lisbon, Portugal, 17–21 September 2015, pages 938–948.

Jeffrey Pennington, Richard Socher, and Christopher D. Manning. 2014. Glove: Global vectors for word representation. In *Proceedings of the 2014 Conference on Empirical Methods in Natural Language Processing,* Doha, Qatar, 25–29 October 2014, pages 1532–1543.

Isaac Persing and Vincent Ng. 2015. Modeling argument strength in student essays. In *Proceedings of the Joint Conference of the 53th Annual Meeting of the Association for Computational Linguistics and the 7th International Joint Conference on Natural Language Processing,* Beijing, China, 26–31 July 2015, pages 543–552.

Isaac Persing and Vincent Ng. 2016. End-to-end argumentation mining in student essays. In *Proceedings of the 2016 Conference of the North American Chapter of the Association for Computational Linguistics: Human Language Technologies,* San Diego, California, 12–17 June 2016, pages 1384–1394.

Hoifung Poon and Pedro Domingos. 2008. Joint unsupervised coreference resolution with Markov Logic. In *Proceedings of the 2008 Conference on Empirical Methods in Natural Language Processing,* Waikiki, Honolulu, Hawaii, 25–27 October 2008, pages 650–659.

Hoifung Poon and Pedro Domingos. 2010. Unsupervised ontology induction from text. In *Proceedings of the 48th Annual Meeting of the Association for Computational Linguistics,* Uppsala, Sweden, 11–16 July 2010, pages 296–305.

Sebastian Riedel. 2008. Improving the accuracy and efficiency of MAP inference for Markov logic. In *Proceedings of the 24th Conference on Uncertainty in Artificial Intelligence,* Helsinki, Finland, 9–12 July 2008, pages 468–475.

Ruty Rinott, Lena Dankin, Carlos Alzate Perez, Mitesh M. Khapra, Ehud Aharoni, and Noam Slonim. 2015. Show me your evidence - an automatic method for context dependent evidence detection. In *Proceedings of the 2015 Conference on Empirical Methods in Natural Language Processing,* Lisbon, Portugal, 17–21 September 2015, pages 440–450.

Tim Rocktäschel, Edward Grefenstette, Karl Moritz Hermann, Tomas Kocisky, and Phil Blunsom. 2016. Reasoning about entailment with neural attention. In *Proceedings of the 4th International Conference on Learning Representations,* San Juan, Puerto Rico, 2-4 May 2016.

Richard Socher, Alex Perelygin, Jean Wu, Jason Chuang, Christopher D. Manning, Andrew Ng, and Christopher Potts. 2013. Recursive deep models for semantic compositionality over a sentiment treebank. In *Proceedings of the 2013 Conference on Empirical Methods in Natural Language Processing,* Seattle, Wash., 18–21 October 2013, pages 1631–1642.

Swapna Somasundaran and Janyce Wiebe. 2009. Recognizing stances in online debates. In *Proceedings of the Joint Conference of the 47th Annual Meeting of the Association for Computational Linguistics and the 4th International Joint Conference on Natural Language Processing,* Singapore, 2–7 August 2009.

Dhanya Sridhar, James Foulds, Bert Huang, Lise Getoor, and Marilyn Walker. 2015. Joint models of disagreement and stance in online debate. In *Proceedings of the Joint Conference of the 53th Annual Meeting of the Association for Computational Linguistics and the 7th International Joint Conference on Natural Language Processing,* Beijing, China, 26–31 July 2015, pages 116–125.

Christian Stab and Iryna Gurevych. 2014. Identifying argumentative discourse structures in persuasive essays. In *Proceedings of the 2014 Conference on Empirical Methods in Natural Language Processing,* Doha, Qatar, 25–29 October 2014, pages 46–56.

Chenhao Tan, Vlad Niculae, Cristian Danescu-Niculescu-Mizil, and Lillian Lee. 2016. Winning arguments: Interaction dynamics and persuasion strategies in good-faith online discussions. In *Proceedings of the 25th World Wide Web Conference,* Montréal, Québec, Canada, 11 – 15 April, 2016, pages 613–624.

Simone Teufel. 1999. *Argumentative zoning: Information extraction from scientific text.* Ph.D. thesis, University of Edinburgh.

Matt Thomas, Bo Pang, and Lillian Lee. 2006. Get out the vote: Determining support or opposition from congressional floor-debate transcripts. In *Proceedings of the 2006 Conference on Empirical Methods in Natural Language Processing,* Sydney, Australia, 22–23 July 2006, pages 327–335.

Marilyn A. Walker, Pranav Anand, Robert Abbott, and Ricky Grant. 2012. Stance classification using dialogic properties of persuasion. In *Proceedings of the 2012 Conference of the North American Chapter of the Association for Computational Linguistics: Human Language Technologies,* Montréal, Québec, Canada, 3–8 June 2012, pages 592–596.

Theresa Wilson, Janyce M. Wiebe, and Paul Hoffmann. 2005. Recognizing contextual polarity in phrase-level sentiment analysis. In *Proceedings of the Human Language Technology Conference and the 2005 Conference on Empirical Methods in Natural Language Processing,* Vancouver, B.C., Canada, 6–8 October 2005, pages 347–354.

Justine Zhang, Ravi Kumar, Sujith Ravi, and Cristian Danescu-Niculescu-Mizil. 2016. Conversational flow in Oxford-style debates. In *Proceedings of the 2016 Conference of the North American Chapter of the Association for Computational Linguistics: Human Language Technologies,* San Diego, California, 12–17 June 2016, pages 136–141.

Projection of Argumentative Corpora from Source to Target Languages

Ahmet Aker
University of Duisburg-Essen
a.aker@is.inf.uni-due.de

Huangpan ZHANG
University of Duisburg-Essen
huangpan.zhang@stud.uni-due.de

Abstract

Argumentative corpora are costly to create and are available in only few languages with English dominating the area. In this paper we release the first publicly available Mandarin argumentative corpus. The corpus is created by exploiting the idea of comparable corpora from Statistical Machine Translation. We use existing corpora in English and manually map the claims and premises to comparable corpora in Mandarin. We also implement a simple solution to automate this approach with the view of creating argumentative corpora in other less-resourced languages. In this way we introduce a new task of multi-lingual argument mapping that can be evaluated using our English-Mandarin argumentative corpus. The preliminary results of our automatic argument mapper mirror the simplicity of our approach, but provide a baseline for further improvements.

1 Introduction

Identifying argument, i.e. claims and their associated pieces of evidence (premises) in large volumes of textual data has the potential to revolutionarise our access to information. Argument based search for information would for example facilitate individual and organisational decision-making, make learning more efficient, enable quicker reporting on present and past events, to name just a few broad applications. Even more important is argument mining in the multi-lingual context, by which argument based search would be available to people in the language of their preference.

Argument mining is a new, but rapidly growing area of research within Computational Linguistic that has gained a great popularity in the last five years. For instance, since 2014 the meeting of the Association for Computational Linguistics (ACL) is hosting a workshop specifically dedicated to Argument Mining.[1] Current studies report methods for argument mining in legal documents (Reed et al., 2008), persuasive essays (Nguyen and Litman, 2015), Wikipedia articles (Levy et al., 2014; Rinott et al., 2015), discussion fora (Swanson et al., 2015), political debates (Lippi and Torroni, 2016) and news (Sardianos et al., 2015; Al-Khatib et al., 2016). In terms of methodology, supervised machine learning is a central technique used in all these studies. This assumes the availability of data sets – argumentative texts – to train and test the argument mining models. Such data sets are readily available in English and – although in comparably smaller quantities – in very few European languages such as German or Italian. Languages other than these are currently neglected. We are only aware of the study conducted by Chow (2016) who manually annotated Chinese news editorial paragraphs about whether they contain an argument or not. However, the boundaries of the arguments and their claims and premises were not annotated. Due to this lack of data the research and development of argumentation mining outside English and few European languages is very limited, rendering multi-lingual argument mining and language independent argument based search impossible.

In this research we aim to fill this gap. We aim to map existing argument annotations from a source language to a target language. For this purpose an ideal situation would be if there existed parallel documents where the source docu-

---

[1]http://argmining2016.arg.tech/

67

Proceedings of the 4th Workshop on Argument Mining, pages 67–72
Copenhagen, Denmark, September 8, 2017. ©2017 Association for Computational Linguistics

ments are annotated for arguments and where every sentence in the source document had a translation in the target document. In this case one could easily map any argumentative annotation from the source language to the target one. However, parallel data are sparse. In particular there exist no annotated argumentative corpora with parallel documents in any other language, expect the one described by Peldszus and Stede (2015) who report argumentative microtexts corpora in German that is also translated into English. Instead, inspired by the statistical machine translation (SMT) methods, we explore the idea of comparable corpora to obtain argumentative data sets. A comparable corpus contains pairs of documents written in two different languages. The document pairs usually share the same topic but the documents in a pair are not necessarily entirely translations of each other. However, they may share few sentences that are translation of each other. Related work has shown the usefulness of such corpora for training SMT system for under-resourced languages, cross-lingual information retrieval and assisted machine translation (Marton et al., 2009; Aker et al., 2013; Hashemi and Shakery, 2014; Kumano et al., 2007; Sharoff et al., 2006; Aker et al., 2012; Skadiņa et al., 2012; Munteanu and Marcu, 2005, 2002; Rapp, 1999). Given the difficulty and the cost of creating an argumentative corpus, extracting arguments from comparable corpora by automatically mapping arguments from the source language corpus to their translations in the target language seems an attractive avenue. In this work, we take a preliminary step to evaluating the viability of such an approach.

This paper reports on the first Mandarin argumentative corpus that is obtained using comparable corpora. We make use of the existing corpora, in which English documents are annotated for arguments, i.e. where sentences within the documents are marked as claims and premises. We manually map these English sentences to the target documents, by determining sentences in Mandarin that are translations of the English argumentative sentences. In addition, we report the results of our attempt to automatise this manual process of cross-lingual argument mapping. This data set will be publicly available for the research community.

Overall the paper contributes the following:

- We make available a first freely available argumentative corpus of Mandarin, also containing projected argumentative sentences from English to Mandarin comparable articles.

- We introduce a new task of creating multilingual argumentative corpora based on the idea of mapping argumentative sentences between articles that are comparable. Our manually generated data can be used to evaluate performance of automatic approaches.

- We establish and evaluate the possibility of obtaining argumentative corpora in any language with lower cost. To this end we propose a first baseline system for mapping English argumentative sentences into Mandarin.

2 Data

We work with the argumentative data published by Aharoni et al. (2014). The data contains the annotation of English Wikipedia articles for topic specific claims called Context Dependent Claims (CDCs) and premises referred as Context Dependent Evidence (CDE). A topic is a short phrase and frames the discussion within the article (Levy et al., 2014). A CDC is a general, concise statement that directly supports or contests the given topic (Levy et al., 2014). A CDE is a text segment that directly supports a claim in the context of the topic (Rinott et al., 2015). The data released in 2014 contains 1392 labeled claims for 33 different topics, and 1291 labeled premises for 350 distinct claims in 12 different topics (Aharoni et al., 2014). The average number of premises for each claim is 3.69.

To create the comparable corpora we used the inter-language links provided by Wikipedia to link the English articles to the articles in the target language Mandarin. The original data has 315 English articles of which have 160 corresponding Mandarin articles. These 160 pairs of English-Mandarin articles build the basis for mapping arguments from the English to Mandarin.

3 Manual mapping

In our manual process we first mapped Context Dependent Claims (CDCs) and then for each successfully mapped CDC its Context Dependent Evidence (CDEs). To do this we first automatically determined the sentences within the English Wikipedia articles that contained those CDCs and

Language	CDC	CDE
Only English	1392	1291
English-Mandarin	79	27

Table 1: Statistics about the CDCs and CDEs.

CDEs.[2] Next, we manually marked sentences that convey the same meaning as the English argumentative sentences. This process was performed by an annotator who is a native speaker of Mandarin and fluent in English.[3]

Table 1 summarizes the results of this process. In total 79 CDCs out of 1392 (5.7%) were mapped. These mappings were found in 34 English-Mandarin article pairs. The remaining 126 article pairs did not share any argumentative sentences. For the 79 CDCs we also analysed their premises (CDEs) and repeated the mapping process to determine corresponding Mandarin CDEs. In total we found 27 CDEs belonging to 18 CDCs. Table 2 shows an example CDC along with its CDEs in both languages.

Compared to the English the number of CDCs and CDEs mapped into Mandarin is substantially smaller. We have noted three major reasons for this data reduction:

- **No article to match an English one:** In this case there is no Mandarin article to match an English one. In most cases this is due to the topic of the article being very specific, so there are only limited language versions available. This is the reason why only 160 Mandarin articles could be identified for 315 English articles.

- **Dissimilar contents:** In this case there is a matched Mandarin article for the English one, but the contents of the article are not similar. This happens in articles which talk about topics whose content is country specific. Like Google China (`https://en.wikipedia.org/wiki/Google_China`) that talks about country specific events or government control wheres the corresponding English version does not contain any of Mandarin topics.

- **Missing sections:** The matched Mandarin article has missing sections. When the English claims are in those missing parts then there is no corresponding Mandarin mapping.

In a final step it was important to verify that the matched argument pairs are indeed comparable. This assessment was performed by three native Mandarin speakers fluent in English educated to post-graduate level. Their task was to indicate whether the sentences containing claims and premises in English translate into Mandarin claims and premises identified by our annotator. These assessors worked independently of each other. Only one argument was judged as not being an identified translation. The assessors agreed on all identified translation with our annotator and with each other, leading to the inter-annotator agreement of $kappa = 1$ based on Cohen's kappa.

4 Automatic mapping

As our manual effort indicates, there is a substantial reduction in data set, when comparable corpora are used to identify arguments that match in source and target languages. For this reason, an automatic approach to argument matching is mandatory in order to achieve larger data set sizes for multi-lingual argument mining approaches. In addition, successfull automatation of matching would open up the possibiity of creation argumentative corpora from any less-resourced language for which comparable corpora are available.

To evaluate the viability of an automatic approach and create a first benchmark we also performed a simple automatic mapping of English CDCs and CDEs into Mandarin. Our approach relies on automatic machine translation using MOSES (Koehn et al., 2007) and Google translate[4].

We trained MOSES using the publicly available parallel corpora from the HIT IR-lab[5]. For each English article we first translate all CDCs and CDEs into Mandarin. Next, we compare each of those translated argumentative pieces of text with every sentence from the corresponding Mandarin article. Our comparison is based on cosine similarity without stop-word removal. To perform tokenisation we used THULAC[6] an efficient Chi-

---

[2] In the data of (Aharoni et al., 2014) few CDCs and CDEs go over sentence boundaries. We ignore such cases and focus only on those that are bordered by a single sentence.

[3] Note that the annotation or mapping does not contain exact boundary information of the actual argument but only that the Mandarin sentence conveys similar meaning as its English counterpart.

[4] https://translate.google.com/
[5] `http://ir.hit.edu.cn/demo/ltp/Sharing_Plan.htm`
[6] `https://github.com/thunlp/THULAC`

	English	**Mandarin**
CDC	there was a connection between video games and violence	暴力事件与电子游戏之间有着必然的联系
CDE 1	Academic studies have attempted to find a connection between violent video games and the rate of violence and crimes from those that play them; some have stated a connection exists	不少学术研究试图找出一些人的犯罪行为同他们玩电子游戏行为之间的联系，有些研究表明这种联系是存在的
CDE 2	Incidents such as the Columbine High School massacre in 1999 have heightened concerns of a potential connection between video games and violent actions	如在1999年的科伦拜校园事件中，有人认为凶手的暴力行为与电子游戏之间就存在潜在的联系

Table 2: Example CDCs and CDEs.

nese lexical analyser.

We evaluate the performance using accuracy of our automatic mapping solution in retrieving correct pairs. For each CDC and CDE we check whether the most similar Mandarin sentence (according to cosine similarity) is also the correct pair. If yes, this is regarded as correct mapping, otherwise it is marked as wrong. Our evaluation results give us an accuracy of 24% for MOSES based translation and 49% for Google based translation. The Google based results are substantially better than those obtained through MOSES translation. This is because the MOSES decoder fails to translate many cases correctly.

5 Discussion

Our simple approach to tackling the automatic mapping of CDCs and CDEs achieves very low accuracy scores. Although the accuracy of the argument mapper based on the Google translation is substantially higher than the one achieved through MOSES translation, 49% of correct matches are still not satisfactory. This indicates that the task of argument matching in comparable corpora requires more sophisticated methods. One venue for improvement could be to extract richer features capturing sequential translations. Another direction for improvement could be towards a two phases approach. In the first phase one could reduce the Mandarin sentences by using an argumentative cue filter. In the second phase rich features could be extracted from the remaining candidates to perform the final pairing.

In terms of size the closest corpus to the one presented in this work is the one reported by Boltužić and Šnajder (2014) with 300 sentences. However, despite its small size at present, our corpus has important potential applications. Apart from training initial Mandarin argument mining solutions it can serve as a benchmark data for the task of mapping argumentative sentences from English to Mandarin. Systems performing with high precision on this data can be used to extend the given corpus by (1) determining annotated documents in the source language, (2) finding comparable documents in Mandarin and (3) using the mapping tool to map the source annotations to Mandarin.

6 Conclusion

In this paper we release the first Mandarin argumentative corpus containing Context Dependent Claims (CDCs) and Context Dependent Evidence (CDE). We obtained the corpus by manually mapping existing CDCs and CDEs from English Wikipedia articles to corresponding Mandarin articles. With this corpus we provide the basis for developing first argumentation mining solutions for Mandarin. The data can be downloaded from git-hub.[7]

By tackling the need for multi-lingual arguments in this paper we also introduced a new task: mapping argumentative sentences from one language to another. With this task we open up possibilities for obtaining argumentative resources in less-resourced languages with substantially lower cost than the manual effort.

Finally, we introduced a simple automatic tool for performing the argument mapping between English and Mandarin. The modest accuracy results achieved by this simple approach indicate that more sophisticated methods are necessary for argument mapping. We plan to improve the performance of our tool by investigating richer features and also the idea of filtering out sentences in the Mandarin languages that bare no argumentation. Our method reported in this work is a baseline system for argument mapping, and its scores can serve as a benchmark for further more sophisticated methods.

---

[7]`https://github.com/ahmetaker/MandarinArguments`

Acknowledgements

This work was supported by the Deutsche Forschungsgemeinschaft (DFG) under grant No. GRK 2167, Research Training Group "User-Centred Social Media".

References

Ehud Aharoni, Anatoly Polnarov, Tamar Lavee, Daniel Hershcovich, Ran Levy, Ruty Rinott, Dan Gutfreund, and Noam Slonim. 2014. A benchmark dataset for automatic detection of claims and evidence in the context of controversial topics. In *Proceedings of the First Workshop on Argumentation Mining*. pages 64–68.

Ahmet Aker, Evangelos Kanoulas, and Robert J Gaizauskas. 2012. A light way to collect comparable corpora from the web. In *LREC*. Citeseer, pages 15–20.

Ahmet Aker, Monica Lestari Paramita, and Robert J Gaizauskas. 2013. Extracting bilingual terminologies from comparable corpora. In *ACL (1)*. pages 402–411.

Khalid Al-Khatib, Henning Wachsmuth, Johannes Kiesel, Matthias Hagen, and Benno Stein. 2016. A news editorial corpus for mining argumentation strategies. In *Proceedings of the 26th International Conference on Computational Linguistics*.

Filip Boltužić and Jan Šnajder. 2014. Back up your stance: Recognizing arguments in online discussions. In *Proceedings of the First Workshop on Argumentation Mining*. Citeseer, pages 49–58.

Marisa Chow. 2016. Argument identification in chinese editorials. In *Proceedings of NAACL-HLT*. pages 16–21.

Homa B Hashemi and Azadeh Shakery. 2014. Mining a persian–english comparable corpus for cross-language information retrieval. *Information Processing & Management* 50(2):384–398.

Philipp Koehn, Hieu Hoang, Alexandra Birch, Chris Callison-Burch, Marcello Federico, Nicola Bertoldi, Brooke Cowan, Wade Shen, Christine Moran, Richard Zens, et al. 2007. Moses: Open source toolkit for statistical machine translation. In *Proceedings of the 45th annual meeting of the ACL on interactive poster and demonstration sessions*. Association for Computational Linguistics, pages 177–180.

Tadashi Kumano, Hideki Tanaka, and Takenobu Tokunaga. 2007. Extracting phrasal alignments from comparable corpora by using joint probability smt model. *Proceedings of TMI*.

Ran Levy, Yonatan Bilu, Daniel Hershcovich, Ehud Aharoni, and Noam Slonim. 2014. Context dependent claim detection .

Marco Lippi and Paolo Torroni. 2016. Argument mining from speech: Detecting claims in political debates. In *AAAI*. pages 2979–2985.

Yuval Marton, Chris Callison-Burch, and Philip Resnik. 2009. Improved statistical machine translation using monolingually-derived paraphrases. In *Proceedings of the 2009 Conference on Empirical Methods in Natural Language Processing: Volume 1-Volume 1*. Association for Computational Linguistics, pages 381–390.

Dragos Stefan Munteanu and Daniel Marcu. 2002. Processing comparable corpora with bilingual suffix trees. In *Proceedings of the ACL-02 conference on Empirical methods in natural language processing-Volume 10*. Association for Computational Linguistics, pages 289–295.

Dragos Stefan Munteanu and Daniel Marcu. 2005. Improving machine translation performance by exploiting non-parallel corpora. *Computational Linguistics* 31(4):477–504.

Huy V Nguyen and Diane J Litman. 2015. Extracting argument and domain words for identifying argument components in texts. In *Proceedings of the 2nd Workshop on Argumentation Mining*. pages 22–28.

Andreas Peldszus and Manfred Stede. 2015. An annotated corpus of argumentative microtexts. In *Proceedings of the First Conference on Argumentation, Lisbon, Portugal, June. to appear*.

Reinhard Rapp. 1999. Automatic identification of word translations from unrelated english and german corpora. In *Proceedings of the 37th annual meeting of the Association for Computational Linguistics on Computational Linguistics*. Association for Computational Linguistics, pages 519–526.

Chris Reed, Raquel Mochales Palau, Glenn Rowe, and Marie-Francine Moens. 2008. Language resources for studying argument. In *Proceedings of the 6th conference on language resources and evaluation-LREC 2008*. ELRA, pages 91–100.

Ruty Rinott, Lena Dankin, Carlos Alzate Perez, Mitesh M Khapra, Ehud Aharoni, and Noam Slonim. 2015. Show me your evidence-an automatic method for context dependent evidence detection. In *EMNLP*. pages 440–450.

Christos Sardianos, Ioannis Manousos Katakis, Georgios Petasis, and Vangelis Karkaletsis. 2015. Argument extraction from news. *NAACL HLT 2015* page 56.

Serge Sharoff, Bogdan Babych, and Anthony Hartley. 2006. Using comparable corpora to solve problems difficult for human translators. In *Proceedings of the COLING/ACL on Main conference poster sessions*. Association for Computational Linguistics, pages 739–746.

Inguna Skadiņa, Ahmet Aker, Nikos Mastropavlos, Fangzhong Su, Dan Tufis, Mateja Verlic, Andrejs Vasiļjevs, Bogdan Babych, Paul Clough, Robert Gaizauskas, et al. 2012. Collecting and using comparable corpora for statistical machine translation. In *Proceedings of the 8th International Conference on Language Resources and Evaluation (LREC), Istanbul, Turkey*.

Reid Swanson, Brian Ecker, and Marilyn Walker. 2015. Argument mining: Extracting arguments from online dialogue. In *Proceedings of 16th Annual Meeting of the Special Interest Group on Discourse and Dialogue (SIGDIAL 2015)*. pages 217–227.

Manual Identification of Arguments with Implicit Conclusions Using Semantic Rules for Argument Mining

Nancy L. Green
University of North Carolina Greensboro
Greensboro, N.C. 27402, U.S.A.
nlgreen@uncg.edu

Abstract

This paper describes a pilot study to evaluate human analysts' ability to identify the argumentation scheme and premises of an argument having an implicit conclusion. In preparation for the study, argumentation scheme definitions were crafted for genetics research articles. The schemes were defined in semantic terms, following our proposal to use semantic rules to mine arguments in that literature.

1 Introduction

Surface text-level approaches to argument mining in the natural sciences literature face various problems (Green, 2015b). The premises and conclusion of an argument are not necessarily expressed in adjacent phrasal units. Components of different arguments may be interleaved in the text. Even more challenging, some of the premises or the conclusion of an argument may be implicit. For example, the following excerpt can be interpreted as expressing an argument having the implicit, tentative conclusion that a certain mutation within the Itpr1 gene may be the cause of the affected mice's movement disorder: *Our initial observations suggested that the affected mice suffered from an apparently paroxysmal movement disorder ... Sequencing ... revealed a single mutation within Itpr1 ...* (Van de Leemput et. al., 2007).

Argumentation schemes (Walton et al., 2008) describe acceptable, often defeasible, patterns of reasoning. The schemes place additional constraints on the relation between an argument's premises and its conclusion than do discourse coherence models such as Rhetorical Structure Theory (Mann and Thompson, 1988) and similar models used to annotate scientific corpora (e.g. Prasad et al., 2011). Recognizing the argumentation scheme underlying an argument is an important task. First, each argument scheme has an associated set of *critical questions*, or potential challenges, so recognizing the scheme can provide information for generating or recognizing challenges. Second, and most relevant to the concerns of this paper, the constraints of the scheme can provide information for inferring an implicit argument component, such as the conclusion of the argument in the above excerpt.

The above problems suggest that a semantics-informed approach to argument mining in this genre would be desirable. We have proposed an approach to argument mining within genetics research articles using semantic argumentation scheme definitions implemented in a logic programming language (Green, 2016). A significant advantage of that approach is that implicit conclusions of arguments can be recognized.

To evaluate such an approach, it would be useful to have a corpus of genetics research articles whose arguments (i.e., argumentation scheme, implicit and explicit premises, and implicit or explicit conclusion) have been identified by human analysts. Note that there is no such corpus currently available, and creating such a corpus will be expensive. To contribute to the creation of such a corpus, we created a draft manual of argumentation scheme definitions in the genetics domain for use by

73

Proceedings of the 4th Workshop on Argument Mining, pages 73–78
Copenhagen, Denmark, September 8, 2017. ©2017 Association for Computational Linguistics

human analysts, and ran a pilot study to evaluate human analysts' ability to apply the definitions to text containing arguments with *implicit* conclusions. As far as we know, no such study has been performed with text from the natural sciences research literature. The main contribution of this paper is to present the study. However, to motivate our interest in using semantic definitions of argumentation schemes in argument mining, we present additional background in the next section. Section 3 describes the study, and Section 4 outlines plans for future work.

2   Background

This section explains how semantic rules could be used in argument mining as proposed in (Green, 2016) and compares it to current approaches. The first step in our proposal is to preprocess a text to extract semantic entities and relations specific to the domain. For example, to mine articles on genetic variants that may cause human disease, we proposed extracting a small set of semantic predicates, such as those describing an organism's genotype and phenotype. Although automatically identifying entities and relations in biomedical text is very challenging, it is the object of much current research (Cohen and Demner-Fushman, 2014), and we assume that BioNLP tools will be able to automate this in the near future. Current BioNLP relation extraction tools include OpenMutation-Minder (Naderi and Witte, 2012) and DiMeX (Mahmood et al., 2016). The extracted relations would populate a Prolog knowledge base (KB).

Next, Prolog rules implementing argument schemes, such as the following, would be applied to the KB to produce instances of arguments, i.e., including the semantic relations comprising the premises and the conclusion, as well as the name of the underlying argumentation scheme.

```
argument(
  scheme('Method of Agreement'),
  premise(have_phenotype(G, P)),
  premise(have_genotype(G, M)),
  conclusion(cause(M, P))) :-
  group(G), have_phenotype(G, P),
  have_genotype(G, M).
```

As a proof-of-concept, the rules were implemented and tested on a manually-created KB. An advantage of this approach is that implicit conclusions of arguments are recognized automatically and can be added to the KB. The added conclusions can then serve as implicit premises of subsequent arguments given in the text.

A semantics-informed approach is in contrast to today's machine learning approaches that use only surface-level text features. Among those approaches, there has been little concern with argument scheme recognition, except for (Feng and Hirst, 2011; Lawrence and Reed, 2016). Saint-Dizier (2012) uses manually-derived rules for argument mining, but the rules are based on syntactic patterns and lexical features. None of these approaches is capable of identifying implicit argument components.

A possible limitation of a semantic rule-based approach is the necessity to first extract semantic relations. However in BioNLP domains, where relation extraction tools are being developed for other purposes and the size of the targeted literature is huge and constantly growing, the benefits may outweigh the cost. Another possible limitation is "scalability", or the cost of manually deriving rules for topics not covered by the current rules. However, the rules are specializations of argumentation schemes that have been previously cited as applicable to the natural sciences in general (Walton et al., 2008; Jenicek and Hitchcock, 2005), so it is plausible that the effort to create rules for other topics in the natural sciences will not be significantly higher than the cost of formulating the current rule set.

3   Pilot Study

3.1   Preparation

The author created a draft document defining argumentation schemes in terms of the domain concepts used in the Prolog implementation of Green's argumentation schemes (2016). Note that in an earlier study (Green, 2015a) we provided definitions of argumentation schemes found in the genetics research literature, but the definitions were abstract and did not refer to   domain-specific concepts used in (Green, 2016). It was decided to redefine the schemes in terms of domain concepts to more closely align with the implementation in (Green, 2016).

A team consisting of the author, a biology doctoral student with research experience in genetics, and a computer science graduate student with an undergraduate degree in philosophy collaborated on identifying the arguments in the Results section of two articles (Van de Leemput et al., 2007; Lloyd et al., 2005) from the CRAFT corpus (Bada et al., 2012; Verspoor et al. 2012). The CRAFT corpus is open access and has already been linguistically annotated. During this process, the argumentation scheme definitions were refined. The goal of the pilot study reported here was to determine if other researchers could apply the resulting definitions with some consistency, and to test the feasibility of this type of study before conducting a larger study.

3.2 Procedure and Materials

Human identification of an argument's premises, conclusion, and scheme in this genre is a very challenging task, requiring some domain knowledge as well as training on argumentation schemes. Thus, it was decided to focus on certain aspects of the problem in this study. The study materials consisted of the draft document of argumentation scheme definitions, and a set of five problems. The problems were constructed to test identification of five different argumentation schemes that we have frequently seen used in this genre and whose definitions are similar to the Prolog rules given in (Green, 2016). The schemes are paraphrased below in a more compact form than that presented to participants. Definitions of domain-specific predicates such as *genotype* and *phenotype* also were included in materials given to participants.

Method of Agreement: If a group has an abnormal genotype G and abnormal phenotype P then G may be the cause of P.

Method of Difference: If a group has an abnormal genotype G and abnormal phenotype P and a second group has neither, then G may be the cause of P.

Analogy: If a group has abnormal genotype G and abnormal phenotype P and G may be the cause of P, and a second group has abnormal genotype G' similar to G and abnormal phenotype P' similar to P, then G' may be the cause of P'.

Consistent with Predicted Effect: If a group has abnormal genotype G and abnormal phenotype P and there is a causal mechanism that predicts that G could cause P, then G may be the cause of P.

Consistent Explanation: If a group has an abnormal genotype G, abnormal gene product Prot, and abnormal phenotype P, and G produces Prot, and Prot may cause P (and thus G may cause P), then if a second group has an abnormal genotype G' similar to G, abnormal gene product Prot' similar to Prot, and abnormal phenotype P' similar to P, then G' may be the cause of P'.

Each problem included a short excerpt containing an argument with an *implicit* conclusion (such as the example given in the Introduction of this paper), three to five sentences of background information on genetics that the intended audience, having domain expertise, would be expected to know, and a paraphrase of the conclusion of the argument. Participants were asked to select (1) the name of the applicable argument scheme from a list of nine scheme names (defined in the other document), and (2) the relevant premises from a list of five possible premises. One reason for designing the problems in this way was that we can envision an application of argument mining as finding an argument for a given conclusion, whether or not it has been stated explicitly. A sample problem is shown in Appendix A.

Invitations to participate in the study were emailed to researchers in biology and (mainly) in computer science, and responses were returned by email. No incentives were offered. Given the difficulty of the task due to the unfamiliarity of the domain to most participants, the lack of training other than receiving the draft document of argumentation scheme definitions, and the length of time required to participate, we were pleased to receive six responses.

3.3 Results and Discussion

The rows of Table 1 show the number of participants who selected each argumentation scheme (Anlg: Analogy, Agr: Agreement, Diff: Difference, CPr: Consistent with Predicted Effect, CEx: Consistent Explanation), and the diagonal shows the number who selected the correct answer. For example, Analogy was correctly selected by four of the six participants; the other two confused it with Consistent with Predicted Effect and Consistent Explanation. Note that one participant selected both Difference and Consistent Explanation as the answer to the problem whose answer was Difference, thus we scored that as 0.5 for each. However, that participant commented that by selecting Consistent Explanation he actually meant Difference Consistent Explanation, an argumentation scheme defined in the other document but not listed among the choices.

	Anlg	Agr	Diff	CPr	CEx
Anlg	4			1	1
Agr		5			1
Diff			5.5		0.5
CPr				5	1
CEx				1	5

Table 1: Confusion Matrix

The table shows that the two schemes that were incorrectly applied the most times (CPr and CEx) were those with the most complicated definitions involving explicit causal explanations. Nevertheless, the results suggest that with careful revision of the definitions and more training than was provided to the participants, humans will be able to identify these schemes consistently.

Table 2 shows the data for each of the six participants. The first row shows the number of premises marked correctly out of 25 choices in all (five choices for each of the five problems). The average number of correctly marked premises was 21/25 or 84 percent. The second row shows that the number of correctly identified schemes

was on average 4/5 or 80 percent. Participants 3, 4, and 5 had the lowest accuracy.

Partic.	1	2	3	4	5	6
Premises	24	23	16	20	20	25
Schemes	5	5	4	2.5	3	5

Table 2: Participant Data

4 Future Work

The long-term goal of the pilot study was to enable us to document arguments in a corpus of scientific research articles. An earlier proposal of ours (Green, 2015b) was to annotate text spans as argument components. In contrast, our current plan is to semantically annotate the arguments in a two-step process. The first step will be to identify the entities and relations in the text. This could be done manually, or better, using BioNLP tools. For example, the result of this step might be an annotated segment like this: *Sequencing ...* <entity id="e1"> *affected mice from the current study* </entity> *revealed a single mutation ...* <entity id="e9"> *Itpr1Δ18/Δ18* </entity> <relation id= "r1" predicate= "genotype" entity1="e1" entity2="e9" />.

The second step would be to manually document the arguments in terms of the entities and relations annotated in the first step, e.g.,
<argument scheme="Agreement"
  premise="genotype(e1,e9)"
  premise="phenotype(e1, e2)"
  conclusion="cause(r1, r4)" />

The documented arguments then could be compared to the arguments mined by the semantic approach proposed in (Green, 2016).

Acknowledgments

The analysis of argument schemes was done with the help of Michael Branon and Bishwa Giri, who were supported by a UNCG 2016 Summer Faculty Excellence Research Grant.

References

M. Bada, M. Eckert, D. Evans, et al. 2012. Concept Annotation in the CRAFT corpus. *BMC Bioinformatics* 13:161.

K. Cohen and D. Demner-Fushman. 2014. *Biomedical Natural Language Processing.* John Benjamins Publishing Company, Amsterdam.

V.W. Feng and G. Hirst, 2011. Classifying Arguments by Scheme. In *Proceedings of the 49th Annual Meeting of the Association for Computational Linguistics,* Portland, OR, 987-996.

N.L. Green. 2015a. Identifying Argumentation Schemes in Genetics Research Articles. In *Proc. Second Workshop on Argumentation Mining.* North American Conference of the Association for Computational Linguistics (NAACL).

N.L. Green. 2015b. Annotating Evidence-Based Argumentation in Biomedical Text. In *Proc. 2015 IEEE International Conference on Bioinformatics and Biomedicine, 2015 International Workshop on Biomedical and Health Informatics.*

N.L. Green. 2016. Implementing Argumentation Schemes as Logic Programs. In *Proc. of Computational Models of Natural Argument (CMNA-16)*, CEUR Workshop Vol-1876.

D. Lloyd, F.W. Halt, L.M. Tarantino, and N. Gekakis. 2005. Diabetes Insipidus in Mice with a Mutation in Aquaporin-2. *PLoS Genetics*, August 2005, Vol. 1, Issue 2, e20, 0171-0178.

M. Jenicek and D.Hitchcock. 2005. *Logic and Critical Thinking in Medicine.* American Medical Association Press.

J. Lawrence and C. Reed. 2016. Argument Mining Using Argumentation Scheme Structures. In Baroni, P. et al. (eds.) *Computational Models of Argument: Proceedings of COMMA 2016.* Amsterdam, IOS Press, 379-90.

A.S. Mahmood, T.J. Wu, R. Mazumder and K. Vijay-Shanker. 2016. DiMeX: A Text Mining System for Mutation-Disease Association Extraction. *PLoS One.*

W. Mann and S. Thompson. 1988. Rhetorical Structure Theory: Towards a Functional Theory of Text Organization. *Text* 8(3): 243-281.

N. Naderi and R. Witte. 2012. Automated extraction and semantic analysis of mutation impacts from the biomedical literature. *BMC Genomics*, 13(Suppl 4):510.

R. Prasad, S. McRoy, N. Frid, A. Joshi, and H. Yu. 2011. The Biomedical Discourse Relation Bank. *BMC Bioinformatics* 2011, 12:188.

P. Saint-Dizier. 2012. Processing natural language arguments with the <TextCoop> platform. *Argument and Computation* 3(1), March 2012, 49-82.

J. Van de Leemput, J. Chandran, M. Knight, et al. Deletion at ITPR1 Underlies Ataxia in Mice and Spinocerebellar Ataxia 15 in Humans. *PLoS Genetics*, 2007, Volume 3, Issue 6, e108, pp. 113-129.

K. Verspoor, K.B. Cohen, A. Lanfranchi, et al. 2012. A corpus of full-text journal articles is a robust evaluation tool for revealing differences in performance of biomedical natural language processing tools. *BMC Bioinformatics* 2012, 13:207.

D. Walton, C. Reed, and F. Macagno. 2008. *Argumentation Schemes.* Cambridge University Press.

Appendix A.   Sample Problem Used in Pilot Study.

2. Excerpt:
"Our initial observations suggested the affected mice suffered from an apparently paroxysmal movement disorder ... At initial examination, a human movement disorder specialist ... likened the disorder to episodic intermittent ataxia ... Sequencing of all exons and intron-exon boundaries of Itpr1 [gene] in affected mice from the current study revealed a single mutation within Itpr1: a novel in-frame deletion of 18 bp within exon 36 (Itpr1Δ18/Δ18)."

Extra background information:
- The phrase "Itpr1Δ18/Δ18" refers to the Itpr1 gene mutation found in the affected mice.
- Exons include genetic sequences that code for proteins; introns do not.
- A deletion is a type of mutation in which part of a DNA sequence is lost.

Using information from the excerpt and from the extra background information, what type of argument could you give for the following conclusion? Circle the best answer:
The Itpr1Δ18/Δ18 mutation may be the cause of the affected mice's movement disorder.
- Agreement
- Failed Method of Agreement
- Analogy
- Consistent Explanation
- Consistent with Predicted Effect
- Difference
- Failed Method of Difference
- Effect to Cause
- Eliminate Candidates

Circle all and only the argument's premises:
- The affected mice suffered from a movement disorder.
- The movement disorder of the mice was likened to episodic intermittent ataxia in humans.
- All exons and intron-exon boundaries of Itpr1 were sequenced.
- The affected mice were found to have a single mutation within Itpr1 (Itpr1Δ18/Δ18).
- A deletion is a type of mutation in which part of a DNA sequence is lost.

Unsupervised corpus-wide claim detection

Ran Levy
Shai Gretz[*]
Benjamin Sznajder
Shay Hummel
Ranit Aharonov
Noam Slonim
IBM Research - Haifa, Israel
{ranl, avishaig, benjams, shayh, ranita, noams}@il.ibm.com

Abstract

Automatic claim detection is a fundamental argument mining task that aims to automatically mine claims regarding a topic of consideration. Previous works on mining argumentative content have assumed that a set of relevant documents is given in advance. Here, we present a first corpus–wide claim detection framework, that can be directly applied to massive corpora. Using simple and intuitive empirical observations, we derive a *claim sentence query* by which we are able to directly retrieve sentences in which the prior probability to include topic-relevant claims is greatly enhanced. Next, we employ simple heuristics to rank the sentences, leading to an unsupervised corpus–wide claim detection system, with precision that outperforms previously reported results on the task of claim detection given relevant documents and labeled data.

1 Introduction

Decision making typically relies on the quality of the arguments being presented and the process by which they are resolved. A common component in all argument models (e.g., (Toulmin, 1958)) is the *claim*, namely the assertion the argument aims to prove. Given a topic of interest, suggesting a diverse set of persuasive claims is a demanding cognitive goal. The corresponding task of *automatic* claim detection was first introduced in (Levy et al., 2014), and is considered a fundamental task in the emerging field of argument mining (Lippi and Torroni, 2016). To illustrate some of the subtleties involved, Table 1 lists examples of sentences related

---

*First two authors contributed equally.

to the topic of whether we should end affirmative action.

S1	*Opponents claim <u>that</u> **affirmative action has undesirable side-effects and that it fails to achieve its goals**.*
S2	*The European Court of Justice held <u>that</u> **this form of positive discrimination is unlawful**.*
S3	*Clearly, **qualifications should be the only determining factor when competing for a job**.*
S4	*In 1961, John F. Kennedy became the first to utilize the term affirmative action in its contemporary sense.*

Table 1: Example sentences for the topic 'End affirmative action': 3 sentences containing claims (in bold), and a non–argumentative sentence which is still relevant to the topic.

Previous works on claim detection have assumed the availability of a relatively small set of articles enriched with relevant claims (Levy et al., 2014). Similarly, other argument–mining works have focused on the analysis of a small set of argumentative essays (Stab and Gurevych, 2014). This paradigm has two limitations. First, it relies on a manual, or automatic (Roitman et al., 2016), process to retrieve the relevant set of articles, which is non-trivial and prone to errors. In addition, when considering large corpora, relevant claims may spread across a much wider and diverse set of articles compared to those considered by earlier works. Here, we present a first corpus–wide claim detection framework, that can be directly applied to massive corpora, with no need to specify a small set of documents in advance.

We exploit the empirical observation that relevant claims are typically (i) semantically related to the topic; and (ii) reside within sentences with identifiable structural properties. Thus, we aim to pinpoint single sentences within the corpus that satisfy both criteria.

Semantic relatedness can be manifested via a rich set of linguistic mechanisms. E.g., in Table 1,

Proceedings of the 4th Workshop on Argument Mining, pages 79–84
Copenhagen, Denmark, September 8, 2017. ©2017 Association for Computational Linguistics

$S1$ mentions the main concept (MC) of the topic (i.e., affirmative action) explicitly; $S2$ mentions the MC using a different surface form – 'positive discrimination'; while $S3$ contains a valid claim without explicitly mentioning the MC. Here, we suggest to use a mention detection tool (Ferragina and Scaiella, 2010), which maps surface forms to Wikipedia titles (a.k.a Wikification), to focus the mining process on sentences in which the MC is detected. Thus, we keep the potential to detect sentences in which different surface forms are used to express the MC. Moreover, using a Wikification tool can help prevent drift in the meaning of the topic. For example, consider the topic *Marriage is outdated* for which the MC is *Marriage*. Had we searched the corpus for all sentences with the word *Marriage*, we would have found many sentences that mention the term *Same sex marriage* which tends to appear more often in argumentative content within the corpus. The risk in this case, is to have the claim detection system drift towards this related but quite different topic. By using a Wikification tool, and assuming it works reasonably well, we avoid this problem. Searching for sentences with the concept *Marriage* will not return sentences in which the Wikification tool found the concept *Same sex marriage*.

However, as mentioned, semantic relatedness is not enough; e.g., $S4$ mentions the MC explicitly, but does not include a claim. To further distinguish such sentences from those containing claims, we observe that the token 'that' is often used as a precursor to a claim; as in $S1$, $S2$ and in the sentence "we observe **that** *the token 'that' is often used as a precursor to a claim*." The usage of 'that' as a feature was first suggested in (Levy et al., 2014). Thus, we use the presence of 'that' as an initial weak label, and further identify unigrams enriched in the suffixes of sentences containing 'that' followed by the MC, compared to sentences containing the MC *without* a preceding 'that'. This yields a *Claim Lexicon* (CL), from which we derive a *Claim Sentence Query* (CSQ) composed of the following ordered triplet: *that* → MC → CL, i.e., the token 'that', the MC as identified by a Wikification tool, and a unigram from the CL, in that order.

We demonstrate empirically over Wikipedia, that for sentences satisfying this query, the prior probability to include a relevant claim is enhanced compared to the background distribution. Further-more, by applying simple unsupervised heuristics to sort the retrieved sentences, we obtain precision results outperforming (Levy et al., 2014), while using no labeled data, and tackling the presumably more challenging goal of corpus–wide claim detection. Our results demonstrate the practical value of the proposed approach, in particular for topics that are well covered in the examined corpus.

2 Related Work

Context dependent claim detection (i.e. the detection of claims that support/contest a given topic) was first suggested by (Levy et al., 2014). Next, (Lippi and Torroni, 2015) proposed the context independent claim detection task, in which one attempts to detect claims without having the topic as input. Thus, if the texts contain claims for multiple topics, all should be detected. Both works used the data in (Aharoni et al., 2014) for training and testing their models.

(Levy et al., 2014) have first described 'that' as an indicator for sentences containing claims. Other works have identified additional indicators of claims, such as discourse markers, and have used them within a rule-based, rather than a supervised, framework (Eckle-Kohler et al., 2015; Ong et al., 2014; Somasundaran and Wiebe, 2009; Schneider and Wyner, 2012).

The usage we make in this work of the word 'that' as an initial weak label is closely related to the idea of distant supervision (Mintz et al., 2009). In the context of argument mining, (Al-Khatib et al., 2016) also used noisy labels to train a classifier, albeit for a different task. They exploited the manually curated idebate.org resource to define – admittedly noisy – labeled data, that were used to train an argument mining classification scheme. In contrast, our approach requires no data curation and relies on a simple linguistic observation of the typical role of 'that' in argumentative text. Our use of the token 'that' as a weak label to identify a relevant lexicon, is also reminiscent of the classical work by (Hearst, 1992) who suggested to use lexico-syntactic patterns to identify various lexical relations. However, to the best of our knowledge, the present work is the first to use such a paradigm in the context of argument mining.

3 System Description

3.1 Sentence Level Index

Corpus-wide claim detection requires a run-time efficient approach. Thus, although the context surrounding a sentence may hint whether it contains a claim, we focus solely on single sentences and the information they contain. Correspondingly, we built an inverted index[1] of sentences for the Wikipedia May 2015 dump, covering $\sim 4.9M$ articles. After text cleaning and sentence splitting using OpenNlp[2] we obtained a sentence–level index that contains $\sim 83M$ sentences. We then used TagMe (Ferragina and Scaiella, 2010) to Wikify each sentence, limiting the context used by TagMe for disambiguation, to the examined sentence.

3.2 Topics

We started with a manually curated list of 431 debate topics that are often used in debate-related sites like idebate.org. We limit our attention to debate topics that focus on a single concept, denoted here as the MC, which is further identified by a corresponding Wikipedia page, e.g., Affirmative Action, Doping in Sport, Boxing, etc. In addition, we focus on topics that are well covered in Wikipedia, which we formally define as topics for which the query $q1 = MC$ has at least $1,000$ matches. This criterion is satisfied in $212/431$ topics, of which we randomly selected 100 as a development set (termed dev-set henceforth) and 50 topics as a test set, used solely for evaluation. The complete list of topics is given in the Supplementary Material (SM).

3.3 Claim Sentence Query (CSQ)

For the 100 dev-set topics we obtained a total of $\sim 1.86M$ sentences that match the query $q1$, hence are assumed to be semantically related to their respective topic. We refer to this set of sentences as the *q1-set*. Using 'that' as a weak label, we divide the q1-set into two classes – the sentences that contain the token 'that' before the MC, and the sentences that do not – denoted c_1 and c_2, respectively. The class c_1 consists of $\sim 183K$ sentences, hence we define the estimated prior probability of a sentence from q1-set to be included in c_1 as $P(c_1) = 0.0986$.

Based on these classes, we are interested in constructing a lexicon of claim-related words that

will enable designing a query with a relatively high prior for detecting claim–containing sentences. We start with standard pre-processing including tokenization, stop-word removal, lower-casing, pos-tagging using OpenNlp, and removal of tokens mentioned in $<$ 10 sentences in q1-set. Preliminary analysis – described in detail in the SM – suggested that we should focus on the *suffixes* of the sentences in c_1, where the suffix is defined as the part of the sentence that follows the MC. Note, that in our setting the claim is expected to occur after the token 'that' with the MC usually being the subject, hence the suffix as defined above seems like a natural candidate to search for words characteristic of claims. Formally, we define n_1 as the number of sentences in c_1 that contain w in the sentence suffix; n_2 as the number of sentences in c_2 that contain w; and $P_{suff}(c_1|w) = n1/(n1 + n2)$. Finally, we define the Claim Lexicon (CL) as the set of words which satisfy $P_{suff}(c_1|w) > P(c_1)$, namely the set of words that are characteristic of the suffixes of sentences in the class c_1. To put it differently, the set of words that, when they appear in the sentence suffix, make the sentence more likely to be in c_1 than expected by the prior.

A desirable feature of the CL is that it contains words which are indicative of claims in the general sense, i.e., in the context of many different topics. Since the resulting lexicon included some topic-specific words, mostly nouns, we applied straightforward cleansing of removing all nouns, as well as numbers, single-character tokens, and country–specific terms from the CL, ending up with a lexicon consisting of 586 words, listed in the SM.

We then use the CL to construct the *claim sentence query* (CSQ): *that* $\rightarrow$ MC $\rightarrow$ CL, where CL denotes any word from the CL. We assessed the prior probability to contain a claim for sentences matching different queries by randomly selecting at most 3 sentences that match the query per dev-set topic, and annotating the resulting sentences by 5 human annotators. We find that, as expected, the prior associated with the query *that* $\rightarrow$ MC is higher than the background prior of sentences matching $q1 = MC$, 4.8% vs. 2.4%, respectively. Using the CSQ further enhances the prior to 9.8%, a factor of 4 compared to the background. Table 2 summarizes the prior and number of matches per query.

---

[1] See Supplementary Material (SM) for details.

[2] https://opennlp.apache.org/

Query	Prior	#Matches
MC	2.4	4872
$that \rightarrow MC$	4.8	493
$that \rightarrow MC \rightarrow CL$	9.8	74

Table 2: Summary of query evaluation. The "Prior" column shows the percentage of claim sentences estimated by the annotation experiment. The "#Matches" column shows the median number of query matches across the dev-set topics.

3.4 From CSQ to Claim Detection

Based on the sentences that match the CSQ, we are now ready to define a system that performs corpus–wide claim detection by adding sentence re-ranking, boundary detection, and simple filters.

Naturally, we are interested to present higher confidence predictions first. Remaining within the unsupervised framework, we rank the sentences by the average of two simple scores: (i) *w2v*: The CSQ only aims to ensure that the MC is present in the examined sentence. Hence, it seems reasonable to assume that considering the semantic similarity of the *entire* candidate claim to the topic will improve the ranking. Thus, we compare the word2vec representation (Mikolov et al., 2013) of each word in the sentence part following the first 'that' to each word in the MC to find the best cosine-similarity match, and average the obtained scores; (ii) *slop*: The number of tokens between 'that' and the first match to the CL. This assumes that the closer the elements appear in the sentence, the higher the probability that it contains a claim.

To perform claim detection, the claim itself should be extracted from the surrounding sentence. From the way the CSQ is constructed, it follows that the claim is expected to start right after the 'that'. The end of the claim is harder to predict. An approach to boundary detection was described in (Levy et al., 2014), but here we employ a simple heuristic, which does not require labeled data, namely ending the claim at the sentence end. Finally, sentences containing location/person named–entities after the 'that' are filtered out.

4 Results

To evaluate the performance of the proposed system we applied crowd labeling[3] on the predicted claims for all 150 topics in the dev- and test-set. For each topic we labeled the top 50 predictions, or all predictions if there were less. A prediction

was considered correct if the majority of the annotators marked it as a claim[4]. The average pairwise Kappa agreement on the dev-set was 0.38, which is similar to the Kappa of 0.39 reported in this context by (Aharoni et al., 2014).

Table 3 depicts the obtained results. Using our approach – that requires no labeling and is applied over the entire Wikipedia corpus – we obtain results that outperform those reached using a supervised approach over a manually pre-selected set of articles (Levy et al., 2014) (see 'Levy' Row), though we note that we consider a different set of topics because of the restrictions we impose on the topic structure (section 3.2). In addition, the test set results are better compared to the dev-set results, suggesting that the system is able to generalize to entirely new topics.

When considering only topics for which $> K$ sentences match the CSQ, the precision increases considerably. For example, for topics that have at least 50 sentences matching the CSQ, $P@50$ is 24% and 34% in the dev- and test-set, respectively. Thus, for topics well covered in the corpus, the precision of the system is even more promising.

The precision results in table 3 are not directly comparable to "classical" argumentation mining tasks, e.g. (Stab and Gurevych, 2014), since our task involves detecting claims over a full corpus in which the ratio of positive cases is much lower (2.4% of sentences containing the MC).

	$P@5$	$P@10$	$P@20$	$P@50$
Dev	31	27	21	15
Test	32	32	28	22
Levy	23	20	16	12
	$P@5'$	$P@10'$	$P@20'$	$P@50'$
Dev	33 (94)	30 (86)	27 (70)	24 (47)
Test	33 (96)	33 (96)	31 (86)	34 (56)

Table 3: System performance in percentages. Levy - Precision as quoted in (Levy et al., 2014), $P@K$ - Precision of the top K candidates per topic, averaged over all topics (following (Levy et al., 2014)), $P@K'$ - same as $P@K$, considering only topics for which there are at least K candidate claims; number in parenthesis denotes the percentage of such topics.

5 Limitations

In this work, we only considered topics that focus on a single concept which has a corresponding

[3] via the CrowdFlower platform: www.crowdflower.com/, see details in supplementary material

[4] We require a minimum of 10 annotators per candidate. After 10 annotations, further annotations are collected until either 90% agreement is reached or 15 annotations.

Wikipedia page. Expanding the proposed framework to more complex queries, covering more than a single concept, merits further investigation. Yet, even without such an expansion, we note that controversial topics are often characterized by a corresponding Wikipedia page.

Our approach targets claims in which the MC is identified by a Wikification tool. While this allows mining claims in which the MC is expressed via different surface forms, Wikification errors also propagate to our performance. Thus, improvements in available Wikification tools are expected to improve the results of the approach. In addition, claims that do not explicitly refer to the MC are out of the radar of the proposed system, limiting its recall. Expanding the CSQ with concepts related to the MC, may mitigate this issue.

Finally, we focused on sentences matching the pattern *that* $\rightarrow$ MC. Exploring the same methodology for additional patterns characterizing claim–containing sentences is left for future work.

6 Discussion

We present an unsupervised simple framework for corpus-wide claim detection, which relies on features that are quick to compute. Exploiting the token 'that' as a weak signal, or as distant supervision (Mintz et al., 2009) for claim–containing sentences, we obtain results that outperform a supervised claim detection system applied to a limited set of documents (Levy et al., 2014). Extending this approach to other computational argumentation tasks like evidence detection (Rinott et al., 2015) is a natural direction for future work.

Notably, the system precision is clearly superior to the precision of the initial 'that' label, indicating the existence of characteristics of claim–containing sentences which may further enhance the signal embodied in this label. Thus, we hypothesize that supervised learning based on labeling the predictions of the unsupervised system can further improve the system results, e.g., by obtaining better ranking schemes and/or stronger methods to determine claim boundaries.

Finally, we demonstrated our approach over the Wikipedia corpus. We speculate that the proposed approach holds even greater potential for mining larger and more argumentative corpora such as newspapers aggregates; in particular, when considering controversial topics that are widely discussed in the media, for which it is natural to expect that relevant claims are mentioned across a very large set of typically short articles.

References

Ehud Aharoni, Anatoly Polnarov, Tamar Lavee, Daniel Hershcovich, Ran Levy, Ruty Rinott, Dan Gutfreund, and Noam Slonim. 2014. A benchmark dataset for automatic detection of claims and evidence in the context of controversial topics. In *Proceedings of the First Workshop on Argumentation Mining*, pages 64–68.

Khalid Al-Khatib, Henning Wachsmuth, Matthias Hagen, Jonas Köhler, and Benno Stein. 2016. Cross-domain mining of argumentative text through distant supervision. In *Proceedings of the 2016 Conference of the North American Chapter of the Association for Computational Linguistics: Human Language Technologies*, pages 1395–1404, San Diego, California. Association for Computational Linguistics.

Judith Eckle-Kohler, Roland Kluge, and Iryna Gurevych. 2015. On the role of discourse markers for discriminating claims and premises in argumentative discourse. In *Proceedings of the 2015 Conference on Empirical Methods in Natural Language Processing*, pages 2236–2242, Lisbon, Portugal. Association for Computational Linguistics.

Paolo Ferragina and Ugo Scaiella. 2010. Tagme: on-the-fly annotation of short text fragments (by wikipedia entities). In *Proceedings of the 19th ACM international conference on Information and knowledge management*, pages 1625–1628. ACM.

Marti A Hearst. 1992. Automatic acquisition of hyponyms from large text corpora. In *Proceedings of the 14th conference on Computational linguistics-Volume 2*, pages 539–545. Association for Computational Linguistics.

Ran Levy, Yonatan Bilu, Daniel Hershcovich, Ehud Aharoni, and Noam Slonim. 2014. Context dependent claim detection. In *Proceedings of COLING 2014, the 25th International Conference on Computational Linguistics: Technical Papers*, pages 1489–1500, Dublin, Ireland. Dublin City University and Association for Computational Linguistics.

Marco Lippi and Paolo Torroni. 2015. Context-independent claim detection for argument mining. In *Proceedings of the 24th International Conference on Artificial Intelligence*, IJCAI'15, pages 185–191. AAAI Press.

Marco Lippi and Paolo Torroni. 2016. Argumentation mining: State of the art and emerging trends. *ACM Transactions on Internet Technology (TOIT)*, 16(2):10.

Tomas Mikolov, Kai Chen, Greg Corrado, and Jeffrey Dean. 2013. Efficient estimation of word representations in vector space. *arXiv preprint arXiv:1301.3781*.

Mike Mintz, Steven Bills, Rion Snow, and Dan Jurafsky. 2009. Distant supervision for relation extraction without labeled data. In *Proceedings of the Joint Conference of the 47th Annual Meeting of the ACL and the 4th International Joint Conference on Natural Language Processing of the AFNLP: Volume 2-Volume 2*, pages 1003–1011. Association for Computational Linguistics.

Nathan Ong, Diane Litman, and Alexandra Brusilovsky. 2014. Ontology-based argument mining and automatic essay scoring. In *Proceedings of the First Workshop on Argumentation Mining*, pages 24–28, Baltimore, Maryland. Association for Computational Linguistics.

Ruty Rinott, Lena Dankin, Carlos Alzate Perez, Mitesh M. Khapra, Ehud Aharoni, and Noam Slonim. 2015. Show me your evidence - an automatic method for context dependent evidence detection. In *Proceedings of the 2015 Conference on Empirical Methods in Natural Language Processing*, pages 440–450, Lisbon, Portugal. Association for Computational Linguistics.

Haggai Roitman, Shay Hummel, Ella Rabinovich, Benjamin Sznajder, Noam Slonim, and Ehud Aharoni. 2016. On the retrieval of wikipedia articles containing claims on controversial topics. In *Proceedings of the 25th International Conference Companion on World Wide Web*, WWW '16 Companion, pages 991–996, Republic and Canton of Geneva, Switzerland. International World Wide Web Conferences Steering Committee.

Jodi Schneider and Adam Z Wyner. 2012. Identifying consumers' arguments in text. In *SWAIE*, pages 31–42.

Swapna Somasundaran and Janyce Wiebe. 2009. Recognizing stances in online debates. In *Proceedings of the Joint Conference of the 47th Annual Meeting of the ACL and the 4th International Joint Conference on Natural Language Processing of the AFNLP*, pages 226–234, Suntec, Singapore. Association for Computational Linguistics.

Christian Stab and Iryna Gurevych. 2014. Identifying argumentative discourse structures in persuasive essays. In *EMNLP*, pages 46–56.

Stephen Toulmin. 1958. The uses of argumentcambridge university press. *Cambridge, UK*.

Using Question-Answering Techniques to Implement a Knowledge-Driven Argument Mining Approach

Patrick Saint-Dizier
CNRS-IRIT
118 route de Narbonne,
31062 Toulouse Cedex, France
stdizier@irit.fr

Abstract

This short paper presents a first implementation of a knowledge-driven argument mining approach. The major processing steps and language resources of the system are surveyed. An indicative evaluation outlines challenges and improvement directions.

1 Introduction

This paper presents a first implementation of a knowledge-driven argument mining approach based on the principles developed in (Saint-Dizier 2016). This knowledge based approach to argument mining was felt to be challenging because of the heavy load put on knowledge description and acquisition, inference pattern development and implementation complexity. The aim of this paper is to introduce an architecture for the implementation, to structure the different sources of data: lexical, knowledge base and inferences, and to explore how the data can be specified or acquired. We feel that this approach allows to develop in the middle and long term an accurate argument mining system that can identify arguments in any type of text given a standpoint or a controversial issue and to explain what facets of the issue are attacked or supported, why, how and how much. It also allows, as shown in (Saint-Dizier 2016b), the construction of a synthesis of arguments based on domain knowledge, which is convenient for users and domain experts. An original rule-based approach to argument mining is introduced in this contribution. We feel that this analysis, due to the diversity of knowledge, is difficult to develop with statistical-based methods. However, our approach is in a very early development stage: this makes comparisons with statistical systems premature and not of mush use.

The implementation principles and the development of the associated data and inferences raise major challenges in NLP and AI. We propose here an initial experiment which nevertheless produces interesting results. We show how the concepts proper to a controversial issue can be extracted and expanded for the purpose of argument mining. Then, patterns that encode the structure of arguments are developed in association with an approach to measure their relatedness to the issue. An linguistic analysis of the structure of standpoints and arguments is proposed. This paper ends by an indicative evaluation that analyzes challenges, e.g. such as those developed in (Feng et al. 2011), (Peldsusz et al. 2016), and identifies the necessary improvement directions. Due to its limited size, this paper outlines the main features of the implementation, while references point to additional material.

2 Controversial Issue Analysis

In this experiment, a controversial issue is formulated as an evaluative statement and interpreted as a query. The general form is:

`NP, VerbExp, Evaluative.`

The initial `NP`, which may be simple or a compound, is the focus of the issue. It contains the **root** concepts that play a role in the argument mining process. The `VerbExp` symbol is composed of a main verb (be, have, verb particle constructions associated with state verbs or factives such as *is based on, relies upon*, etc.) possibly modified by a modal (*must, should, ought to*). The `Evaluative` symbol covers a variety of evaluative forms typical of consumer evaluations: Adjective Phrase (AP), adverbs (e.g. *necessary*), evaluatives with the right-adjunction of an NP or a PP (e.g. *expensive for a 2 stars hotel*). Attacks and supports are based on this structure. This simple

Proceedings of the 4th Workshop on Argument Mining, pages 85–90
Copenhagen, Denmark, September 8, 2017. ©2017 Association for Computational Linguistics

format should cover, possibly via reformulation, quite a large number of situations.

The concepts used in the arguments for or against a controversial issue are basically the issue root concepts or those derived from them. In (Saint-Dizier 2016), it is shown that these root and derived concepts are appropriately defined and structured in the constitutive, agentive and telic roles of the Qualia structures of the Generative Lexicon (Pustejovsky 1995). In general, arguments indeed support or attack purposes, functions, goals (in the telic role) or parts (in the constitutive role) of these concepts, or the way they have been created (agentive role). In the author's previous works, a concept network is constructed from these Qualias.

Root concepts extraction: these concepts are the nouns in the initial NP, e.g. in *Vaccine against Ebola is necessary*, root concepts are 'vaccine' and 'Ebola'. The relational term *against* appears in the telic role of the head noun of 'vaccine', whose purpose is to protect 'against' a disease.

Structure of a Qualia: our implementation is carried out in Prolog, Qualias are facts:

```
qualia(Concept, role-name([list of
Related-Concepts])).
```

Related-Concepts are constants or predicates. Their lexical realizations are given in a lexicon, where Related-Concept matches with Concept:

```
lex([Word], Category, SemanticFeature,
Concept).
```

Qualia structures are considered here as a knowledge and lexical data repository appropriate for argument mining independently of the theoretical aims behind the Generative Lexicon.

Qualia acquisition and description: at the moment there is no available repository of Qualia structures. Therefore, Qualias must be constructed for each application and domain. (Claveau et al. 2013) investigated ways to automatically acquire the basic information which should appear in Qualias. In our case, and this is a temporary situation, we develop Qualia by a combination of manual descriptions and bootstrapping techniques to acquire e.g. uses, purposes or functions of the concepts at stake in a controversial issue. For example, bootstrapping based on patterns such as 'X is used for Y' allows to get uses Y of concept X. In (Saint-Dizier 2016), it is shown that the number of Qualias for an issue is very limited, to a maximum of 20 structures; this facilitates the task and

improves its feasibility. In our perspective, Qualia structures are a formalism that is appropriate to represent the required knowledge. In addition and prior to bootstrapping, it would be of much interest to investigate how and how much large knowledge bases such as Cyc or Sumo and lexical repositories such as FrameNet can be used to feed Qualia structures of given concepts.

An introduction to the Generative Lexicon

The Generative Lexicon (GL) (Pustejovsky, 1995) is an attempt to structure lexical semantics knowledge in conjunction with domain knowledge. In the GL, the Qualia structure of an entity is both a lexical and knowledge repository composed of four fields called roles:

- **the constitutive role** describes the various parts of the entity and its physical properties, it may include subfields such as material, parts, shape, etc.

- **the formal role** describes what distinguishes the entity from other objects, i.e. the entity in its environment.

- **the telic role** describes the entity functions, uses, roles and purposes,

- **the agentive role** describes the origin of the entity, how it was created or produced.

To illustrate this conceptual organization, let us consider the controversial issue (1):
The vaccine against Ebola is necessary.
The main concepts in the Qualia structure of the head term of (1), *vaccine* are organized as follows:

$$
\text{Vaccine(X):} \begin{bmatrix} \text{CONSTITUTIVE:} \begin{bmatrix} \text{ACTIVE\_PRINCIPLE,} \\ \text{ADJUVANT} \end{bmatrix}, \\ \text{TELIC:} \begin{bmatrix} \text{MAIN: PROTECT\_FROM(X,Y,D),} \\ \text{AVOID(X,DISSEMINATION(D)),} \\ \text{MEANS: INJECT(Z,X,Y)} \end{bmatrix}, \\ \text{FORMAL:} \begin{bmatrix} \text{MEDICINE, ARTIFACT} \end{bmatrix}, \\ \text{AGENTIVE:} \begin{bmatrix} \text{DEVELOP(T,X), TEST(T,X),} \\ \text{SELL(T,X)} \end{bmatrix} \end{bmatrix}
$$

Construction of a network of concepts: This network is constructed following the recursive principle described in (Saint-Dizier 2016), for a depth of three, to preserve a certain conceptual proximity with the root concepts (Mochales et al 2009). It is a tree where root concepts appear at the root, and concepts derived from the initial Qualias appear at levels 2 or 3. This network partly characterizes the **generative expansion of arguments w.r.t. an issue**.

3 The argument mining process

The argument mining model and implementation are structured in five phases which are briefly described below. These are adapted from question-answering techniques (Maybury 2004), in particular factoid and comparative questions..

A. The context of the experiment: For this experiment, three relatively concrete controversial issues have been selected:
(Issue 1) Vaccination against Ebola is necessary,
(Issue 2) Nuclear plants must be banished,
(Issue 3 Car traffic must be reduced.
A set of 21 texts dealing with these topics has been manually searched on the web using the keywords of the issues to get relevant texts. These texts do not contain any technical considerations and are therefore accessible to most readers. Besides arguments, these texts contain a lot of additional considerations, which are definitions, descriptions, historical considerations, etc. One challenge is therefore to identify arguments among other types of data. The accuracy of the different steps of the automatic mining process is evaluated on this set of texts and compared to our manual analysis (section 4).

B. Discourse analysis: Argumentative units are assumed to be sentences. The first step is to make a discourse analysis of each sentence in the 21 texts. This is realized using TextCoop (Saint-Dizier 2012). Discourse structures which are identified are those usually found associated with arguments: conditions, circumstances, causes, goal and purpose expressions, contrasts and concessions. The goal is to identify the kernel of the argument, in general the main proposition of the sentence, and its sentential modifiers. In addition, the discourse structures may give useful indications on the argumentation strategy that is used.

C. Analysis of argument kernels: similarly to the controversial issue, argument kernels are specific forms of evaluative statements. The following forms are recognized by our parser:
(1) **evaluative expressions** in attribute-value form, where the attribute is one of the concepts of the controversial issue concept lattice: *Vaccine development is very expensive, car exhaust is toxic.*
(2) use of **comparatives**, e.g. *nuclear wastes are more dangerous than coal wastes.*
(3) **facts related to the uses, consequences or purposes** of the main concept of the issue e.g.: *vaccine prevents bio-terrorism*
(4) Structures (1) to (3) described above may be embedded into report or epistemic structures such as *the authorities claimed that the adjuvant is not toxic.* The main proposition is the proposition in the scope of thes constructions.
Specific language patterns to identify these constructions have been developed by means of Prolog rules or TextCoop patterns. The result is an additional tagging that identifies the argument topic and the evaluation structure (see example below).

D. Relatedness detection: the next step is to identify those sentences whose kernel is conceptually related to the controversial issue that is considered. In a first stage, a simple strategy, similar to factoid question analysis, identifies argument candidates on the basis of the set of lexicalizations *Lex* of the concepts in the issue concept network. The kernels whose subject or object NP head term (the argument topic) belongs to *Lex* are considered as potential arguments. The closer they are to the root, the more relevant they are a priori. Object NPs are also processed to account for cases where the subject is neutral w.r.t. the issue, e.g.: *car manufacturers provide incorrect pollution rates*. In a further stage, more advanced question-answering techniques will be used, including constraint relaxation and terminological inference.

The annotation of each of the selected sentences includes an attribute that indicates the comprehensive conceptual path that links it to the controversial issue. This annotation clarifies the relation(s) that hold between the argument and the issue, and what facets of the concept(s) are supported or attacked.

E. Argument polarity identification: w.r.t. the issue. From C-(1) above, the following constructions are frequently observed:
(1) The pattern contains a subject with no specific polarity followed by verb with a polarity specified in the lexicon (e.g. *protects, prevents* are positive whereas *pollutes* is negative), followed by either:
(1a) the negation of the VP; (1b) the use of adverbs of frequency, completion, etc. possibly combined with a negation: *never, almost never, sel-*

dom, rarely, not frequently, very frequently, fully, systematically, or (1c) the use of modals expressing doubt or uncertainty: *seem, could, should*. The polarity of the argument is an equation that includes the lexical elements polarities. For example a verb with a negative polarity combined with a negation results in a positive polarity. Polarity could also be neutral if the strength of each term can be specified a priori. Finally, this polarity is combined with the issue orientation in order to determine if the argument is an attack or a support. (2) When the subject head noun and the verb are neutral, then language realizations involve attribute structures with one or more adjectives that evaluate the concept: *toxic, useless, expensive*, etc., which can be modified by intensifiers such as: *100%, totally*. Those adjectives have a clear polarity in the context at stake. The polarity of the adjective is combined with the polarity induced by the intensifier, e.g. *rarely toxic* has a positive polarity, since it combines two negative polarities.

A comprehensive representation for an argument mined from issue (1) is:

<argument Id= 11, polarity= negative , conceptualPath= vaccine/agentive/test/constitutive/protocol >
<concession> Even if the vaccine seems 100% efficient and without any side effects on the tested population,
< /concession>
<kernel arg> <topic> more elaborated test protocols </topic><eval> are necessary < /eval>. < /kernel arg>
<elaboration> The national authority of Guinea has approved the continuation of the tests on targeted populations.</elaboration> < /argument>.

4   An indicative evaluation

We consider that the evaluation carried out at this stage gives indications on the feasibility and accuracy of the process and suggests a number of improvement directions. The evaluation presented below is developed by components so that the difficulties of each of them can be identified. It is too early, but necessary in a later stage, to compare the results of our approach with others on the basis of existing datasets such as those defined by e.g. (Stab and Gurevych 2014) or (Aharoni et ali. 2014).

A. Corpus characteristics: Table 1 summarizes the manual annotation process, realized here by ourselves on the 21 texts advocated in section 3A. Annotation by several annotators is planned and necessary, but requires some in depth training

Issue nb.	nb of texts + size (words)	nb of annotated arguments
Issue 1	9 (3900)	27
Issue 2	6 (3100)	21
Issue 3	6 (1500)	18
Total	21 (8500)	66

Table 1: Corpus characteristics.

Issue	nb of Qualias	nb of concepts
Issue 1	12	38
Issue 2	9	35
Issue 3	15	41
Total	36	114

Table 2: Qualia development.

and competence in knowledge representation.

All the arguments found have been annotated, including redundant ones over different texts. Redundant arguments (between 40% to 50% of the total because authors often copy-paste each other) have been eliminated from the analysis below, but kept for further tests. Table 1 indicates the total of different arguments per issue. On average, 22 different arguments for or against a given issue have been found, this is quite large for this type of issue.

B. Knowledge and lexical representation evaluation: The head terms of issues (1) to (3) are: *vaccination, Ebola, nuclear plants, car traffic*. The last two terms are compound terms: they are treated as a a specialization of *plant* and *traffic* respectively, with their own Qualias, some of which being inherited from the generic terms *plant* and *traffic*. Table 2 presents the number of Qualia structures that have been developed for this experiment and the total number of concepts included in the telic, agentive and constitutive roles, which can potentially serve to identify arguments (D. above). To each of these concepts correspond one or more lexical entries. It is clear that a principled and partly automatic development of Qualia structures is a cornerstone to this approach. For this experiment, for each issue, it took about a half day to develop the Qualias.

Table 3 presents the distribution of the concepts over the three levels of the concept network. Level 2 has several terminal concepts, with no associated Qualia, therefore, level 3 has less concepts.

C. Argument kernel identification: This step is realized using TextCoop, which is well-suited for the relatively simple structures found in these texts. In this experiment, there is no manual discourse structure analysis, since this is not the task that is investigated here. In this type of text,

Concept network levels	nb of concepts
Level 1 (root)	16
Level 2	53
Level 3	45
Total	114

Table 3: The concept network.

Issue	nb args. recognized - accuracy rate	nb of concepts from levels 1 / 2 / 3
Issue 1	20 - 74%	4 / 8 / 2
Issue 2	13 - 62%	4 / 11 / 7
Issue 3	11 - 61%	5 / 9 / 3
Total	44 - 66%	13 / 28 / 12

Table 4: Indicative accuracy.

TextCoop has an accuracy of about 90% (Saint-Dizier 2012). Manual annotation begins after the discourse analysis of each sentence of the 21 texts.

D. Relatedness: Table 4 summarizes the accuracy of the analysis w.r.t. the manual analysis. Correctly identified arguments are given in column 2. Column 3 gives indications on the concept level used in the concept network. An argument can be selected on the basis of several concepts. Non-overlapping arguments may also use the same concept(s).

Table 5 indicates the rate of incorrectly recognized arguments (noise) and of arguments not found w.r.t. to the manual annotation (silence).

The size of the corpus that is investigated is rather modest but for each issue we feel we have quite a good coverage in terms of argument diversity: adding new texts does not produce any new, critical, argument. The main reasons for noise and silence are the following, which need to be taken into account to extend the system, and to deal with more abstract issues:

- **noise:** (1) some sentences are selected because they are related to the issue, but they are rather comments, general rules or explanation, not arguments, in spite of their main proposition evaluative structure; (2) some sentences involve level 3 concepts in the network, and have been judged to be too weak or remote in the manual annotation.

- **silence:** (1) some sentences which have been manually annotated require additional inferences

Issue	noise: nb args.	silence: nb or args.
Issue 1	6 - 22%	7 - 26%
Issue 2	4 - 19%	8 - 38%
Issue 3	3 - 16%	7 - 39%
Total	13 - 19%	22 - 34%

Table 5: noise- silence.

such as those developed in (Saint-Dizier 2012) and cannot be reduced to a concept network traversal; (2) other sentences have arguments which are not related to the concept network (e.g. *vaccine prevents bio-terrorism*), these are of much interest but difficult to relate to the issue at stake.

- **over-performing humans**: in a few cases, the automatic analysis can over-perform human annotators. For example, *7 persons died under the Ebola vaccine tests* is manually annotated as an attack of issue (1). However, in our implementation, the concept 'test' is in the agentive role of the Qualia of vaccine (how the vaccine was created), it is pre-telic and cannot be an attack of the issue which considers the uses and functions (telic) of the vaccine. The system correctly ignored this statement. This can be modeled by an axiomatization of the semantics of the Qualia roles.

These limitations of our implementation raise additional knowledge representation and inference features which are of much scientific and practical interest for the evolution of this approach.

E. Polarity: Polarity analysis is based on the equations developed in section 3, E. above. The system is rather simple at the moment, but seems to be relatively satisfactory, with 39 correctly assigned polarity over the 44 correctly recognized arguments (accuracy of 88%).

5 Conclusion

Although this implementation for a knowledge-based argument mining approach, based on question-answering techniques, is rather simple, it shows the architecture of the system, the required resources and the type of extensions, in terms of knowledge and inferences, which may be needed.

The system is fully implemented in Prolog and TextCoop. For the moment, the implementation is quite simple, however, we are exploring ways to limit the non-determinism by reducing a priori the search space. Linguistic resource structures are quite standard, the main current corner stone of the approach is the acquisition of the relevant roles (telic and constitutive) of Qualia structures. An exploration of the use of existing knowledge resources may be helpful in this respect when the exact nature of the required resources for argument mining has been identified and modelled.

A demo by component could be made at the workshop if appropriate. The code is not (yet) available due to university property regulations.

References

Ehud Aharoni, Anatoly Polnarov, Tamar Lavee, Daniel Hershcovich, Ran Levy, Ruty Rinott, Dan Gutfreund and Noam Slonim. 2014. *A Benchmark Dataset for Automatic Detection of Claims and Evidence in the Context of Controversial Topics* . 1st workshop on Agument Mining, Baltimore.

Vincent Claveau and Pascale Sebillot. 2013. *Automatic Acquisition of GL Resources, Using an Explanatory, Symbolic Technique*, ch 19. Advances in Generative Lexicon Theory, Springer.

Alan Cruse. 1986. *Lexical Semantics*. Cambridge University Press, Cambridge, UK.

Vincent W. Feng and Graeme Hirst. 2011. *Classifying arguments by scheme*, In Proceedings of the 49th ACL: Human Language Technologies, Portland, USA.

Alan Fiedler and Helmut Horacek. 2007. *Argumentation within deductive reasoning*, 22(1):49-70. International Journal of Intelligent Systems.

Cristina Kirschner, Johan Eckle-Kohler and Iryna Gurevych. 2015. *Linking the Thoughts: Analysis of Argumentation Structures in Scientific Publications*, Proceedings of the 2nd Workshop on Argumentation Mining, Denver

Mark Maybury (ed). 2004. *New Directions in Question Answering.*, MIT Press.

Rachel Mochales Palau and Marie-Francine Moens. 2009. *Argumentation mining: the detection, classification and structure of arguments in text.*, Twelfth international ICAIL'09, Barcelona.

Hung Nguyen and Diane Litman. 2015. *Extracting Argument and Domain Words for Identifying Argument Components in Texts*. Proc of the 2nd Workshop on Argumentation Mining, Denver.

Andreas Peldszus and Manfred Stede. 2016. *From argument diagrams to argumentation mining in texts: a survey*. International Journal of Cognitive Informatics and Natural Intelligence (IJCINI).

James Pustejovsky. 1995. *The Generative Lexicon.*. MIT Press.

Patrick Saint-Dizier. 2012. *Processing natural language arguments with the TextCoop platform*. vol 3(1). journal of Argumentation and Computation.

Patrick Saint-Dizier. 2016. *Argument Mining: The bottleneck of knowledge and language resources*. LREC16, Portoroz.

Patrick Saint-Dizier. 2016.(b) *A Two-Level Approach to Generate Synthetic Argumentation Reports*. CMNA17, London.

Christian Stab,Iryna Gurevych. *Identifying Argumentative Discourse Structures in Persuasive Essays*. COLING'14, Dublin.

What works and what does not: Classifier and feature analysis for argument mining

Ahmet Aker, Alfred Sliwa, Yuan Ma, Ruishen Liu
Niravkumar Borad, Seyedeh Fatemeh Ziyaei, Mina Ghbadi
University of Duisburg-Essen
`a.aker@is.inf.uni-due.de`
`alfred.sliwa.92, yuan.ma, ruishen.liu, niravkumar.borad`
`seyedeh.ziyaei, mina.ghobadi@stud.uni-due.de`

Abstract

This paper offers a comparative analysis of the performance of different supervised machine learning methods and feature sets on argument mining tasks. Specifically, we address the tasks of extracting argumentative segments from texts and predicting the structure between those segments. Eight classifiers and different combinations of six feature types reported in previous work are evaluated. The results indicate that overall best performing features are the structural ones. Although the performance of classifiers varies depending on the feature combinations and corpora used for training and testing, Random Forest seems to be among the best performing classifiers. These results build a basis for further development of argument mining techniques and can guide an implementation of argument mining into different applications such as argument based search.

1 Introduction

Argument mining refers to the automatic extraction of arguments from natural texts. An argument consists of a claim (also referred to as the conclusion of the argument) and several pieces of evidence called premises that support or reject the claim (Lippi and Torroni, 2016).

As a research area argument mining has seen a rapid progress in the last three-to-five years (Lippi and Torroni, 2015). Current studies report methods for argument mining in legal documents (Moens et al., 2007; Reed et al., 2008), persuasive essays (Nguyen and Litman, 2015; Stab and Gurevych, 2014b), Wikipedia articles (Levy et al., 2014), user comments (Park and Cardie, 2014),

online products (Wyner et al., 2012), social media (Goudas et al., 2014) and news articles (Sardianos et al., 2015).

Argument mining is a process that involves the following steps, each of which is a research area in itself addressed by several studies: *identifying argumentative segments in text* (Moens et al., 2007; Wyner et al., 2012; Park and Cardie, 2014; Goudas et al., 2014; Levy et al., 2014; Lippi and Torroni, 2015; Swanson et al., 2015; Sardianos et al., 2015; Lawrence et al., 2014), *clustering recurring arguments* (Boltužić and Šnajder, 2015; Misra et al., 2015), *classification of premises as supporting (pro) or rejecting (contra)* (Stab and Gurevych, 2014b; Nguyen and Litman, 2015), *determining argument structure* (Cabrio and Villata, 2012; Lawrence et al., 2014; Ghosh et al., 2014) and *mapping arguments into pre-defined argument schemas* (Feng and Hirst, 2011).

In terms of methods all these studies rely on supervised machine learning. Among the different classification approaches applied Support Vector Machines, Naïve Bayes and Logistic Regression are the most common ones. Also different feature types have been investigated for the different steps of the argument mining task. Among the features types the prominent ones are *structural, lexical, syntactic, indicators* and *contextual* features as summarized by Stab and Gurevych (2014b).

Given this variety of work on argument mining time is ripe for an extensive comparative analysis of the performance of different machine learning techniques on different argument mining tasks using different data sets. Such an analysis should serve as a basis for further development of argument mining techniques and also inform those who want to implement argument mining components into other applications.

In this paper we offer such a comparative analysis of machine learning methods and features with

91

Proceedings of the 4th Workshop on Argument Mining, pages 91–96
Copenhagen, Denmark, September 8, 2017. ©2017 Association for Computational Linguistics

respect to two argument mining tasks: (1) identifying argumentative segments in text, i.e. the classification of textual units (usually sentences) into claims, premises or none and (2) the prediction of argument structure, i.e. connecting claims and premises. We re-implement a rich set of features reported by related work and evaluate eight different classification systems. We perform our investigation on two different well-known corpora: (1) the persuasive essays corpus reported by Stab and Gurevych (2016) and (2) the Wikipedia claim and premise data reported by Aharoni et al. (2014).

2 Experimental Settings

2.1 Data

We investigate the feature and classifier performances on two corpora. The first corpus consists of over 400 persuasive essays where arguments are annotated as claim, premise or major claim (Stab and Gurevych, 2016). For our purposes we consider each major claim as a claim to keep the argumentation model as simple as possible and ensure comparability between data sets. The second corpus consists of over 300 Wikipedia articles in which arguments are annotated as either Context Dependent Claim (CDC) or Context Dependent Evidence (CDE) in the context of a given topic (Aharoni et al., 2014).

2.2 Features

We evaluate several feature types proposed in previous work (Stab and Gurevych, 2014b): *Structural features* consider statistics about tokens and punctuation. *Lexical features* capture information on unigram frequency, as well as salient verbs and adverbs. *Syntactic features* incorporate occurrences of frequent POS-Sequences. *Indicators introduce* a list of argumentative keywords. *Contextual features* take into account structural and lexical features of surrounding sentences. In terms of data preprocessing we performed lemmatization before feature extraction step but left out removing stopwords as they are relevant for determining arguments. For instance stopwords like because, therefore, etc. are indeed good indicators for argumentative text.

Each feature set is scaled to a range between 0 and 1 and normalized by tf-idf. Furthermore, we also investigated *word embeddings* as an additional feature type by using the pre-trained

Google News corpus consisting of 3 million 300-dimension English word vectors [1].

2.3 Tasks

2.3.1 Detection of Argumentative Sentences

The first classification task involves identifying argumentative sentences in natural texts. This is considered as a three-class classification task, where sentences are classified as claim, premise and none. The gold standard data contains texts annotated either as premise or claim. To determine the non-argumentative sentences, which are necessary for developing a classifier to distinguish between positive and negative examples, we include sentences for which there is no annotations.

2.3.2 Prediction of Argumentative Structures

The second classification task aims to identify the relationship between claims and premises. This task is treated as a binary classification task: a claim and a premise can be in a linked or unlinked relation. All annotated pairs of claims and premises are taken as linked examples. To determine the unlinked examples we take a subset of both annotated premises and claims and calculate the cross product of these two sets.[2] The selection of negative pairs is a randomized process where repetition of single arguments are possible but not as a complete pair.

2.4 Classifiers

We investigate 8 classifiers, some of which have been used by previous studies (LinearSVC, Logistic Regression, Random Forest, Multinominal Naïve Bayes (MNB)) and some of which we implement for the first time for the above tasks: Nearest Neighbor, AdaBoosted Decision Tree (AdaBoost), Gaussian Naïve Bayes (GNB) and Convolutional Neural Networks (CNNs)). Each classifier, except the CNN, has been trained and tested on each possible combination of the six feature types.

3 Results

For each corpus we performed stratified 10-fold cross validation. The results are reported using macro F1-score.

---

[1] https://code.google.com/archive/p/word2vec/
[2] All linked pairs are discarded from this set.

Feature Type Combination	MNB	LinearSVC	Log. Regr.	Random Forest	AdaBoost	Near. Neigh.	GNB
Structural	.62/.6	.69/.65	.68/.65	.76/.64	.58/.64	.76/.61	.51/.58
Lexical	.41/.37	.53/.37	.53/.37	.48/.51	.39/.5	.42/.48	.48/.37
Indicators	.28/.41	.29/.44	.28/.44	.3/.47	.27/.44	.29/.42	.26/.4
Syntactic	.23/.37	.23/.37	.23/.37	.29/.37	.23/.37	.34/.37	.39/.3
Contextual	.23	.48	.48	.47	.48	.47	.48
Word Embeddings	.23/.37	.51/.45	.36/.37	.42/.42	.48/.45	.45/.44	.48/.48
All	.65/.55	**.81**/.59	.79/.62	.75/.5	.76/.58	.71/.56	.63/.43
All without Embeddings	.64/.55	.76/.63	.76/.63	.78/.65	.76/**.66**	.71/.57	.62/.43
All without Contextual	.64	.79	.76	.72	.58	.7	.63
All without Syntactic	.64/.55	.8/.59	.78/.62	.75/.51	.76/.58	.72/.56	.63/.43
All without Indicators	.64/.57	.8/.6	.78/.64	.75/.5	.76/.58	.73/.62	.7/.52
All without Lexical	.61/.55	.8/.59	.77/.62	.76/.5	.76/.58	.73/.57	.56/.43
All without Structural	.39/.43	.65/.47	.61/.45	.55/.46	.6/.49	.47/.53	.39/.41

Table 1: F1-scores of 7 classifiers for different feature combinations for the persuasive essay corpus. The results are shown as X/Y where X refers to the score for the task of detecting argumentative sentences and Y refers to the score for argument structure prediction task.

3.1 Results for Persuasive Essays

In the corpus of persuasive essays we have 3832 premise examples, 2256 claim examples and 1317 non-argumentative examples for the sentence detection task. For structure prediction task we obtained 3117 positive examples for support relations between premises and claims and 2200 negative examples for non-supporting relations.

The classification results are reported in Table 1. CNN results for both corpora are presented in Section 3.3.

For the task of argumentative sentence detection the best overall result on persuasive essays is achieved by combining all six feature sets yielding an F1-score of 81% achieved by the Linear SVC classifier. The structural features achieve the best results among the single feature types. Similar results have been also reported in (Stab and Gurevych, 2014a) for a smaller corpus of 90 persuasive essays. Also in the leave-one-out setting removing the structural features leads to the largest loss in performance. Lexical features are the next most useful feature for separating argumentative sentences from non-argumentative ones. Syntactic features are found to be least useful for this task. The performance of the classifiers based on these features only is low and removing them from a set of features does not lead to a substantial reduction in performance.

For the task of predicting the argument structure the best overall results (66%) are achieved by AdaBoost classifier based on all features without word embeddings. Table 1 indicates that the structural features are again the best performing feature set among the single ones achieving an F1-score of 65% in combination with Logistic Regression and LinearSVC. This single structural feature set even outperforms combined feature sets (excluding the ALL without Word Embeddings feature) showing that inclusion of the other feature types, in particular word embeddings lead only to noise. The other feature types all perform substantially worse than the structural feature type and their overall performance is similar.

Due to the great performance of the structural feature we computed significance test between this feature (took the best results) and all the other single features with their best performance. Results of the significance test are shown in the first two rows (after the table heading) of Table 3.

3.2 Results on Wikipedia Data

For the Wikipedia corpus we extracted 2858 premise and claim examples and 1200 non-argumentative examples for sentence detection classification task.[3] For structure prediction classification task we obtained 1232 positive examples for support relations between premises and claims and 1200 negative examples for non-supporting relations. The negative relational instances are those that bear wrong pairings. The results for the Wikipedia corpus are shown in Table 2.

Table 2 reveals that for argumentative sentence detection the structural features again achieve the best results among the single feature types and

---

[3] We randomly selected 1200 non-argumentative examples that were not annotated. We admit that these negative examples can still have argumentative sentences because the Wikipedia corpus contains only topic dependent claims and premises. Any claim or premise not topic related was not annotated.

Feature Type Combination	MNB	LinearSVC	Log. Regr.	Random Forest	AdaBoost	Near. Neigh.	GNB
Structural	.80/.52	.90/.54	.85/.55	.94/.55	.92/.55	.92/.56	.84/.36
Lexical	.73/.53	.81/.52	.80/.52	.85/.52	.75/.52	.66/.47	.64/.53
Indicators	.38/.47	.52/.47	.52/.47	.58/.50	.53/.54	.29/.44	.33/.36
Syntactical	.20/.33	.33/.33	.33/.33	.45/.33	.44/.33	.43/.33	.41/.33
Contextual	0.18	0.27	0.27	0.74	0.27	0.64	0.31
Word Embeddings	.20/.52	.72/.53	.64/.54	.85/.47	.76/.48	.68/.53	.61/.53
All	.92/.52	.94/.57	.93/.59	.95/.48	.92/.53	.84/.56	.88/.43
All without Embeddings	.92/.49	.93/.54	.93/.53	**.96**/.57	.93/.55	.83/.54	.85/.37
All without Contextual	0.92	0.94	0.93	0.95	0.92	0.84	0.88
All without Syntactic	.92/.53	.94/.58	.93/**.60**	.95/.5	.92/.54	.83/.55	.88/.43
All without Indicators	.92/.53	.94/.55	.93/.57	.94/.48	.92/.48	.85/.6	.9/.55
All without Lexical	.83/.49	.94/.56	.91/.58	.94/.51	.93/.51	.84/.56	.87/.47
All without Structural	.77/.5	.87/.53	.84/.53	.88/.49	.82/.51	.73/.55	.66/.47

Table 2: F1-scores of different classifiers on different feature type combinations for the Wikipedia corpus. The results are shown as X/Y where X refers to score for the task of detecting argumentative sentences and Y refers to the score for predicting argumentative structure.

Feature	Str.	Lex.	Ind.	Syn.	Con.	Emb.
Arg.	-	Y	Y	Y	Y	Y
Str.	-	Y	Y	Y	-	Y
Arg.	-	Y	Y	Y	Y	Y
Str.	-	N	Y	Y	-	N

Table 3: Significance using using Student's t-test between the structural features and the others for the essay (first 2 rows) and the Wikipedia corpus (last 2 rows). When conducting multiple analyses on the same dependent variable, the chance of achieving a significant result by pure chance increases. To correct for this we did a Bonferroni correction. Results are reported after this correction. In the cells Y means yes and N means no-significance.

lead to largest loss in performance when removed from the set of all features. The best scoring classifier is Random Forest, which based on structural features achieves an F1-score of 94%. The best overall result is achieved by random Forest classifier by combining five feature sets without word embeddings. The F1 score in this setting is 96%. As in the persuasive essay corpus, the arguments in Wikipedia corpus are also best identified using structural features. The lexical feature type gains the next best evaluation results in both single and leave-one-out feature settings. Syntactic features do not have a substantial influence in separating argumentative from non-argumentative sentences, which was also observed within the persuasive essay corpus. Overall, the scores for Wikipedia are substantially higher than those obtained for the essay corpus.

For the structure prediction task on the Wikipedia corpus Table 2 indicates that structural feature proved best feature type for argument structure prediction, achieving an F1-score of 56% in Nearest Neighbors classifier. The performance of syntactic features is the lowest, while lexical and word embedding feature types perform in general comparably to the structural features. Best results are achieved when word embeddings, lexical, indicators and structural feature types are combined leading to an F1-score of 60% in combination with Logistic Regression classifier.

Similar to the essay corpus we computed the significance test between the structural feature set with the other single feature sets. The results are shown in the last two rows of Table 3.

3.3 Results with CNN

Finally, for the purpose of detecting argumentative pieces of text as well as structure prediction we have adopted the Convolutional Neural Network (CNN) architecture described by Kim (2014), who applied it to the task of sentiment analysis. Apart from changing the inputs from sentimental sentences to argumentative pieces of text, we kept the original architecture, as well as all settings used for training as described by Kim (2014).

Table 4 shows the results of our adopted CNN classifier for both corpora. We can see the CNN has a good performance in argumentative sentence detection, it achieves an F1-score of 74% for the persuasive essay corpus and an F1-score of 75% for the Wikipedia data.[4] In terms of structure pre-

---

[4]Note that in case of the CNN we do not distinguish between claim, premise but rather argumentative or non-argumentative. We tried to run CNN to perform the claim, premise and none class classification however, the results

diction it leads to an F1-score of 73% for the persuasive essay corpus and 52% for the Wikipedia corpus.

Data Source	argumentative or not	structure
Essays-CNN	0.74	0.73
Wikipedia-CNN	0.75	0.52

Table 4: F1-scores of CNN on both persuasive essay and Wikipedia corpora

4 Conclusion

In this paper we presented a comparative analysis of supervised classification methods for two argument mining tasks. Specifically, we investigated six feature types proposed by previous work implemented in 8 classifiers, some of which have been proposed before and some of which were new. We addressed two argument mining tasks: (1) the detection of argumentative pieces of text and (2) predicting the structure between claims and premises. We performed our analysis on two different corpora: persuasive essays and Wikipedia articles. The most robust result in our analysis was the contribution of structural features. For both corpora and both tasks, these features were consistently the most relevant ones. Likewise, syntactic features were not useful in any of the experimental settings. The classifier performance varied across features and corpora and we did not get a robust result for one classifier consistently outperforming others. However, Random Forest classifier showed best results on the Wikipedia Corpus and results comparable to the best ones for the essays corpus. In our future work we plan to expand our investigation by including other corpora to test on as well as Recurrent Neural Networks. Also note for the final version of the paper we plan to include an extensive error analysis which we omit now due to space limitations.

Acknowledgements

This work was supported by the Deutsche Forschungsgemeinschaft (DFG) under grant No. GRK 2167, Research Training Group "User-Centred Social Media".

---

were substantially lower than what is reported in Table 4.

References

Ehud Aharoni, Anatoly Polnarov, Tamar Lavee, Daniel Hershcovich, Ran Levy, Ruty Rinott, Dan Gutfreund, and Noam Slonim. 2014. A benchmark dataset for automatic detection of claims and evidence in the context of controversial topics. In *Proceedings of the First Workshop on Argumentation Mining*. pages 64–68.

Filip Boltužić and Jan Šnajder. 2015. Identifying prominent arguments in online debates using semantic textual similarity. In *2nd Workshop on Argumentation Mining (ArgMining 2015)*.

Elena Cabrio and Serena Villata. 2012. Combining textual entailment and argumentation theory for supporting online debates interactions. In *Proceedings of the 50th Annual Meeting of the Association for Computational Linguistics: Short Papers-Volume 2*. Association for Computational Linguistics, pages 208–212.

Vanessa Wei Feng and Graeme Hirst. 2011. Classifying arguments by scheme. In *Proceedings of the 49th Annual Meeting of the Association for Computational Linguistics: Human Language Technologies-Volume 1*. Association for Computational Linguistics, pages 987–996.

Debanjan Ghosh, Smaranda Muresan, Nina Wacholder, Mark Aakhus, and Matthew Mitsui. 2014. Analyzing argumentative discourse units in online interactions. In *Proceedings of the First Workshop on Argumentation Mining*. pages 39–48.

Theodosis Goudas, Christos Louizos, Georgios Petasis, and Vangelis Karkaletsis. 2014. Argument extraction from news, blogs, and social media. In *Hellenic Conference on Artificial Intelligence*. Springer, pages 287–299.

Yoon Kim. 2014. Convolutional neural networks for sentence classification. *arXiv preprint arXiv:1408.5882* .

John Lawrence, Chris Reed, Colin Allen, Simon McAlister, Andrew Ravenscroft, and David Bourget. 2014. Mining arguments from 19th century philosophical texts using topic based modelling. In *Proceedings of the First Workshop on Argumentation Mining*. Citeseer, pages 79–87.

Ran Levy, Yonatan Bilu, Daniel Hershcovich, Ehud Aharoni, and Noam Slonim. 2014. Context dependent claim detection .

Marco Lippi and Paolo Torroni. 2015. Context-independent claim detection for argument mining. In *Proceedings of the Twenty-Fourth International Conference on Artificial Intelligence*. pages 185–191.

Marco Lippi and Paolo Torroni. 2016. Argumentation mining: State of the art and emerging trends. *ACM Transactions on Internet Technology (TOIT)* 16(2):10.

Amita Misra, Pranav Anand, JEF Tree, and MA Walker. 2015. Using summarization to discover argument facets in online idealogical dialog. In *NAACL HLT*. pages 430–440.

Marie-Francine Moens, Erik Boiy, Raquel Mochales Palau, and Chris Reed. 2007. Automatic detection of arguments in legal texts. In *Proceedings of the 11th international conference on Artificial intelligence and law*. ACM, pages 225–230.

Huy V Nguyen and Diane J Litman. 2015. Extracting argument and domain words for identifying argument components in texts. In *Proceedings of the 2nd Workshop on Argumentation Mining*. pages 22–28.

Joonsuk Park and Claire Cardie. 2014. Identifying appropriate support for propositions in online user comments. In *Proceedings of the First Workshop on Argumentation Mining*. pages 29–38.

Chris Reed, Raquel Mochales Palau, Glenn Rowe, and Marie-Francine Moens. 2008. Language resources for studying argument. In *Proceedings of the 6th conference on language resources and evaluation-LREC 2008*. ELRA, pages 91–100.

Christos Sardianos, Ioannis Manousos Katakis, Georgios Petasis, and Vangelis Karkaletsis. 2015. Argument extraction from news. *NAACL HLT 2015* page 56.

Christian Stab and Iryna Gurevych. 2014a. Annotating argument components and relations in persuasive essays. In *COLING*. pages 1501–1510.

Christian Stab and Iryna Gurevych. 2014b. Identifying argumentative discourse structures in persuasive essays. In *EMNLP*. pages 46–56.

Christian Stab and Iryna Gurevych. 2016. Parsing argumentation structures in persuasive essays. *arXiv preprint arXiv:1604.07370* .

Reid Swanson, Brian Ecker, and Marilyn Walker. 2015. Argument mining: Extracting arguments from online dialogue. In *Proceedings of 16th Annual Meeting of the Special Interest Group on Discourse and Dialogue (SIGDIAL 2015)*. pages 217–227.

Adam Wyner, Jodi Schneider, Katie Atkinson, and Trevor JM Bench-Capon. 2012. Semi-automated argumentative analysis of online product reviews. *COMMA* 245:43–50.

Unsupervised Detection of Argumentative Units though Topic Modeling Techniques

Alfio Ferrara and **Stefano Montanelli**
Dipartimento di Informatica, Università degli Studi di Milano
Via Comelico 39, 20135 - Milano, Italy
{alfio.ferrara,stefano.montanelli}@unimi.it

Georgios Petasis
Institute of Informatics and Telecommunications,
National Centre for Scientific Research (N.C.S.R.) "Demokritos"
P.O. BOX 60228, Aghia Paraskevi, GR-153 10, Athens, Greece
petasis@iit.demokritos.gr

Abstract

In this paper we present a new *unsupervised* approach, "Attraction to Topics" – $\mathcal{A}2\mathcal{T}$, for the detection of argumentative units, a sub-task of argument mining. Motivated by the importance of topic identification in manual annotation, we examine whether topic modeling can be used for performing unsupervised detection of argumentative sentences, and to what extend topic modeling can be used to classify sentences as claims and premises. Preliminary evaluation results suggest that topic information can be successfully used for the detection of argumentative sentences, at least for corpora used in the evaluation. Our approach has been evaluated on two English corpora, the first of which contains 90 persuasive essays, while the second is a collection of 340 documents from user generated content.

1 Introduction

Argument mining involves the automatic discovery of *argument components* (i.e. claims, premises) and the *argumentative relations* (i.e. supports, attacks) among these components in texts. Primarily aiming to extract arguments from texts in order to provide structured data for computational models of argument and reasoning engines (Lippi and Torroni, 2015a), argument mining has additionally the potential to support applications in various research fields, such as opinion mining (Goudas et al., 2015), stance detection (Hasan and Ng, 2014), policy modelling (Florou et al., 2013; Goudas et al., 2014), legal information systems (Palau and Moens, 2009), etc.

Argument mining is usually addressed as a pipeline of several sub-tasks. Typically the first sub-task is the separation between argumentative and non-argumentative text units, which can be performed at various granularity levels, from clauses to several sentences, usually depending on corpora characteristics. Detection of argumentative units (AU)[1], as discussed in Section 2, is typically modeled as a fully-supervised classification task, either a binary one, where units are separated in argumentative and non-argumentative ones with argumentative ones to be subsequently classified in claims and premises as a second step, or as a multi-class one, where identification of argumentative units and classification into claims and premises are performed as a single step. According to a recent survey (Lippi and Torroni, 2015a), the performance of proposed approaches depends on highly engineered and sophisticated, manually constructed, features.

However, fully-supervised approaches rely on manually annotated datasets, the construction of which is a laborious, costly, and error-prone process, requiring significant effort from human experts. At the same time, reliance on sophisticated features may hinder the generalisation of an approach to new corpora types and domains (Lippi and Torroni, 2015a). The removal of manual supervision through exploitation of *unsupervised approaches* is a possible solution to both of the aforementioned problems.

1.1 Motivations of our work

Topics seem to be related to the task of argument mining, at least for some types of corpora, as topic

---

[1] Also known as "Argumentative Discourse Units – ADUs" (Peldszus and Stede, 2013).

97

Proceedings of the 4th Workshop on Argument Mining, pages 97–107
Copenhagen, Denmark, September 8, 2017. ©2017 Association for Computational Linguistics

identification frequently appears as a step in the process of manual annotation of arguments in texts (Stab and Gurevych, 2014a). However, despite its apparent importance in manual annotation, only a small number of studies have examined the inclusion of topic information in sub-tasks of argument mining. Habernal and Gurevych (2015) have included sentiment and topic information as features for classifying sentences as claims, premises, backing and non-argumentative units. A less direct exploitation of topic information has been presented in (Nguyen and Litman, 2015), where topics have been used to extract lexicons of argument and domain words, which can provide evidence regarding the existence of argument components.

In this paper we propose "Attraction to Topics" – $\mathcal{A}2\mathcal{T}$, an unsupervised approach based on topic modeling techniques for detecting argumentative discourse units at sentence-level granularity (a sub-task known as "argumentative sentence detection"). The goals of $\mathcal{A}2\mathcal{T}$ are twofold. On the one side, $\mathcal{A}2\mathcal{T}$ enforces identification of sentences that contain argument components, by also distinguishing them from the non-argumentative sentences that do not contain argument components. On the other side, $\mathcal{A}2\mathcal{T}$ classifies the discovered argumentative sentences according to their role, as *major claims*, *claims*, and *premises*.

The rest of the paper is organized as follows: Section 2 presents an overview of approaches related to argument mining focusing on the detection of argumentative units, while Section 3 presents our approach on applying topic modeling for identifying sentences that contain argument components. Section 4 presents our experimental setting and evaluation results, with Section 5 concluding this paper and proposing some directions for further research.

2 Related work

Almost all argument mining frameworks proposed so far employ a pipeline of stages, each of which is addressing a sub-task of the argument mining problem (Lippi and Torroni, 2015a). The segmentation of text into argumentative units is typically the first sub-task encountered in such an argument mining pipeline, aiming to segment texts into argumentative and non-argumentative text units (i.e. segments that do contain or do not contain argument components, such as claims or premises). The granularity of argument components is text-

dependant. For example, in Wikipedia articles studied in (Rinott et al., 2015), argument components spanned from less than a sentence to more than a paragraph, although 90% of the cases was up to 3 sentences, with 95% of components being comprised of whole sentences.

Several approaches address the identification of argumentative units at the sentence level, a sub-task known as "argumentative sentence detection", which typically models the task as a binary classification problem. Employing machine learning and a set of features representing sentences, the goal is to discard sentences that are not part (or do not contain a component) of an argument. As reported also by Lippi and Torroni (2015a), the vast majority of existing approaches employ "classic, off-the-self" classifiers, while most of the effort is devoted to highly engineered features. A plethora of learning algorithms have been applied on the task, including Naive Bayes (Moens et al., 2007; Park and Cardie, 2014), Support Vector Machines (SVM) (Mochales and Moens, 2011; Rooney et al., 2012; Park and Cardie, 2014; Stab and Gurevych, 2014b; Lippi and Torroni, 2015b), Maximum Entropy (Mochales and Moens, 2011), Logistic Regression (Goudas et al., 2014, 2015; Levy et al., 2014), Decision Trees and Random Forests (Goudas et al., 2014, 2015; Stab and Gurevych, 2014b).

However, approaches addressing this task in a semi-supervised or unsupervised manner are still scarce. In (Petasis and Karkaletsis, 2016) an unsupervised approach is presented, which addresses the sub-task of identifying the main claim in a document by exploiting evidence from an extractive summarization algorithm, TextRank (Mihalcea and Tarau, 2004). In an attempt to study the overlap between graph-based approaches and approaches targeting extractive summarization with argument mining, evaluation results suggest a positive effect on the sub-task, achieving an accuracy of 50% on the corpus compiled by Hasan and Ng (2014) from online debate forums and on a corpus of persuasive essays (Stab and Gurevych, 2014a). Regarding semi-supervised approaches, Habernal and Gurevych (2015) propose new unsupervised features that exploit clustering of unlabeled argumentative data from debate portals based on word embeddings, outperforming several baselines. This work employs also topic modeling as one of its features, by including as features the distributions of sentences from LDA (Blei et al., 2003).

Topic modeling has been mainly exploited for identification of argumentative relations and for extraction of argument and domain lexicons. In Lawrence et al. (2014), LDA is used to decide whether a proposition can be attached to its previous proposition in order to identify non directional relations among propositions detected through classifiers based on words and part-of-speech tags. LDA has been also used to mine lexicons of argument (words that are topic independent) and domain words (Nguyen and Litman, 2015), by post-processing document topics generated by LDA. These lexicons have been used as features for supervised approaches for argument mining (Nguyen and Litman, 2016a,b). However, to the best of our knowledge, no prior approach has applied topic modeling to argumentative sentence detection in an unsupervised setting, which is the featuring aspect of the proposed $\mathcal{A}2\mathcal{T}$ approach presented in the following.

3 Topic modeling for argument mining

Given a document corpus, topic modeling techniques can be employed to discover the most representative topics throughout the corpus, and to provide an assignment of documents to topics, meaning that the higher is the assignment value of a document to a certain topic, the higher is the probability that the document is "focused" on that topic.

The idea of $\mathcal{A}2\mathcal{T}$ is that an argumentative unit is a sentence highly focused on a specific topic, namely a sentence with high assignment value to a certain topic and low assignment value to the other topics. To this end, $\mathcal{A}2\mathcal{T}$ introduces the notion of *attraction* with the aim at recognizing the sentences highly focused on specific topics, that represent the recognized argumentative units. In the following, the $\mathcal{A}2\mathcal{T}$ approach and related techniques are described in detail.

3.1 $\mathcal{A}2\mathcal{T}$ approach

The schema of the $\mathcal{A}2\mathcal{T}$ approach is shown in Figure 1. Consider a corpus of texts $\mathcal{C} = \{c_1, \ldots, c_n\}$, where a text $c_i \in \mathcal{C}$ is a sequence of sentences, like for example an essay, a web page/post, or a scientific paper. The ultimate goal of the $\mathcal{A}2\mathcal{T}$ approach is to derive a set of argumentative units $\mathcal{U} = \{\langle s_1, c, l\rangle, \ldots, \langle s_h, c, l\rangle\}$, where

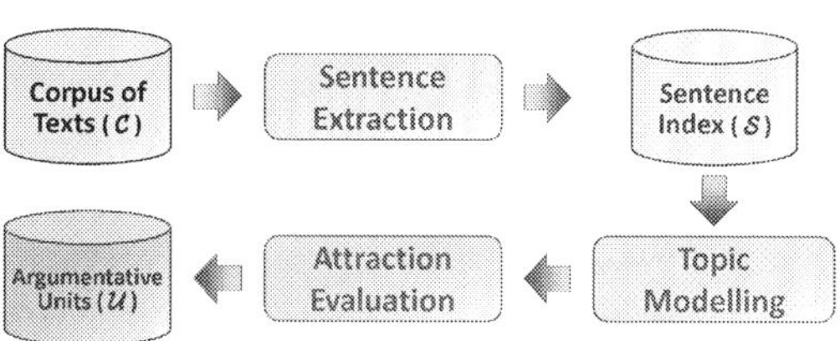

Figure 1: Schema of the $\mathcal{A}2\mathcal{T}$ approach

s_i is a sentence containing an argumentative unit, c is the text containing s, and l is the argumentative role expressed by the unit (e.g., major claim, claim, premise). The $\mathcal{A}2\mathcal{T}$ approach is articulated in the following activities:

Sentence extraction. $\mathcal{A}2\mathcal{T}$ approach is characterized by the use of topic modeling at sentence-level granularity. For this reason, a pre-processing step of the corpus $\mathcal{C}$ is enforced based on conventional techniques for sentence tokenization, words tokenization, normalization, and indexing (Manning et al., 2008). The result is a sentence set $S = \{\langle \vec{s_1}, c, pos_1\rangle, \ldots, \langle \vec{s_m}, c, pos_m\rangle\}$, where $\vec{s_i}$ is the vector representation of the sentence s_i and c, pos are text and position in the text where the sentence appears, respectively. The sentence set is stored in a sentence index for efficient access of S elements.

Topic modeling. The set of extracted sentences S is used as the document corpus on which topic modeling is applied. The result of this activity is twofold. First, topic modeling returns a set of topics $\mathcal{T} = \{t_0, \ldots, t_k\}$ representing the latent variables that are most representative for the sentences S. Second, topic modeling returns a distribution of sentences over topics $\theta = \{\theta_{s_1}, \ldots, \theta_{s_m}\}$. In particular, $\theta_{s_i} = [p(t_0|s_i), \ldots, p(t_k|s_i)]$ is the probability distribution of the sentence s_i over the set of topics $\mathcal{T}$, where $p(t_j|s_i)$ represents the probability of the topic t_j given the sentence s_i (i.e., the so-called assignment value of s_i to t_j).

Attraction evaluation. The notion of attraction is introduced to measure the *degree of focus* that characterizes sentences with respect to the emerged topics. To this end, the distribution of sentences over topics θ is exploited with the aim at determining the best topic assignment for each sentence of S. The result is an attraction set $\mathcal{A} = \{\langle s_1, a_1\rangle, \ldots, \langle s_m, a_m\rangle\}$ where s_i is a sentence of S and a_i is its corresponding attraction value.

Sentence labeling. By exploiting the attraction set $\mathcal{A}$, labeling has the goal to determine the sentences of $\mathcal{S}$ that are more focused on a specific topic, according to the hypothesis that those sentences are the argumentative units. In a basic scenario, labeling consists in distinguishing between sentences that are argumentative units ($l = au$) and sentences that are not argumentative units ($l = \overline{au}$). In a more articulated scenario, labeling consists in assigning a role to sentences that are recognized as argumentative units. For instance, it is possible to distinguish argumentative-unit sentences that are claims ($l = cl$), major claims ($l = mc$), or premises ($l = pr$). A sentence s recognized as argumentative unit is inserted in the final set $\mathcal{U}$ with the assigned label and it is returned as a result of $\mathcal{A}2\mathcal{T}$.

3.2 $\mathcal{A}2\mathcal{T}$ techniques

In $\mathcal{A}2\mathcal{T}$, the *sentence extraction* step is enforced by relying on standard techniques for representing documents in terms of feature vectors and bag of words (using *tf-idf* as weighting scheme) (Castano et al., 2017). Probabilistic topic modeling is exploited to enforce the subsequent *topic modeling* step. Probabilistic topic models are a suite of algorithms whose aim is to discover the hidden thematic structure in large archives of documents, namely *sentences* in $\mathcal{A}2\mathcal{T}$. The idea is that documents are represented as random mixtures over latent topics, where each topic is characterized by a distribution over words (Blei et al., 2003). Probabilistic topic modeling algorithms infer the distribution θ of documents over topics and the distribution ϕ of words over topics, by sampling from the bag of words of each document. In our approach, we choose to exploit the Hierarchical Dirichlet Process (HDP). With respect to other algorithms (such as LDA), HDP has the advantage to provide the optimal number of topics instead of requiring to set such a number as input (Teh et al., 2006).

Attraction evaluation. The notion of *attraction* is introduced in $\mathcal{A}2\mathcal{T}$ to capture the intuition that argumentative units are related to the distribution of sentences over topics. Consider a set of sentences $\mathcal{S}$ and the distribution θ of sentences over the set of topics $\mathcal{T}$. The more the distribution θ_{s_i} of a sentence s_i over the topics is unequal, the more s_i is *focused* on a topic, thus suggesting s_i

as a possible argumentative unit. A further feature that attraction aims to capture is that argumentative units often appear either at the beginning or at the end of texts. The attraction a_i of a sentence s_i is calculated as follows:

$$a_i = K\varphi_{s_i} + (1 - K)\frac{\rho_{s_i}}{\sum\limits_{s_j \in c} \rho_{s_j}},$$

$\varphi_{s_i} = \max(\theta_{s_i})$ is a measure of how much s_i is focused on a topic and $\rho_{s_i} = \alpha f(pos_i)^2 + \beta f(pos_i) + \gamma$ is a parabolic function over the position of the sentence in c. In particular, given $L(c)$ as the number of sentences in c, $f(pos_i) = \left| \frac{L(c)}{2} - pos_i \right|$ such that $f(pos_i)$ is higher when s_i appears either at the beginning or at the end of c. The parameters α, β, γ determine the shape of ρ_{s_i}. $K \in [0, 1]$ is a constant value used to balance the role of focus and position in calculating the attraction. The attraction a_i can be interpreted as the probability of a sentence s_i to contain an argumentative unit. According to this interpretation, given s_i, also the contiguous sentences s_{i-1} and s_{i+1} have a chance to be argumentative units. As a result, given the calculated attraction set $\mathcal{A}$, we update the attraction values a_i through an interpolation mechanism based on the Savitzky-Golay smoothing filter (SGF) (Savitzky and Golay, 1964), so that $\mathcal{A} := SGF(\mathcal{A})$.

In Figure 2, an example of attraction evaluation is provided by showing the values of φ, ρ, attraction, and interpolated attraction for all the sentences within one considered student essays included in the corpus from (Stab and Gurevych, 2014a) (see Section 4).

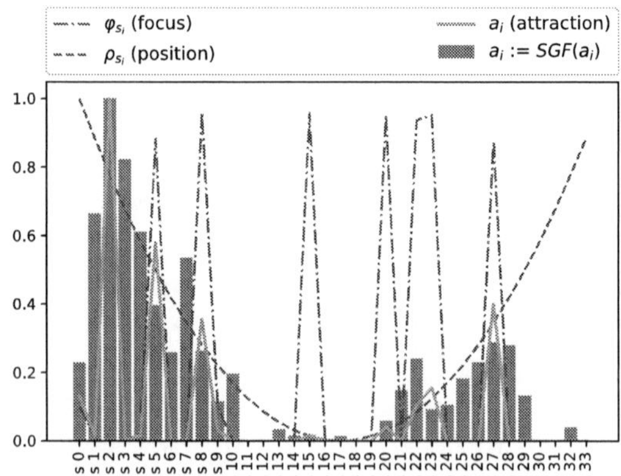

Figure 2: Attraction evaluation for the sentences of a considered text

100

Sentence labeling. Sentence labeling has the goal to turn attraction values into labeled categories. Consider a set of possible labels $\mathcal{L} = \{l_1, \ldots, l_g\}$, each one denoting a possible argumentative role that can be assigned to a sentence. Given a set of attraction values $\mathcal{A}$, a threshold-based mechanism is enforced to assign labels to sentences according to the following scheme:

$$
\begin{aligned}
a_i < \tau_1 \quad &: \quad s_i \leftarrow l_1 \\
\tau_1 \leq a_i < \tau_2 \quad &: \quad s_i \leftarrow l_2 \\
\ldots \quad & \quad \ldots \quad \ldots \\
a_i \geq \tau_{g-1} \quad &: \quad s_i \leftarrow l_g
\end{aligned}
$$

where $\tau_1 < \tau_2 < \ldots < \tau_{g-1}$ ($\tau_1, \ldots \tau_{g-1} \in (0,1]$) are prefixed threshold values. The result of sentence labeling is a partition of S into g categories with associated labels.

In the experiments, we discuss two different strategies for sentence labeling. The first one is a *two-class labeling* strategy where the possible labels for a sentence are argumentative unit (au) and non-argumentative unit ($\overline{au}$. The second strategy is a *multi-class labeling* in which the possible labels of a sentence are non-argumentative unit $\overline{au}$, premise (pr), claim (cl), and major claim (mc).

4 Experimental results

For evaluation of the proposed $\mathcal{A}2\mathcal{T}$ approach, we have used two English corpora. The first corpus (C1 in the following) is a collection of 90 student persuasive essays (Stab and Gurevych, 2014a) which has been manually annotated with major claims (one per essay), claims and premises at the clause level. In addition, the corpus contains manual annotations of argumentative relations, where the claims and premises are linked, while claims are linked to the major claim either with a support or an attack relation. Inter-annotation agreement has been measured to unitized alpha (Krippendorff, 2004) $\alpha_U = 0.724$. These 90 essays consist of a total of $1,675$ sentences (from which 19.3% contain no argument components), with an average length of 18.61 ± 7 sentences per essay, while the 5.4% of sentences contain a major claim, 26.4% contain a claim, and 61.1% contain a premise.

The second corpus (C2 in the following) has been compiled and manually annotated as described in (Habernal and Gurevych, 2017). This corpus focuses on user generated content, including user comments, forum posts, blogs, and newspaper articles, covering several thematic domains from educational controversies, such as home-schooling, private vs. public schools, or single-sex education. Containing in total 340 documents, the corpus has been manually annotated with an argument scheme based on extended Toulmin's model, involving claims, premises, and backing, rebuttal, refutation argument units. The corpus contains documents of various sizes, with a mean size of 11.44 ± 11.70 sentences per document, while the inter-annotator agreement was measured as $\alpha_U = 0.48$. The corpus consists of 3,899 sentences, from which 2,214 sentences (57%) contain no argument components.

Both corpora have been preprocessed with NLTK (Loper and Bird, 2002) in order to identify tokens and sentences. Then, each sentence was annotated as argumentative or non-argumentative, depending on whether it contained an argument unit (i.e. a text fragment annotated as major claim, claim, or premise). In addition, each argumentative sentence was further annotated with one of *major claim*, *claim*, and *premise*, based on the type of the contained argumentative unit. For the second corpus, which utilizes a richer argument scheme, we have considered backing, rebuttal and refutation units as premises. This second corpus does not contain units annotated as major claims. The following three tasks have been executed:

- Task 1: Argumentative sentence identification – given a sentence, classify whether or not it contains an argument component.
- Task 2: Major claim identification – given a argumentative sentence, classify whether or not it contains a major claim.
- Task 3: Argumentative sentence classification – given a sentence, classify the sentence as *major claim*, *claim*, *premise*, or *non-argumentative*.

Baseline. As a baseline for comparison against our approach, we created a probabilistic classifier of sentences which evaluates the probability $p(l = au|s_i)$ as follows. Given the text c containing $L(c)$ sentences s_i, let be $\zeta_c \sim Dir(\boldsymbol{\alpha})$ the probability distribution of the sentences in c, such that $\zeta_c^{s_i} \sim p(l = au|s_i)$. The $L(c)$ parameters $\boldsymbol{\alpha}$ used to generate ζ_c are defined such that $\alpha_i = \left| \frac{L(c)}{2} - pos_i \right|$. The rationale of this procedure is to bias the random assignment of a sentence to the au label in favor of sentences appearing either in the beginning or in the end of a text. This bias attempts to model empirical evidence that in several types of documents, the density of argumentative units in various sections of documents depends on the structure of documents. The beginning and end of a document are expected to contain argumentative units in structured documents like news, scientific publications, or argumentative essays (Stab and Gurevych, 2017), where major claims and supporting premises are frequently found in the beginning of documents, with documents frequently ending with repeating the major claims and supporting evidence.

4.1 Task 1: Argumentative sentence identification

The goal of Task 1 is to associate each sentence of the corpora to a label in $\mathcal{L} = \{au, \overline{au}\}$ by following a two-class labeling strategy (see Section 3). As a first experiment, we performed sentence labeling with different threshold ranging from 0 to 1 with step 0.05. In Figure 3, we report the precision, recall, and F1-measure for $\mathcal{A}2\mathcal{T}$ and for the baseline. In addition, we report also the results of applying sentence labeling based on φ and ρ (the components of attraction) separately. The parameter K for attraction calculation has been set to 0.5. Since $\mathcal{A}2\mathcal{T}$ is an unsupervised method, there is no easy way to define the threshold parameter τ, which has been empirically defined to $\tau = 0.3$. The different behavior of $\mathcal{A}2\mathcal{T}$ with respect to the baseline is shown in the confusion matrices reported in Figures 4 and 5.

From Figure 3, we can see that $\mathcal{A}2\mathcal{T}$ is significantly better than the baseline, especially for the C1 corpus. A characteristic of this corpus is that argumentative units are frequently located in the introduction or the conclusion of an essay, which is also reflected by the baseline that achieved an F1-measure of 0.35 for a threshold of $\tau = 0.05$ (with the baseline being particularly precise, suggesting that argumentative units are very frequently at the beginning and end of essays). Both components of attraction (φ and ρ) perform well, with the topic component φ being slightly better than position information ρ, both in precision and recall. The results are similar for corpus C2, with $\mathcal{A}2\mathcal{T}$ surpassing the baseline, although $\mathcal{A}2\mathcal{T}$ advantage in precision is smaller. As shown in the confusion matrix of Figure 5, the main source of error is the large number of false positives for the au class, proposing more argumentative units than what have been manually identified in corpus C2. This can be attributed to the sparseness of argumentative units in the C2 corpus, with almost 60% of the sentences being non-argumentative.

4.2 Task 2: Major claim identification

As a second experiment, we exploited probabilities associated with sentences to perform a ranked evaluation. In particular, we calculated two measures, namely P that is the area the under the precision-recall curve and R that is the area under the receiver operating characteristic (ROC) curve. In this experiments, we used different criteria for defining the true labels: in PCM, an annotated sentence in the corpus is considered a true argumentative unit if it is either a premise, a claim, or a major claim; in CM only claims and major claims are taken as valid au; in M only major claims are taken into account. Results are reported in Table 1.

Table 1: Area under the precision-recall (P) and the ROC (R) curves

	C1			C2	
P	PCM	CM	M	PCM	CM
$\mathcal{A}2\mathcal{T}$	0.79	0.31	0.08	0.26	0.19
φ	0.84	0.29	0.06	0.19	0.1
ρ	0.68	0.29	0.09	0.24	0.19
Baseline	0.68	0.31	0.11	0.16	0.06
R	PCM	CM	M	PCM	CM
$\mathcal{A}2\mathcal{T}$	0.4	0.52	0.62	0.7	0.76
φ	0.52	0.51	0.53	0.58	0.57
ρ	0.16	0.52	0.77	0.69	0.77
Baseline	0.16	0.53	0.79	0.31	0.18

4.3 Task 3: Argumentative sentence classification

The goal of Task 3 is to associate each sentence of the corpora to a label in $\mathcal{L} = \{\overline{au}, pr, cl, mc\}$ by following a multi-class labeling strategy (see Section 3). In particular, we adopted the thresholds $[0.1, 0.3, 0.5]$. This task is challenging since it is required to distinguish the different role played in argumentation by sentences that are often very similar from the terminological point of view. The confusion matrix for corpus C1 is shown in Figure 6, while Figure 7 shows the confusion matrix for corpus C2. Both $\mathcal{A}2\mathcal{T}$ and the baseline achieve low results, but the accuracy of $\mathcal{A}2\mathcal{T}$ is 0.3 against the 0.1 of the baseline. From Figure 6 we see that $\mathcal{A}2\mathcal{T}$ achieved good results for premises, and quite good results for claims, although distinguishing between claims and premises is challenging for the $\mathcal{A}2\mathcal{T}$ approach. In particular, the role

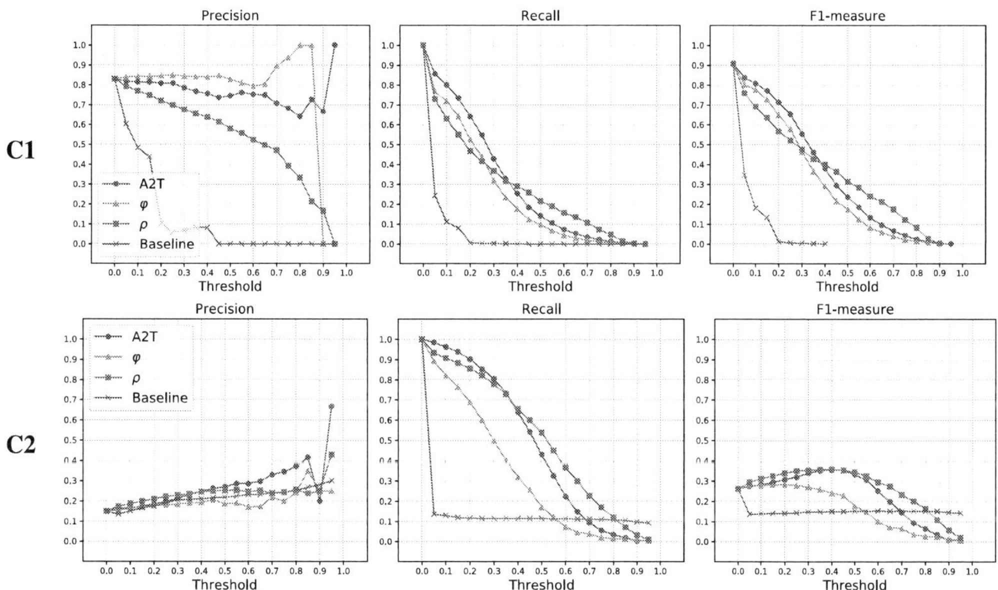

Figure 3: Precision, Recall and F1-measure with different thresholds

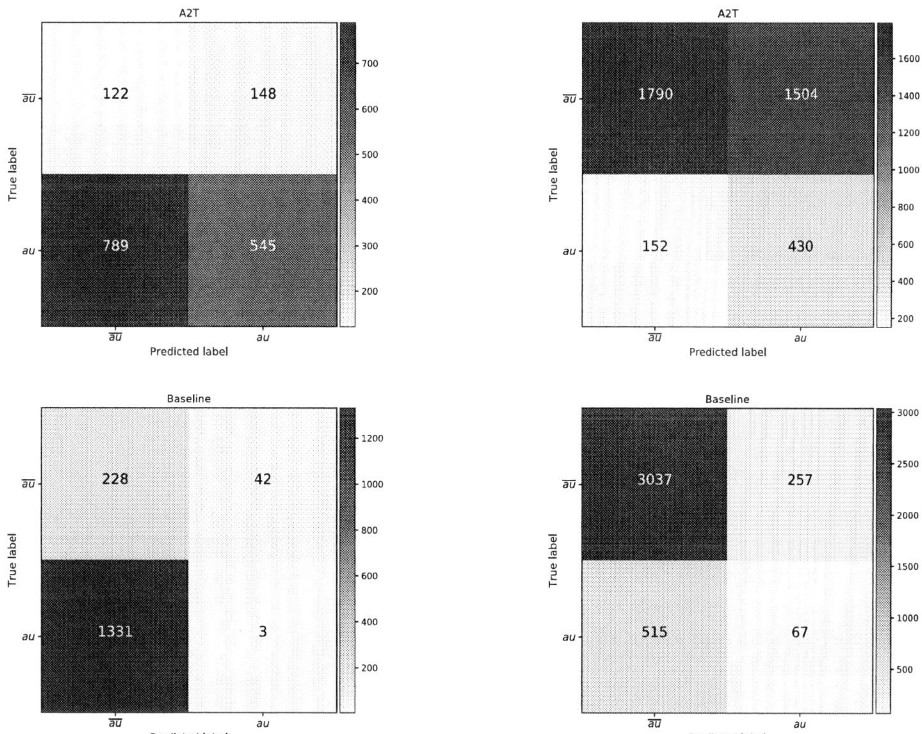

Figure 4: Two-class confusion matrices for corpus C1 (Threshold $\tau = 0.3$)

Figure 5: Two-class confusion matrices for corpus C2 (Threshold $\tau = 0.3$)

of sentences may change in different texts so that claims in one context are premises in another. This kind of contextual shift is only partially addressed by $\mathcal{A}2\mathcal{T}$, because the only contextual information we take into account is topic distribution. To the end of improving the understanding of the context,

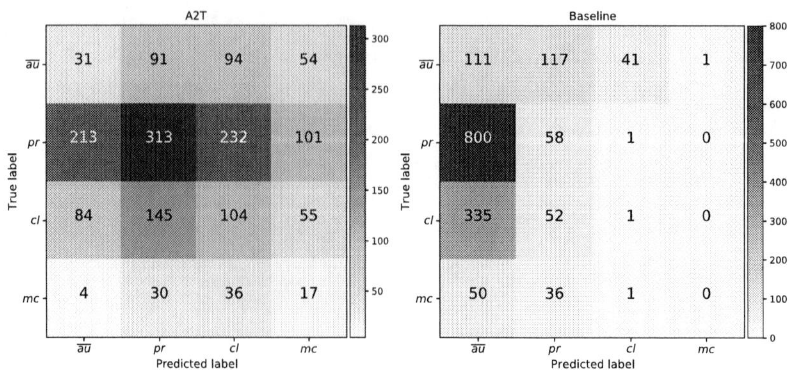

Figure 6: Multi-class confusion matrices for corpus C1

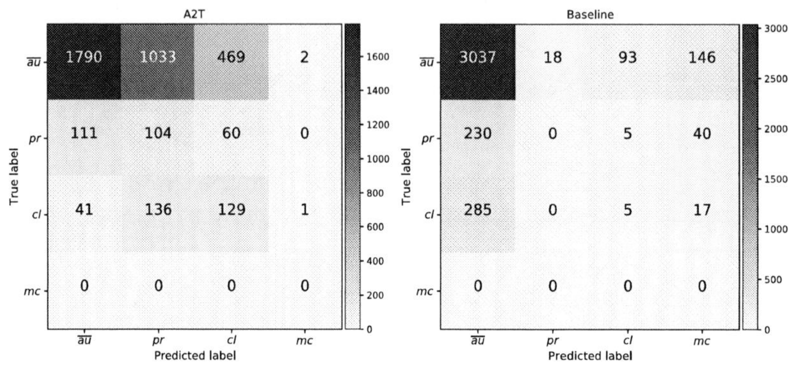

Figure 7: Multi-class confusion matrices for corpus C2

it may be useful to work also on semantic relations holding among sentences. This is actually one of the future tasks in our research work.

Another specific challenge emerges when we consider the corpus C2. Indeed, C2 contains a limited number of argumentative sentences with respect to the corpus size. In this case, since we analyze all the sentences according to their bag of words, we tend to overestimate the number of argumentative units, collecting a relatively high number of false positives.

4.4 Lessons learned from error analysis

A first evidence emerging from the analysis of confusion matrices for both corpora C1 and C2 is that the role of sentences is strictly dependent on the type of documents. C1 contains structured essays of various topics, while C2 provides conversational texts extracted from blogs and chats. In the first case, the number of argumentative units is higher than in the second one. In particular, for C2 we overestimated the probability of sentences to be an argumentative unit. This is mainly due

to the fact that those sentences contain words that are semantically related to the main topic of the conversation although they are not playing a role in the argumentation. An example is the following sentence, taken from a document associated with the topic "school": *"why do some parents not think their kids can attain?"*. The sentence is clearly part of a conversation and it has been annotated as a non argumentative unit because it is a question. However, since it contains words that are relevant for the topic (i.e., parents, kids, attain), $\mathcal{A2T}$ associates the sentence with a good level of attraction, labeling it as a premise. In order to address this kind of false positives, we aim in our future work to study the dependency relations among sentences in text (such as question-answers) to the goal of achieving a better insight of the sentences role.

A second lesson learned from error analysis concerns the distinction between claims and premises. This confusion is evident especially when dealing with corpus C1. An example is given by the following two sentences, taken from an essay about the role of sports in favor of peace.

- (s1) *for example, when Irak was hardly struck by the second gulf war, its citizens tried to catch any incoming news about the football-world cup through their portable receivers.*

- (s2) *thus, world sports events strongly participate in eventually pulling back people towards friendship and peace*

The sentence (s1) has been annotated as a premise, while (s2) as a claim. In our classification, they are both claims. The reason is that they both contain topic-related words and their position in text is similar. The main distinction is the presence of the expression "for example" in the first sentence which qualifies it as a premise. To this end, in our future work we aim at adding some special words (such as "for example", "therefore") in the background knowledge of the classifier, in order to improve the capability of discriminating premises and claims.

5   Concluding remarks

In this paper, we present the "Attraction to Topics" – $A2T$ unsupervised approach for detecting argumentative discourse units, at sentence-level granularity. Motivated by the observation that topic information is frequently employed as a sub-task in the process of manual annotation of arguments, we propose an approach that exploits topic modeling techniques in order to identify argumentative units. Since manual supervision is not required, $A2T$ has the potential to be applicable on documents of various genres and domains. Preliminary evaluation results on two different corpora are promising. First, $A2T$ performs significantly better than the baseline on argumentative sentence detection on both corpora. Second, $A2T$ exhibits good results for classifying argumentative sentences as major claims, claims, premises, and non-argumentative units, at least for the first corpus, which has a low rate of non-argumentative sentences (20%).

Regarding directions for further research, there are several axes that can be explored. Evaluation on a larger set of annotation corpora will provide enhanced insights about the performance of the proposed approach on different document types. Our preliminary results showed that despite good recall on multiple corpora, achieving also good precision can be a challenging task in documents where argumentative units are sparse, and false positives can be an issue. In this context, we would like to also exploit other types of relations, and extend our method with other kinds of similarities over sentences.

References

David M. Blei, Andrew Y. Ng, and Michael I. Jordan. 2003. Latent dirichlet allocation. *J. Mach. Learn. Res.* 3:993–1022. http://dl.acm.org/citation.cfm?id=944919.944937.

Silvana Castano, Alfio Ferrara, and Stefano Montanelli. 2017. Exploratory analysis of textual data streams. *Future Generation Computer Systems* 68:391–406.

Eirini Florou, Stasinos Konstantopoulos, Antonis Koukourikos, and Pythagoras Karampiperis. 2013. Argument extraction for supporting public policy formulation. In Piroska Lendvai and Kalliopi Zervanou, editors, *Proceedings of the 7th Workshop on Language Technology for Cultural Heritage, Social Sciences, and Humanities, LaTeCH@ACL 2013, August 8, 2013, Sofia, Bulgaria.* The Association for Computer Linguistics, pages 49–54. http://aclweb.org/anthology/W/W13/W13-2707.pdf.

Theodosis Goudas, Christos Louizos, Georgios Petasis, and Vangelis Karkaletsis. 2014. Argument extraction from news, blogs, and social media. In Aristidis Likas, Konstantinos Blekas, and Dimitris Kalles, editors, *Artificial Intelligence: Methods and Applications: 8th Hellenic Conference on AI, SETN 2014, Ioannina, Greece, May 15-17, 2014. Proceedings*, Springer International Publishing, Cham, pages 287–299. https://doi.org/10.1007/978-3-319-07064-3_23.

Theodosis Goudas, Christos Louizos, Georgios Petasis, and Vangelis Karkaletsis. 2015. Argument extraction from news, blogs, and the social web. *International Journal on Artificial Intelligence Tools* 24(05):1540024. https://doi.org/10.1142/S0218213015400242.

Ivan Habernal and Iryna Gurevych. 2015. Exploiting debate portals for semi-supervised argumentation mining in user-generated web discourse. In *Proceedings of the 2015 Conference on Empirical Methods in Natural Language Processing.* Association for Computational Linguistics, Lisbon, Portugal, pages 2127–2137. http://aclweb.org/anthology/D15-1255.

Ivan Habernal and Iryna Gurevych. 2017. Argumentation mining in user-generated web discourse. *Computational Linguistics* 43(1):125–179. https://doi.org/10.1162/COLI_a_00276.

Kazi Saidul Hasan and Vincent Ng. 2014. Why are you taking this stance? identifying and classifying reasons in ideological debates. In *Proceedings of the 2014 Conference on Empirical Methods in Natural Language Processing (EMNLP)*. Association for Computational Linguistics, Doha, Qatar, pages 751–762. http://www.aclweb.org/anthology/D14-1083.

Klaus Krippendorff. 2004. Measuring the reliability of qualitative text analysis data. *Quality and Quantity* 38(6):787–800. https://doi.org/10.1007/s11135-004-8107-7.

John Lawrence, Chris Reed, Colin Allen, Simon McAlister, and Andrew Ravenscroft. 2014. Mining arguments from 19th century philosophical texts using topic based modelling. In *Proceedings of the First Workshop on Argumentation Mining*. Association for Computational Linguistics, Baltimore, Maryland, pages 79–87. http://www.aclweb.org/anthology/W/W14/W14-2111.

Ran Levy, Yonatan Bilu, Daniel Hershcovich, Ehud Aharoni, and Noam Slonim. 2014. Context dependent claim detection. In Jan Hajic and Junichi Tsujii, editors, *COLING 2014, 25th International Conference on Computational Linguistics, Proceedings of the Conference: Technical Papers, August 23-29, 2014, Dublin, Ireland*. ACL, pages 1489–1500. http://aclweb.org/anthology/C/C14/C14-1141.pdf.

Marco Lippi and Paolo Torroni. 2015a. Argument mining: A machine learning perspective. In Elizabeth Black, Sanjay Modgil, and Nir Oren, editors, *Theory and Applications of Formal Argumentation: Third International Workshop, TAFA 2015, Buenos Aires, Argentina, July 25-26, 2015, Revised Selected Papers*. Springer International Publishing, Cham, pages 163–176. https://doi.org/10.1007/978-3-319-28460-6_10.

Marco Lippi and Paolo Torroni. 2015b. Context-independent claim detection for argument mining. In *Proceedings of the 24th International Conference on Artificial Intelligence*. AAAI Press, IJCAI'15, pages 185–191. http://dl.acm.org/citation.cfm?id=2832249.2832275.

Edward Loper and Steven Bird. 2002. Nltk: The natural language toolkit. In *Proceedings of the ACL-02 Workshop on Effective Tools and Methodologies for Teaching Natural Language Processing and Computational Linguistics - Volume 1*. Association for Computational Linguistics, Stroudsburg, PA, USA, ETMTNLP '02, pages 63–70. https://doi.org/10.3115/1118108.1118117.

Christopher D Manning, Prabhakar Raghavan, and Hinrich Schütze. 2008. *Introduction to information retrieval*, volume 1. Cambridge university press Cambridge.

Rada Mihalcea and Paul Tarau. 2004. Textrank: Bringing order into texts. In Dekang Lin and Dekai Wu, editors, *Proceedings of EMNLP 2004*. Association for Computational Linguistics, Barcelona, Spain, pages 404–411. http://www.aclweb.org/anthology/W/W04/W04-3252.pdf.

Raquel Mochales and Marie-Francine Moens. 2011. Argumentation mining. *Artificial Intelligence and Law* 19(1):1–22. https://doi.org/10.1007/s10506-010-9104-x.

Marie-Francine Moens, Erik Boiy, Raquel Mochales Palau, and Chris Reed. 2007. Automatic detection of arguments in legal texts. In *Proceedings of the 11th International Conference on Artificial Intelligence and Law*. ACM, New York, NY, USA, ICAIL '07, pages 225–230. https://doi.org/10.1145/1276318.1276362.

Huy Nguyen and Diane J. Litman. 2015. Extracting argument and domain words for identifying argument components in texts. In *Proceedings of the 2nd Workshop on Argumentation Mining, ArgMining@HLT-NAACL 2015, June 4, 2015, Denver, Colorado, USA*. The Association for Computational Linguistics, pages 22–28. http://aclweb.org/anthology/W/W15/W15-0503.pdf.

Huy Nguyen and Diane J. Litman. 2016a. Context-aware argumentative relation mining. In *Proceedings of the 54th Annual Meeting of the Association for Computational Linguistics, ACL 2016, August 7-12, 2016, Berlin, Germany, Volume 1: Long Papers*. The Association for Computer Linguistics. http://aclweb.org/anthology/P/P16/P16-1107.pdf.

Huy Nguyen and Diane J. Litman. 2016b. Improving argument mining in student essays by learning and exploiting argument indicators versus essay topics. In Zdravko Markov and Ingrid Russell, editors, *Proceedings of the Twenty-Ninth International Florida Artificial Intelligence Research Society Conference, FLAIRS 2016, Key Largo, Florida, May 16-18, 2016.*. AAAI Press, pages 485–490. http://www.aaai.org/ocs/index.php/-FLAIRS/FLAIRS16/paper/view/12791.

Raquel Mochales Palau and Marie-Francine Moens. 2009. Argumentation mining: The detection, classification and structure of arguments in text. In *Proceedings of the 12th International Conference on Artificial Intelligence and Law*. ACM, New York, NY, USA, ICAIL '09, pages 98–107. https://doi.org/10.1145/1568234.1568246.

Joonsuk Park and Claire Cardie. 2014. Identifying appropriate support for propositions in online user comments. In *Proceedings of the First Workshop on Argumentation Mining*. Association for Computational Linguistics, Baltimore, Maryland, pages 29–38. http://www.aclweb.org/anthology/W/W14/W14-2105.

Andreas Peldszus and Manfred Stede. 2013. From argument diagrams to argumentation mining in texts: A survey. *Int.*

J. Cogn. Inform. Nat. Intell. 7(1):1–31. https://doi.org/10.4018/jcini.2013010101.

Georgios Petasis and Vangelis Karkaletsis. 2016. Identifying argument components through textrank. In *Proceedings of the 3rd Workshop on Argument Mining (ArgMining2016)*. Association for Computational Linguistics, Berlin, Germany, pages 56–66. http://aclweb.org/anthology/W/W16/W16-2811.pdf.

Ruty Rinott, Lena Dankin, Carlos Alzate Perez, Mitesh M. Khapra, Ehud Aharoni, and Noam Slonim. 2015. Show me your evidence - an automatic method for context dependent evidence detection. In *Proceedings of the 2015 Conference on Empirical Methods in Natural Language Processing*. Association for Computational Linguistics, Lisbon, Portugal, pages 440–450. http://aclweb.org/anthology/D15-1050.

Niall Rooney, Hui Wang, and Fiona Browne. 2012. Applying kernel methods to argumentation mining. In G. Michael Youngblood and Philip M. McCarthy, editors, *Proceedings of the Twenty-Fifth International Florida Artificial Intelligence Research Society Conference, Marco Island, Florida. May 23-25, 2012.* AAAI Press. http://www.aaai.org/ocs/index.php/-FLAIRS/FLAIRS12/paper/view/4366.

Abraham Savitzky and Marcel JE Golay. 1964. Smoothing and differentiation of data by simplified least squares procedures. *Analytical chemistry* 36(8):1627–1639.

Christian Stab and Iryna Gurevych. 2014a. Annotating argument components and relations in persuasive essays. In Junichi Tsujii and Jan Hajic, editors, *Proceedings of the 25th International Conference on Computational Linguistics (COLING 2014)*. Dublin City University and Association for Computational Linguistics, Dublin, Ireland, pages 1501–1510. http://www.aclweb.org/anthology/C14-1142.

Christian Stab and Iryna Gurevych. 2014b. Identifying argumentative discourse structures in persuasive essays. In *Proceedings of the 2014 Conference on Empirical Methods in Natural Language Processing (EMNLP)*. Association for Computational Linguistics, Doha, Qatar, pages 46–56. http://www.aclweb.org/anthology/D14-1006.

Christian Stab and Iryna Gurevych. 2017. Parsing argumentation structures in persuasive essays. *Computational Linguistics* 0(ja):1–62. https://doi.org/10.1162/COLI_a_00295.

Yee Whye Teh, Michael I Jordan, Matthew J Beal, and David M Blei. 2006. Hierarchical dirichlet processes. *Journal of the American Statistical Association* 101(476):1566–1581. https://doi.org/10.1198/016214506000000302.

Using Complex Argumentative Interactions to Reconstruct the Argumentative Structure of Large-Scale Debates

John Lawrence and **Chris Reed**
Centre for Argument Technology,
University of Dundee, UK

Abstract

In this paper we consider the insights that can be gained by considering large scale argument networks and the complex interactions between their constituent propositions. We investigate metrics for analysing properties of these networks, illustrating these using a corpus of arguments taken from the 2016 US Presidential Debates. We present techniques for determining these features directly from natural language text and show that there is a strong correlation between these automatically identified features and the argumentative structure contained within the text. Finally, we combine these metrics with argument mining techniques and show how the identification of argumentative relations can be improved by considering the larger context in which they occur.

1 Introduction

Argument and debate form cornerstones of civilized society and of intellectual life. Processes of argumentation elect and run our governments, structure scientific endeavour and frame religious belief. Understanding the nature and structure of these argumentative processes has broad ranging applications including: supporting legal decision making (Palau and Moens, 2009); analysing product reviews to determine not just *what* opinions are being expressed, but *why* people hold those opinions (Wyner et al., 2012); opening up the complex debates in parliamentary records to a wider audience (Hirst and Feng, 2015); and providing in-depth, yet easily digestable, summaries of complex issues (Lawrence et al., 2016).

Argument Mining[1] is the automatic identification of the argumentative structure contained within a piece of natural language text. By automatically identifying this structure and its associated premises and conclusions, we are able to tell not just *what* views are being expressed, but also *why* those particular views are held.

In this paper, we consider the insights that can be gained by considering large scale argument networks as a whole. We present two metrics, *Centrality* and *Divisiveness* which can be viewed as how important an issue is to the argument as a whole (how many other issues are connected to it), and how much an issue splits opinion (how many others issues are in conflict with it and the amount of support which the two sides have).

We first show how these metrics can be calculated from an annotated argument structure and then showing how they can be automatically approximated from the original text. We use this automatic approximation, reversing the original calculation, to determine the argumentative structure of un-annotated text. Finally, we combine this approach with existing argument mining techniques and show how the identification of properties of argumentative relations can be improved by considering the larger context in which these relations occur.

2 Related Work

Despite the rich heritage of philosophical research in argumentation theory (van Eemeren et al., 2014; Chesñevar et al., 2006), the majority of argument mining techniques explored to date have focused on identifying specific facets of the argumentative structure rather than considering the complex network of interactions which occur in real-life debate. For example, existing approaches have considered, classifying sentences as argumentative or non-argumentative (Moens et al., 2007), classify-

---

[1] Sometimes also referred to as argumentation mining

Proceedings of the 4th Workshop on Argument Mining, pages 108–117
Copenhagen, Denmark, September 8, 2017. ©2017 Association for Computational Linguistics

ing text spans as premises or conclusions (Palau and Moens, 2009), classifying the relations between specific sets of premises and their conclusion (Feng and Hirst, 2011), or classifying the different types of premise that can support a given conclusion (Park and Cardie, 2014).

The approach which we present in this paper considers large scale argument networks as a whole, looking at properties of argumentative text spans that are related to their role in the entire argumentative structure. In our automatic determination of *Centrality* and *Divisiveness*, we first construct a graph of semantic similarity between text spans and then use the Textrank algorithm (Mihalcea and Tarau, 2004) to determine those which are most central. For *Divisiveness*, we then look at the sentiment polarity of each text span compared to the rest of the corpus to measure how many others are in conflict with it and the amount of support which the two sides have. TextRank has been successfully applied to many natural language processing applications, including identifying those parts of a text which are argumentative (as opposed to those which are not) (Petasis and Karkaletsis, 2016).

Similarly, Wachsmuth et al. (2017) propose a model for determining the relevance of arguments using PageRank (Brin and Page, 1998). In this approch, the relevance of an argument's conclusion is decided by what other arguments reuse it as a premise. These results are compared to an argument relevance benchmark dataset, manually annotated by seven experts. On this dataset, the PageRank scores are found to beat several intuitive baselines and correlate with human judgments of relevance.

Lawrence and Reed (2015) used semantic similarity to determine argumentative connections between text spans. The intuition being that if a proposition is similar to its predecessor then there exists some argumentative link between them, whereas if there is low similarity between a proposition and its predecessor, the author is going back to address a previously made point or starting a new topic. Using this method a precision of 0.72, and recall of 0.77 are recorded when comparing the resulting connections to a manual analysis, however it should be noted that what is being identified here is merely that an inference relationship exists between two propositions, and no indication is given as to the direction of this inference.

3 Data: The US 2016 Presidential Debate Corpus

The data which we use is taken from transcripts of the 2016 US presidential debates, along with a sampling of the online reaction to these debates. Specifically, the corpus consists of Argument Interchange Format (AIF) (Chesñevar et al., 2006) analyses of the first general presidential head-to-head debate between Donald Trump and Hillary Clinton along with corresponding comments from threads on Reddit (`reddit.com`) dedicated to the debates as they were happening[2].

3.1 The Argument Interchange Format

The Argument Interchange Format is a popular standard for representing argument structures as graphs, founded upon philosophical research in argumentation theory (van Eemeren et al., 2014), implemented as a Semantic Web ontology, and recently extended to handle dialogical interaction (Reed et al., 2010). The AIF distinguishes information, I-nodes, from the schematic ways in which they are related, S-nodes. I-nodes represent propositional information contained in an argument, such as a conclusion, premise etc. A subset of I-nodes refers to propositional reports specifically about discourse events: these are L-nodes (locutions). S-nodes capture the application of *schemes* of three categories: argumentative, illocutionary and dialogical. Amongst argumentative patterns there are inferences or reasoning (RA-nodes), conflict (CA-nodes) and rephrase (MA-nodes). Dialogical transitions (TA-nodes) are schemes of interaction or protocol of a given dialogue game which determine possible relations between locutions. Illocutionary schemes (YA-nodes) are patterns of communicative intentions which speakers use to introduce propositional contents. These node types are summarised in Table 1.

3.2 Annotation

Analysis was performed using the OVA+ (Online Visualisation of Argument) analysis tool (Janier et al., 2014) to create a series of argument maps covering the entire televised debate along with online reaction consisting of sub-threads selected from the Reddit 'megathreads' created during the debate. Annotators were instructed to select sub-

---

[2]The full annotated corpus along with the original text is available at `http://corpora.aifdb.org/US2016G1`

Node	Component	Category	Node	Component
I-node	Information (propositional contents)		I-node but not L-node	contents of locutions
			L-node	locutions
S-node	Schemes (relations between contents)	Argument schemes	RA	inference
			CA	conflict
			MA	rephrase
		Illocutionary schemes	YA	illocutionary connections
		Dialogue schemes	TA	transitions

Table 1: Types and sub-types of nodes in the AIF standard and components of analysed argument data, and the categories of schemes.

threads based on three criteria (a) sub-threads must not be shorter than five turns; (b) sub-threads containing only jokes and wordplays are excluded; (c) technical and non-related threads are excluded. Details of the resulting corpora can be seen in Table 2 and a fragment of the analysed structure can be seen in Figure 1. The total number of RA and CA nodes is greater than the sum of these values for the TV and reddit corpora, this is due to additional connections linking these two corpora which appear in the combined corpus, but not in the individual copora. These connections mean that the total corpus forms a coherent whole where topics discussed in the televised debate are linked argumentatively to points made in the online discussion.

3.3 Inter-Annotator Agreement

Two analysts (A1, A2) completed analysis of televised debate; and a further two analysts (A3 and A4) worked on the reddit reaction. A subset of the dataset (approximately 10%) was randomly selected for duplicate annotation by two analysts and these sets were then used to calculate pairwise inter-annotator agreement. Measures of agreement were calculated using Cohen's kappa κ (Cohen, 1960) ($\kappa = 0.55$) and the Combined Argument Similarity Score version of κ, CASS-κ (Duthie et al., 2016), which refines Cohen's κ to avoid over-penalizing for segmentation differences (CASS-$\kappa = 0.71$)[3]. In the former case, Cohen's κ is difficult to apply directly, because it assumes that the items being categorized are fixed – in this case, the items being categorized are segments, whereas analysts may differ on segmentation boundaries.

---

[3]The most usual interpretation of κ scores is proposed in (Landis and Koch, 1977) which suggest that $0.4 - 0.6$ represents "good agreement"; $0.61 - 0.8$ represents "substantial agreement" and $0.81 - 1.0$ represents "almost perfect agreement"

4 Large Scale Argument Graph Properties

The argument graphs described in the previous section allow us to look at the structure of the debate as a whole rather than focusing on the properties of individual relations between propositions. In this section we look at two measures, *Centrality* and *Divisiveness*, that individual propositions (I-nodes) exhibit which can only be interpreted when considering the broader context in which they occur.

Whilst there are certainly other measures that could be applied to an argument graph highlighting interesting features of the arguments being made, we have selected these two metrics as they can both be calculated as properties of the argument graph and approximations can be determined directly from the original text. In Section 5, we describe methods to determine these approximations directly from the original text. By first calculating them directly we can then reverse the process of determining them from the argumentative structure, cutting the manual analysis out of the loop and allowing us to determine the argumentative structure directly. In Section 6, we look at how this approach can be used to improve the accuracy of extracting the full argumentative structure directly from un-annotated text.

4.1 Centrality

Central issues are those that play a particularly important role in the argumentative structure. For example, in Figure 1, we can see that the node "CLINTON knows how to really work to get new jobs..." is intuitively more central to the dialogue, being the point which all of the others are responding to, than the node "CLINTON's husband signed NAFTA...".

In order to calculate centrality scores for each

	Words	I-nodes	RA-nodes	CA-nodes
Televised Debate	17,190	1,473	505	79
Reddit Reaction	12,694	1,279	377	242
Total (US2016G1 Corpus)	**29,884**	**2,752**	**901**	**347**

Table 2: US 2016 General Presidential Debate Corpora statistics, listing word counts, propositions (I-nodes), supporting arguments (RAs) and conflicts (CAs).

I-node, we adapt eigenvector centrality (used in the Google Pagerank algorithm (Brin and Page, 1998)). This measure is closer to intuitions about claim centrality in arguments than alternative measures such as the Estrada index (Estrada, 2000) despite the latter's wide applicability. We have not found the Estrada index an informative measure for debate structure.

First, we consider the complete AIF structure as a directed graph, $G = (V, E)$, in which vertices (V) are either propositions, locutions or relations between propositions; and those relations are either support, conflict, rephrase, illocution or transition, captured by a function R which maps $V \mapsto \{prop, loc, support, conflict, rephrase, illocution, transition\}$ and edges exist between them $E \subset V \times V$.

From this we build the subgraph corresponding only to vertices connected by support or conflict relationships, which we call $G_l = (V_l, E_l)$, where $V_l = \{v \in V : R(V) \in \{support, conflict\}\}$ and $\forall v_l \in V_l$, if $(v_l, v') \in E$, then, $(v_l, v') \in E_l$ and if $(v', v_l) \in E$, then, $(v', v_l) \in E_l$. We can then define eigencentrality over G_l as in Equation 1, where λ is a constant representing the greatest eigenvalue for which a non-zero eigenvector solution exists.

$$Central(v) =_{def} \frac{1}{\lambda} \sum_{\substack{v' \in V_l \\ \text{s.t. } (v,v') \in E_l}} Central(v') \tag{1}$$

This results in a centrality score for each proposition, from which we can rank the propositions by how central they are to the debate. The top four ranked central propositions are listed below:

- CLINTON could encourage them by giving them tax incentives, for example

- there is/is not any way that the president can force profit sharing

- CLINTON also wants to see more companies do profit-sharing

- CLINTON is hinting at tax incentives

It is encouraging that these issues all concern the economy, which Pew Research identified as the single most important issue to voters (with 84% of voters ranking it as "very important") in the 2016 US presidential elections[4].

4.2 Divisiveness

Divisive issues are those that split opinion and which have points both supporting and attacking them (Konat et al., 2016). Looking again at Figure 1, we can see that the node "CLINTON knows how to really work to get new jobs..." is not only central, but also divisive, with both incoming support and conflict. At the opposite end of the scale, the node "CLINTON has been a secretary of state", is not divisive; such factual statements are unlikely to be disputed by anyone on either side of the debate.

The Divisiveness of an issue measures how many others are in conflict with it and the amount of support which the two sides have. By this measure, every proposition v_2 which is in conflict with v (i.e. for which there is an edge either outgoing from v through a conflict v_c to v_2, or in the other direction, or both) is assessed for its support in comparison to that for v and the sum over all such v_2 yields an overall measure of *Divisiveness* as shown in Equation 2, in which $|v|^{in}_{R(v)}$ refers to the *in* order of vertex v where constraint $R(v)$ is met.

Again we list the top four ranked divisive issues below, and it is certainly easy to see how such statements on the character of the candidates, the validity of their claims and controversial issues such as gun control could easily divide those commenting on the debate:

- TRUMP settled that lawsuit with no admission of guilt

- I still support hand guns though

[4] http://www.people-press.org/2016/07/07/4-top-voting-issues-in-2016-election/

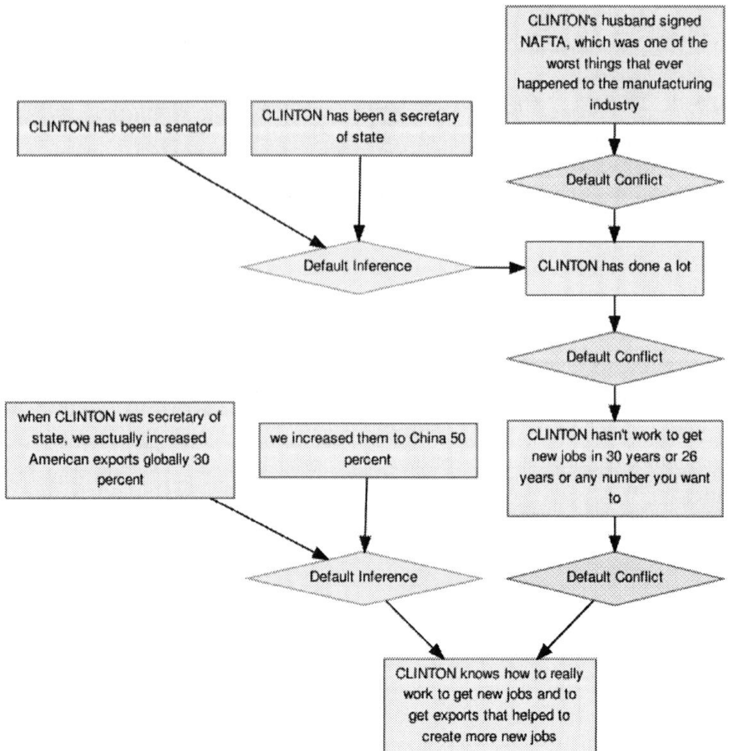

Figure 1: Fragment of Manually Analysed Argumentative Structure from the US 2016 General Presidential Debate Corpus. The nodes shown in this graph have been filtered to display only the propositional text spans (I-nodes shown as rectangles) and the support and conflict relations between them (RA and CA nodes shown as diamonds).

$$Divisive(v) =_{def} \sum_{\substack{\forall v_2 \in V \text{ s.t.} \\ [(v_2,v_c),(v_c,v)\in E \ \vee \\ (v,v_c),(v_c,v_2)\in E] \ \wedge \\ R(v_c)=conflict}} |v|^{in}_{R(v')=support} * |v_2|^{in}_{R(v')=support} \tag{2}$$

- people have looked at both of our plans, have concluded that CLINTON's would create 10 million jobs and TRUMP's would lose us 3.5 million jobs

- CLINTON didn't realize coming off as a snarky teenager isn't a good look either

5 Automating the Identification of Large Scale Argument Graph Properties

In this section we investigate techniques to automatically rank text fragments by their centrality and divisiveness with no prior knowledge of the argumentative structure contained within the text. In each case, we take the manually segmented propositions from our corpus and apply techniques to rank these, we then compare the resulting rankings to the ranking determined from the manually analysed argument structures as described in Section 4.

5.1 Automatic Identification of Centrality

In order to calculate centrality automatically, we first hypothesise that propositions (I-nodes) that are connected by relations of either support or attack in an AIF graph will have a higher semantic similarity than those which have no argumentative connection. We can again see an example of this in Figure 1, where the node "CLINTON knows how to really work to get new **jobs** and to get **exports** that..." is connected via support and attack relations to nodes whose propositional contents are all related to jobs or exports. The remaining nodes in this example fragment all discuss more distant concepts, such as Clinton's experience.

We consider a range of methods for determining semantic similarity and in each case use these as the edge weights in an automatically generated similarity graph. We can then consider centrality to be determined by high similarity to the greatest number of other nodes. As such, we can use TextRank (Mihalcea and Tarau, 2004) to produce a centrality ranking directly from the text and compare this to the ranking obtained from the argumentative structure.

The first approach to determining similarity that we consider is calculated as the number of common words between the two propositions, based on the method proposed by Mihalcea and Tarau (2004) for ranking sentences. Formally, given two propositions P_i and P_j, with a proposition being represented by the set of N_i words that appear in the proposition $P_i = w_1^i, w_2^i, ..., w_{N_i}^i$, the similarity of P_i and P_j is defined as:

$$Similarity(P_i, P_j) = \frac{|\{w_k | w_k \in P_i \wedge w_k \in P_j\}|}{log(|P_i|) + log(|P_j|)}$$

$$(3)$$

Whilst this approach is sufficient to determine similarity in the example discussed above, it is reliant on the exact same words appearing in each proposition. In order to allow for the use of synonyms and related terms in the dialogue, we consider several further measures of semantic similarity.

The first of these approaches uses WordNet (Miller, 1995) to replace the binary matching of words in the method above with the distance between the synsets of each word. This value is inversely proportional to the number of nodes along the shortest path between the synsets. The shortest possible path occurs when the two synsets are the same, in which case the length is 1, giving the same result for exactly matching words.

We also tested two further methods of determining semantic similarity which have both been shown to perform robustly when using models trained on large external corpora (Lau and Baldwin, 2016).

The first of these approaches uses word2vec

(Mikolov et al., 2013), an efficient neural approach to learning high-quality embeddings for words. Due to the relatively small size of our training dataset, we used pre-trained skip-gram vectors trained on part of the Google News dataset[5]. This model contains 300-dimensional vectors for 3 million words and phrases obtained using a simple data-driven approach described in Mikolov et al. (2013).

To determine similarity between propositions, we located the centroid of the word embeddings for each by averaging the word2vec vectors for the individual words in the proposition, and then calculating the cosine similarity between centroids to represent the proposition similarity.

The final approach which we implemented uses a doc2vec (Le and Mikolov, 2014) distributed bag of words (*dbow*) model to represent every proposition as a vector with 300 dimensions. Again, we then calculated the cosine similarity between vectors to represent the proposition similarity.

For each of the methods described above, we applied the ranking algorithm to give an ordered list of propositions, we then compared the ranking obtained by each to the centrality ranking calculated for the manually annotated argument structure, as described in Section 4, by calculating the Kendall rank correlation coefficient (Kendall, 1938). The results for each method are shown in Table 3. In each case the results show a correlation between the rankings ($p < 0.05$) suggesting that all of these methods are able to approximate the centrality of propositions in the argumentative structure. In Section 6 we explore these results further and show that these approximations are in all cases sufficient to improve the automatic extraction of the argumentative structure directly from the original text.

5.2 Automatic Identification of Divisiveness

Whilst divisiveness is a related concept to centrality, it is more challenging to determine directly from the text, as we need to not only locate those nodes that are most discussed, but also to limit this to those which are involved in conflict relations.

Here we implement a method of determining conflict relations using SentiWordNet[6], a lexical resource for opinion mining. SentiWordNet assigns a triple of polarity scores to each synset of

---

[5]https://code.google.com/archive/p/word2vec/
[6]http://sentiwordnet.isti.cnr.it/

Similarity Method	Kendall τ
Common words	0.524
WordNet Synsets	0.656
Word2vec	0.618
Doc2vec	0.620

Table 3: The Kendall rank correlation coefficient (τ) for the rankings determined using TextRank for each method of determining semantic similarity compared to the Centrality ranking obtained from the manually annotated argument structure.

WordNet, a positivity, negativity and objectivity score. The sum of these scores is always 1. For example, the triple (1, 0, 0) (positivity, negativity, objectivity) is assigned to the synset of the word "good".

Each proposition (I-node), is split into words and each word is stemmed and tagged, and stop words are removed. If a stemmed word belongs to one of the word classes "adjective", "verb" or "noun", its polarity scores are looked up in SentiWordNet. Where a word has multiple synsets, each of the polarity scores for that word are averaged across all of its synsets. The scores of all words within a sentence are then summed and divided by the number of words with scores to give a resulting triple of {positivity, negativity, objectivity} values for each proposition.

Having calculated the polarity triples for each proposition, we are then able to calculate the difference in polarity between two propositions, P_i and P_j as in equation 4.

We compute these differences in polarity for each pair of propositions in the corpus and then, for each of the methods of determining similarity discussed in the previous Subsection, multiply the similarity scores by the polarity difference to obtain a value representing the likelihood of conflict between the two. Finally for each proposition, we mirror the method of computing divisiveness from the argument graph. To do this, we look at each proposition, and take the sum of the centrality scores multiplied by the conflict value for each other proposition.

Following this approach for each method of determining similarity again gives us a ranking which we can then compare to the divisiveness ranking calculated for the manually annotated argument structure, as described in Section 4. For each approach, we again calculate the Kendall

rank correlation coefficient. These results are shown in Table 4. We can see from these results that whilst there is still a positive correlation between the rankings, these are substantially less significant than those obtained for the centrality rankings. In the next Section we investigate whether these values are sufficient to have a positive impact on the argument mining task.

Similarity Method	Kendall τ
Common words	0.197
WordNet Synsets	0.284
Word2vec	0.167
Doc2vec	0.133

Table 4: The Kendall rank correlation coefficient (τ) for the Divisiveness rankings for each method of determining semantic similarity compared to the Divisiveness ranking obtained from the manually annotated argument structure.

6 Validation: Applying Automatically Identified Centrality and Divisiveness Scores to Argument Mining

Our final step is to validate both our concepts of centrality and divisiveness as calculated from annotated argument structures and our methods of calculating these same metrics directly from unannotated text. To do this, we adapt the "Topical Similarity" argument mining technique presented in (Lawrence et al., 2014), where it is assumed firstly that the argument structure to be determined can be represented as a tree, and secondly, that this tree is generated depth first. That is, the conclusion is given first and then a line of reasoning is followed supporting this conclusion. Once that line of reasoning is exhausted, the argument moves back up the tree to support one of the previously made points. If the current point is not related to any of those made previously, then it is assumed to be disconnected and possibly the start of a new topic.

Based on these assumptions the argumentative structure is determined by looking at how similar each proposition is to its predecessor. If they are sufficiently similar, it is assumed that they are connected and that the line of reasoning is being followed. If they are not sufficiently similar, then it is first considered whether we are moving back up the tree, and the current proposition is compared to

$$Polarity(P_i, P_j) = \frac{|positivity(P_i) - positivity(P_j)| + |negativity(P_i) - negativity(P_j)|}{2} \quad (4)$$

all of those statements made previously and connected to the most similar previous point. Finally, if the current point is not related to any of those made previously, then it is assumed to be disconnected from the existing structure. This process is illustrated in Figure 2.

Lawrence et al. perform these comparisons using a Latent Dirichlet Allocation (LDA) topic model. In our case, however, the argument structures we are working with are from much shorter pieces of text and as such generating LDA topic models from them is not feasible. To achieve the same task, we use the same semantic similarity measures described in Section 5. As in (Lawrence et al., 2014), the threshold required for two propositions to be considered sufficiently similar can be adjusted, altering the output structure, with a lower threshold giving more direct connections and a higher threshold greater branching and more unconnected components.

We first carried out this process for each method of computing semantic similarity using the same methodology as Lawrence et al. We then adapted Step 2 from Figure 2 by considering all of the previous propositions as potential candidate structures and, having produced these candidate structures calculated the Centrality and Divisiveness rankings for each structure as described in Section 4. Finally we computed the Kendall rank correlation coefficient comparing the centrality ranking of each candidate structure to the ranking computed only using similarity (as described in Section 5) and selected the structure which maximised the rank correlation.

Table 5 shows the precision, recall and F1-scores for automatically determining connections in the argumentative structure using each semantic similarity measure combined with maximising the rank correlations for centrality and divisiveness. We can see from these results that maximising divisiveness results in small increases in accuracy, and in all cases maximising centrality results in increased accuracy in determining connections, with increases of 0.03–0.05 in F1-score demonstrated for all the methods considered.

7 Conclusion

In this paper we have presented two metrics, Centrality and Divisiveness, for describing the nature of propositions and their context within a large scale argumentative structure. We have shown how these metrics can be calculated from annotated argument structures and produced reliable estimations of these metrics that can be extracted directly from un-annotated text, with strong positive correlations between both rankings.

Finally, we have shown how these metrics can be used to improve the accuracy of existing argument mining techniques. By broadening the focus of argument mining from specific facets, such as classifying as premise or conclusion, to look at features of the argumentative structure as a whole, we have presented an approach which can improve argument mining results either as a feature of existing techniques or as a part of a more robust ensemble technique such as that presented in (Lawrence and Reed, 2015).

Similarity Method	p	r	F1
Common words	0.66	0.51	0.58
+ Max Centrality	**0.68**	**0.55**	**0.61**
+ Max Divisiveness	0.67	0.51	0.58
WordNet Synsets	0.75	0.63	0.68
+ Max Centrality	**0.81**	**0.64**	**0.72**
+ Max Divisiveness	0.77	0.63	0.69
Word2vec	0.72	0.74	0.73
+ Max Centrality	**0.78**	**0.78**	**0.78**
+ Max Divisiveness	0.72	0.77	0.74
Doc2vec	0.67	0.66	0.66
+ Max Centrality	**0.73**	**0.70**	**0.71**
+ Max Divisiveness	0.69	0.67	0.68

Table 5: Precision, recall and F1-scores for automatically determining connections in the argumentative structure using each semantic similarity measure combined with Centrality and Divisiveness.

Acknowledgments

This work was funded in part by EPSRC in the UK under grant EP/N014871/1.

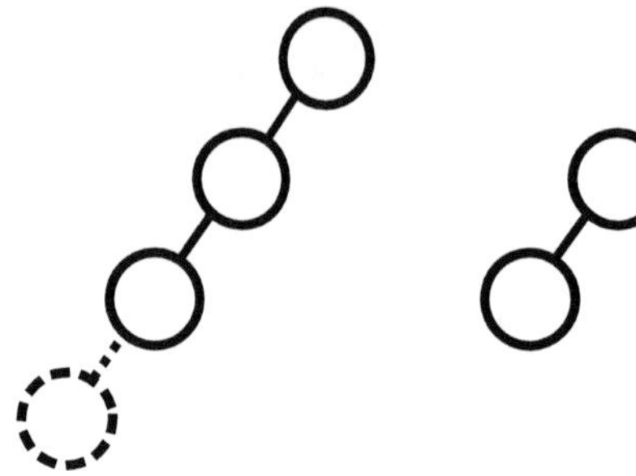
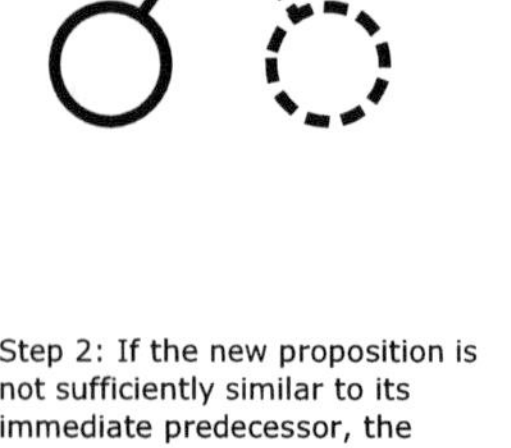
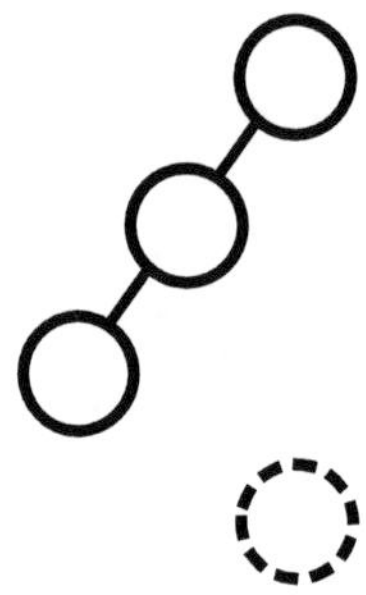

Figure 2: The steps involved in determining how the argument structure is connected using the "Topical Similarity" argument mining technique presented in (Lawrence et al., 2014).

References

S. Brin and L. Page. 1998. The anatomy of a large-scale hypertextual web search engine. *Comput. Net. ISDN Syst.* 30:107–117.

Carlos Chesñevar, Sanjay Modgil, Iyad Rahwan, Chris Reed, Guillermo Simari, Matthew South, Gerard Vreeswijk, Steven Willmott, et al. 2006. Towards an argument interchange format. *The Knowledge Engineering Review* 21(04):293–316.

Jacob Cohen. 1960. A coefficient of agreement for nominal scales. *Edu. Psychol. Meas.* 20:37–46.

Rory Duthie, John Lawrence, Katarzyna Budzynska, and Chris Reed. 2016. The CASS technique for evaluating the performance of argument mining. In *Proceedings of the 3rd Workshop on Argumentation Mining*. Association for Computational Linguistics, Berlin.

Ernesto Estrada. 2000. Characterization of 3d molecular structure. *Chemical Physics Letters* 319(5):713–718.

Vanessa Wei Feng and Graeme Hirst. 2011. Classifying arguments by scheme. In *Proceedings of the 49th Annual Meeting of the Association for Computational Linguistics: Human Language Technologies-Volume 1*. Association for Computational Linguistics, pages 987–996.

Graeme Hirst and Vanessa Wei Feng. 2015. Automatic exploration of argument and ideology political texts. In *1st European Conference on Argumentation (ECA 2015)*. pages 493–504.

Mathilde Janier, John Lawrence, and Chris Reed. 2014. OVA+: An argument analysis interface. In S. Parsons, N. Oren, C. Reed, and F. Cerutti, editors, *Proceedings of the Fifth International Conference on Computational Models of Argument (COMMA 2014)*. IOS Press, Pitlochry, pages 463–464.

Maurice G Kendall. 1938. A new measure of rank correlation. *Biometrika* 30(1/2):81–93.

Barbara Konat, John Lawrence, Joonsuk Park, Katarzyna Budzynska, and Chris Reed. 2016. A corpus of argument networks: Using graph properties to analyse divisive issues. In *Proceedings of the 10th edition of the Language Resources and Evaluation Conference*.

J Richard Landis and Gary G Koch. 1977. The measurement of observer agreement for categorical data. *Biometrics* 3:159–174.

Jey Han Lau and Timothy Baldwin. 2016. An empirical evaluation of doc2vec with practical insights into document embedding generation. *arXiv preprint arXiv:1607.05368* .

John Lawrence, Rory Duthie, Katarzyna Budzysnka, and Chris Reed. 2016. Argument analytics. In P. Baroni, M. Stede, and T. Gordon, editors, *Proceedings of the Sixth International Conference on Computational Models of Argument (COMMA 2016)*. IOS Press, Berlin.

John Lawrence and Chris Reed. 2015. Combining argument mining techniques. In *Proceedings of the 2nd Workshop on Argumentation Mining*. Association for Computational Linguistics, Denver, CO, pages 127–136.

John Lawrence, Chris Reed, Colin Allen, Simon McAlister, and Andrew Ravenscroft. 2014. Mining arguments from 19th century philosophical texts using topic based modelling. In *Proceedings of the*

First Workshop on Argumentation Mining. Association for Computational Linguistics, Baltimore, Maryland, pages 79–87.

Quoc V Le and Tomas Mikolov. 2014. Distributed representations of sentences and documents. In *ICML*. volume 14, pages 1188–1196.

Rada Mihalcea and Paul Tarau. 2004. Textrank: Bringing order into texts. In *Proceedings of EMNLP 2004*. Association for Computational Linguistics, pages 404–411.

Tomas Mikolov, Ilya Sutskever, Kai Chen, Greg S Corrado, and Jeff Dean. 2013. Distributed representations of words and phrases and their compositionality. In *Advances in neural information processing systems*. pages 3111–3119.

George A Miller. 1995. Wordnet: a lexical database for english. *Communications of the ACM* 38(11):39–41.

Marie-Francine Moens, Erik Boiy, Raquel M. Palau, and Chris Reed. 2007. Automatic detection of arguments in legal texts. In *Proceedings of the 11th international conference on Artificial intelligence and law*. ACM, pages 225–230.

Raquel M. Palau and Marie-Francine Moens. 2009. Argumentation mining: the detection, classification and structure of arguments in text. In *Proceedings of the 12th international conference on artificial intelligence and law*. ACM, pages 98–107.

Joonsuk Park and Claire Cardie. 2014. Identifying appropriate support for propositions in online user comments. In *Proceedings of the First Workshop on Argumentation Mining*. Association for Computational Linguistics, Baltimore, Maryland, pages 29–38.

Georgios Petasis and Vangelis Karkaletsis. 2016. Identifying argument components through textrank. In *Proceedings of the 3rd Workshop on Argumentation Mining*. Association for Computational Linguistics, Berlin.

Chris Reed, Simon Wells, Katarzyna Budzynska, and Joseph Devereux. 2010. Building arguments with argumentation: the role of illocutionary force in computational models of argument. In P. Baroni, F. Cerutti, M. Giacomin, and G.R. Simari, editors, *Proceedings of the 3rd International Conference on Computational Models of Argument (COMMA 2010)*. IOS Press, pages 415–426.

Frans H. van Eemeren, Bart Garssen, Eric C.W. Krabbe, A.Francisca Snoeck Henkemans, Bart Verheij, and Jean H.M. Wagemans. 2014. *Handbook of Argumentation Theory*. Springer.

Henning Wachsmuth, Benno Stein, and Yamen Ajjour. 2017. pagerank for argument relevance. In *Proceedings of the 15th Conference of the European Chapter of the Association for Computational Linguistics*. volume 1, pages 1117–1127.

Adam. Wyner, Jodi. Schneider, Katie. Atkinson, and Trevor. Bench-Capon. 2012. Semi-automated argumentative analysis of online product reviews. In *Proceedings of the Fourth International Conference on Computational Models of Argument (COMMA 2012)*. pages 43–50.

Unit Segmentation of Argumentative Texts

Yamen Ajjour, Wei-Fan Chen, Johannes Kiesel, Henning Wachsmuth and **Benno Stein**

Bauhaus-Universität Weimar

99423 Weimar, Germany

`<first name>.<last name>@uni-weimar.de`

Abstract

The segmentation of an argumentative text into argument units and their non-argumentative counterparts is the first step in identifying the argumentative structure of the text. Despite its importance for argument mining, unit segmentation has been approached only sporadically so far. This paper studies the major parameters of unit segmentation systematically. We explore the effectiveness of various features, when capturing words separately, along with their neighbors, or even along with the entire text. Each such context is reflected by one machine learning model that we evaluate within and across three domains of texts. Among the models, our new deep learning approach capturing the entire text turns out best within all domains, with an F-score of up to 88.54. While structural features generalize best across domains, the domain transfer remains hard, which points to major challenges of unit segmentation.

1 Introduction

Argument mining deals with the automatic identification and classification of arguments in a text. It has become an emerging topic of research mainly owing to its many applications, such as writing support tools (Stab and Gurevych, 2014a), intelligent personal assistants (Rinott et al., 2015), and argument search engines (Wachsmuth et al., 2017).

Unit segmentation is often seen as the first task of an argument mining pipeline. It consists in the splitting of a text into its argumentative segments (called *argument units* from here on) and their non-argumentative counterparts. Afterwards, the roles that the argument units play in the argumentative

structure of the text as well as the relations between the units are classified. Conceptually, an argument unit may span a clause, a complete sentence, multiple sentences, or something in between. The size of the units depends on the domain of an argumentative text (in terms of topic, genre, or similar), but can also vary within a text. This makes unit segmentation a very challenging task.

As detailed in Section 2, much existing research on argument mining has skipped the segmentation, assuming it to be given. For applications, however, an automatic segmentation is obligatory. Recently, three approaches have been presented that deal with the unit segmentation of persuasive essays: Persing and Ng (2016) rely on handcrafted rules based on the parse tree of a sentence to identify segments; Stab (2017) uses sequence modeling based on sophisticated features to classify the argumentativeness of each single word based on its surrounding words; and Eger et al. (2017) employ a deep learning architecture that uses different features to do the same classification based on the entire essay. So far, however, it is neither clear what the best segmentation approach is, nor how different features and models generalize across domains and genres of argumentative texts.

In this paper, we carry out a systematic study to explore the major parameters of unit segmentation, reflected in the following three research questions:

1. What features are most effective in unit segmentation?

2. What is the best machine learning model to capture the context of a unit that is relevant to segmentation?

3. To what extent do the features and models generalize across domains?

We approach the three questions on and across three existing argumentation corpora, each repre-

---

The first two authors equally contributed to this paper.

118

Proceedings of the 4th Workshop on Argument Mining, pages 118–128

Copenhagen, Denmark, September 8, 2017. ©2017 Association for Computational Linguistics

senting a different domain (Section 3): the essays corpus of Stab (2017), the editorials corpus of Al-Khatib et al. (2016), and the web discourse corpus of Habernal and Gurevych (2015). All combinations of training and test domain are considered for these corpora, resulting in nine experiments.

Given the corpora, we follow the existing approaches outlined above in tackling unit segmentation as a token-level classification task (Section 4). To capture the context around each token, we analyze different semantic, syntactic, structural, and pragmatic feature types, and we compare three fundamental machine learning techniques based on these features: standard feature-based classification realized as a support vector machine (SVM), sequence modeling realized as linear-chain conditional random field (CRF), and a new deep learning approach realized as a bidirectional long short-term memory (Bi-LSTM). These models correspond to increasingly complex levels of modeling context: The SVM considers only the current token, resulting in an isolated classification for each word. The CRF is additionally able to consider the preceding classifications. The Bi-LSTM, finally, can exploit all words and classifications before and after the current word.

We evaluate all features and models in Section 5. Our results provide clear evidence that the capability of deep learning to model the entire context is beneficial for unit segmentation within domains. The Bi-LSTM achieves the highest effectiveness on each corpus, even outperforming the approach of Stab (2017) on the essays corpus. Across domains, however, all three perform similar and notably drop in effectiveness. Matching intuition, semantic features turn out best to characterize argument units in the in-domain experiments, whereas structural features are more effective across domains. Our findings indicate that the concepts of argument units in the given corpora do not fully match.

Altogether, the contribution of our paper is an extensive analysis of the benefits and limitations of standard approaches to argument unit segmentation. Nevertheless, argument unit segmentation is by far not a solved task yet, which is why we end with a discussion of its major challenges in Section 6, before we finally conclude (Section 7).

2   Related Work

Unit segmentation is a classical segmentation task, that is related to discourse segmentation (Azar, 1999; Green, 2010; Peldszus and Stede, 2013) as for rhetorical structure theory (Mann and Thompson, 1988). Both discourse and argument units are used as building blocks, which are then hierarchically connected to represent the structure of the text. However, argument units are closer to classical logic, with each unit representing a proposition within the author's argumentation.

Much existing work on argument mining skips the segmentation, assuming segments to be given. Such research mainly discusses the detection of sentences that contain argument units (Teufel, 1999; Palau and Moens, 2009; Mochales and Moens, 2011; Rooney et al., 2012), the classification of the given segments into argumentative and non-argumentative classes (Stab and Gurevych, 2014b), or the classification of relations between given units (Stab and Gurevych, 2014b; Peldszus, 2014; Peldszus and Stede, 2015).

A few publications address problems closely related to unit segmentation. Madnani et al. (2012) identify non-argumentative segments, but they do not segment the argumentative parts. Levy et al. (2014), on the other hand, try to detect segments that are argumentatively related to specific topics. However, they do not segment the whole text.

A unit segmentation algorithm has been already applied by Al-Khatib et al. (2016) in the creation of the editorials corpus analyzed in this paper. The authors developed a rule-based algorithm to automatically pre-segment the corpus texts before the manual annotation. The algorithm was tuned to rather split segments in cases of doubt. During the annotation, annotators were then asked to correct the segmentation by merging incorrectly split segments. The authors argue that—even with a simple algorithm—this approach simplifies the annotation process and makes evaluating inter-annotator agreement more intuitive.

In the few publications that fully address unit segmentation, a detailed analysis of features and models is missing. Previous work employs rule-based identification (Persing and Ng, 2016), feature-based classification (Lawrence et al., 2014), conditional random fields (Sardianos et al., 2015; Stab, 2017), or deep neural networks (Eger et al., 2017). Especially the most recent approaches by Stab and Eger et al. rely on sophisticated structural, syntactical, and lexical features. Eger et al. even report that they beat the human agreement in unit segmentation on the one corpus they consider, but the paper does not clarify which linguistic cues are most helpful to reach this performance. To remedy this, we also employ a deep neural network based on Bi-LSTMs, but we perform a detailed comparison of models and feature sets.

Previous work trains and tests unit segmentation algorithms on one single corpus. A frequent choice is one of the two versions of the Argument Annotated Essay Corpus (Stab and Gurevych, 2014a; Stab, 2017), which is studied by Persing and Ng (2016), Eger et al. (2017), Stab (2017) himself, and also by us. However, for a unit segmentation algorithm to be integrated into applications, it has to work robustly also for new texts from other domains. This paper therefor extends the discussion of unit segmentation in this direction.

3 Data

This study uses three different corpora to evaluate the models that we developed to segment argument units. The corpora resprented different domains, particularly in terms of genre. We detail each corpus below, give an overview in Table 1, and provide example excerpts in Figure 1.

Essays The Argument Annotated Essays Corpus (Stab and Gurevych, 2014a; Stab, 2017) includes 402 persuasive essays from `essayforum.com` written by students. All essays have been segmented by three expert annotators into three types of argument units (major claims, claims, and premises) and non-argumentative parts. Each argument unit covers an entire sentence or less. The essays are on average 359.5 tokens long with 70% of tokens being part of an argument unit.[1] We employ the test-training split provided by the authors.

Editorials The Webis-Editorials-16 corpus (Al-Khatib et al., 2016) consists of 300 news editorials from the three online news portals Al Jazeera, Fox News, and The Guardian. Prior to the annotation process, the corpus was automatically pre-segmented based on clauses. After that, three annotators performed the final segmentation by merging segments and distinguishing argument units of six types (common ground, assumption, anecdote, testimony, statistics, and other) from non-argumentative parts. The annotation guidelines define a unit as a segment that spans a proposition (or two or more interwoven propositions) stated by the

---

[1]The percentage of tokens that are part of an argument unit is calculated from Table 1 as (Arg-B + Arg-I)/Total.

There are lots of other effects of growing technology on transportations and communications, which are mentioned as follows. First and for most, email can be count as one of the most benefical results of modern technology. Many years ago, peoples had to pay a great deal of mony to post their letters, and their payments were related to the weight of their letter or boxes, and many accidents may cause problem that the post could not be deliver delivered.

Excerpt of a document in the essays corpus

You have to be made of wood not to laugh at this: a private Russian bank has given a load to France's National Front. The political party, drawn to victory by Marine Le Pen, won the recent French elections by almost three times the number of votes than President Francios Holllande. Although this is news, this wasn't the biggest media reaction of the day.

Excerpt of a document in the editorials corpus

Private schools succeed where public schools fail largely because in a public school the teach's hand are tied by potlitically correct nonsense. They cannot correct errors, cannot encourge high achievers for fear of upsetting the regular students , assign homework, or expect respect from the students. The inmates are running the asylum in many public schools.

Excerpt of a document in the web discourse corpus

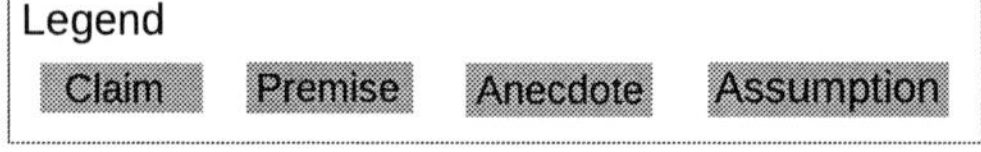

Figure 1: Excerpts of three documents for the essays, editorials and web discourse corpus. Each excerpt is highlighted with argument units as annotated in the original corpus

author to discuss, directly or indirectly, his or her thesis. This corpus contains the longest documents with an average of 957.9 tokens. The editorials are mainly argumentative, with 92% of the tokens in the corpus being part of an argument unit. We employ the provided training-test split.

Web Discourse The Argument Annotated User-Generated Web Discourse corpus (Habernal and Gurevych, 2016) contains 340 user comments, forum posts, blogs, and newspaper articles. Each of these is annotated according to a modified version of Toulmin's model (Toulmin, 1958). In the corpus, argument units belong to one of five types (premise, claim, rebuttal, refutation and backing) and can be arbitrary text spans. Because of the

Corpus	Part	# Documents	Number of tokens				
			Arg-B	Arg-I	Arg-O	Total	Average
Essays	Training	322	4,823	75,621	35,323	115,767	359.5
	Test	80	1,266	18,790	8,699	28,755	359.4
	Total	402	6,089	94,411	44,022	144,522	359.5
Editorials	Training	240	11,323	202,279	17,227	230,829	961.8
	Test	60	2,811	49,102	4,622	56,535	942.3
	Total	300	14,234	251,381	21,849	287,364	957.9
Web Discourse	Training	272	905	32,093	36,731	69,729	256.4
	Test	68	224	7,949	8,083	16,256	239.1
	Total	340	1,129	40,042	44,814	85,985	252.9

Table 1: Number of documents, tokens per class, and average tokens per document per corpus and part.

latter, the units are on average much longer than in the other two corpora: 36.5 tokens compared to 16.5 tokens (essays) and 18.7 tokens (editorials).[2] The complete documents are relatively short though (252.9 tokens on average), and they contain many non-argumentative parts: only 48% of the tokens are part of an argument unit. Since the authors do not provide any split, we randomly split the corpus into a training set (80%) and test set (20%), similar to the other corpora.

The three corpora vary in terms of how arguments are actually annotated in the contained documents. Following Stab (2017), we converted all documents into the BIO format, where each token is labeled according to the position in the segment that it belongs to as *Arg-B* (the first token of an argument unit), *Arg-I* (any other token of an argument unit), or *Arg-O* (not in an argument unit).

4   Method

This paper explores the effectiveness of semantic, syntactic, structural, and pragmatic features when capturing tokens separately, along with their neighbors, or along with the entire text. In line with recent work (see Section 2), we address unit segmentation as a token labeling problem. In the following, we detail each set of features as well as the three machine learning models that we employ. Each model reflects one of the outlined contexts used to classify the tokens. To demonstrate the strengths and weaknesses of the models, we encode the features as analog as possible in each model. However, some variations are necessary due to differences in the way the models utilize the features.

4.1   Features

For every token, we extract the following semantic, syntactic, structural and pragmatic features.

Semantic Features   Semantic features capture the meaning of tokens. This work employs the simple but often effective way of representing meaning by using the occurrence of each token as a feature (bag-of-words). We also tested word embeddings (Pennington et al., 2014) as semantic features, but found that they performed worse for all models introduced below except for the Bi-LSTM.

Syntactic Features   The syntactic features that we employ capture the role of a token in a sentence or argument unit. We resort to standard part-of-speech (POS) tags as produced by the Stanford tagger (Toutanova et al., 2003) for this feature set.

Structural Features   Structural features capture the congruence of argument units with sentences, clauses, or phrases. We employ the Stanford parser (Klein and Manning, 2003) to identify sentences, clauses, and phrases in the text and represent them with token labels. In particular, we use one feature for each token and structural level (sentence, clause, phrase), capturing whether the token is at the beginning, within, or at the end of such a structural span, respectively.

Pragmatic Features   Pragmatic features capture the effects the author of a text intended to have on the reader. We use lists of discourse markers compiled from the Penn Discourse Treebank (Prasad et al., 2008) and from (Stab, 2017) to identify such markers in the text. The latter have been specifically created for detecting argument units. For each token and discourse marker, we use five binary fea-

---

[2] Average length of argument units is calculated from Table 1 as (Arg-B + Arg-I)/Arg-B

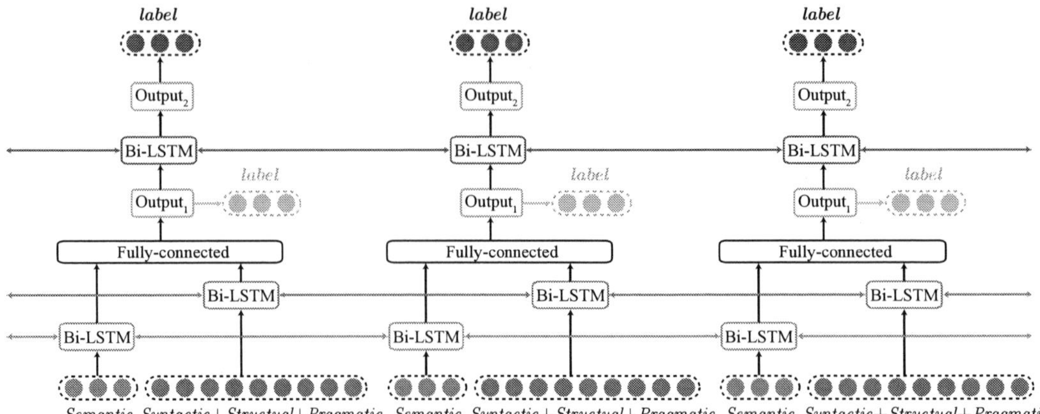

Figure 2: The neural network structure used in our paper with the input feature vectors for three tokens at the bottom. The labels by $Ouput_1$ are estimated without considering label dependency and are not used; instead we report the results for $Output_2$, which considers this dependency.

tures that are 1 iff. the token is before the marker, the beginning of the marker, inside a multi-token marker, the last token of a multi-token marker, or after the marker in the sentence, respectively.

4.2 Models

We make use of three common machine learning models in order to capture an increasing amount of context for the token labeling: a support vector machine (SVM), a conditional random field (CRF), and a bidirectional long short-term memory (Bi-LSTM). To provide a comparison to results from related work, we reimplemented the method of Stab (2017) and use it as a baseline.

Reimplementation   The approach of Stab (2017) is based on a CRF sequence model (Lafferty et al., 2001). It has been specifically developed for the segmentation given in the essays corpus. Since the license of the original implementation prohibited the author from giving us access to the code, we fully reimplemented the approach.

Analog to Stab (2017), we employ the CRF-Suite (Okazaki, 2007) with the averaged perceptron method (Collins, 2002). For the reimplementation, we use the exact feature sets described by Stab (2017): Structural, Syntactic, LexSyn and Prob. Our reimplementation achieves an F-score of 82.7, which is slightly worse than the value reported by Stab (2017) for unit segmentation (86.7). We attribute this difference to implementation details in the employed features.

SVM   We employ a linear SVM model in terms of a standard feature-based classifier that labels each consecutive token independently, disregarding the token's context. In other words, features of neighboring tokens are not considered by the SVM. Accordingly, this model does not capture the transition between labels, as well.

CRF   We implement a CRF sequence model to capture the context around the token for labeling the token. For labeling, the linear-chain CRF that we use considers the labels and features of the surrounding tokens within a certain window, which we chose to be of size 5 for our experiments. We use the same framework and method as for the reimplementation.

Since CRFs explicitly capture the local context of a token, we simplify the pragmatic features for this model and use only binary features for whether the token is at the beginning, inside, at the end, or outside of a discourse marker.

Bi-LSTM   Finally, we also build a Bi-LSTM neural network to capture the entire text as context. The architecture of the model is illustrated in Figure 2 and further explained below.

Compared to the CRF, the Bi-LSTM model does not utilize a window while classifying a token but considers the whole the text at once. Instead of using the tokens directly as semantic features, we use the word embedding of the tokens (Pennington et al., 2014), as this is common for neural networks. In particular, we use the standard pre-trained em-

Features	Models	Test on Essays			Test on Editorials			Test on Web Discourse		
		Essays	Editorials	Web Dis.	Essays	Editorials	Web Dis.	Essays	Editorials	Web Dis.
Semantic	SVM	53.42	40.89	28.89	50.00	53.96	16.20	31.71	26.58	33.34
	CRF	76.56	53.06	26.31	66.30	78.90	8.48	37.51	37.25	42.53
	Bi-LSTM	87.91	**57.11**	36.00	60.70	81.56	24.63	**41.29**	36.44	**54.98**
Syntactic	SVM	49.66	36.14	26.45	49.98	51.36	14.32	28.44	25.33	31.93
	CRF	66.79	48.40	15.48	68.30	76.74	5.05	34.73	38.13	24.25
	Bi-LSTM	83.10	55.70	21.65	64.92	80.35	15.28	36.58	37.40	43.02
Structural	SVM	41.19	36.14	26.45	49.53	77.71	5.96	27.97	37.98	27.52
	CRF	60.12	48.41	15.48	68.96	77.55	5.68	34.64	**38.30**	22.51
	Bi-LSTM	69.77	48.63	**41.19**	61.54	79.62	**38.08**	35.46	37.75	39.51
Pragmatic	SVM	38.75	28.65	30.09	31.33	33.02	22.38	30.85	22.24	35.59
	CRF	40.15	31.66	15.48	37.06	40.20	5.02	24.30	30.30	23.70
	Bi-LSTM	76.47	54.72	15.24	57.66	75.31	5.24	34.88	36.68	22.76
All	SVM	61.40	50.88	31.26	58.84	79.89	22.55	39.14	37.42	42.76
	CRF	79.15	52.50	21.74	**69.80**	81.97	8.00	37.09	37.63	37.74
	Bi-LSTM	**88.54**	**57.11**	36.97	60.69	**84.11**	20.85	39.78	36.56	54.51
Reimplementation		82.70	52.00	20.00	67.00	78.00	6.00	31.66	37.30	49.00

Table 2: The in-domain (gray background) and cross-domain macro F-scores on each test (first header row) after training on one of the training sets (second header row). Each row lists the results of one of the three models (SVM, CRF, and Bi-LSTM) using one of the four feature types (semantic, syntactic, structural, and pragmatic) in isolation or their combination (all). For each column, the highest value is marked in bold. The bottom line shows the F-scores of our reimplementation of the approach of Stab (2017).

bedding of Pennington et al. (2014), which has a dimensionality of 300. For the other feature sets, we concatenate all the boolean features described in the previous section into a sparse feature vector (more precisely, a one-hot vector).

The architecture in Figure 2 should be viewed from bottom to top. We first feed the features into bidirectional LSTMs (Schuster and Paliwal, 1997). Next, we feed the semantic features into a separate Bi-LSTM in order to be able to use a different kernel for the dense feature vector of the semantic features than for the one-hot vectors. The output of the two Bi-LSTM layers is then concatenated and fed into a fully-connected layer. To model label dependencies, we add another Bi-LSTM and another output layer. Both output layers are softmax layers, and they are trained to fit the labels of tokens. We process only the result of the second output layer, though. As we will see in Section 5, the second output layer does indeed better capture the sequential relationship of labels.

5 Experiments

Using the three corpora detailed in Section 3, we conduct in-domain and cross-domain experiments to answer the three research questions from Section 1. In each experiment, we use the training set of one corpus for training the model and the test set of the same or another corpus for evaluating the model. In all cases, we test all four considered feature sets both in isolation and in combination. We report the macro F-score as an evaluation measure, since this allows for a comparison to related work and since we consider all three classes (*Arg-B*, *Arg-I*, and *Arg-O*) to be equally important.

Table 2 lists the macro F-scores of all combinations of features and models as well as of our reimplementation of the approach of Stab (2017) for all combinations of training and test set.

5.1 Comparison to Previous Work

To put our results into context, we also imitate the experiment setting of Stab (2017). For this purpose, we randomly split the test set of the essays corpus into five equally-sized subsets and use the student's t-test to compare the F-scores of our methods on each subset with the result of Stab (2017). We find that our best-performing method, the Bi-LSTM using all features, achieves a significantly better F-score (88.54 versus 86.70) with p-value < 0.001.

	Label	B-B	B-I	B-O	I-B	I-I	I-O	O-B	O-I	O-O
						Prediction				
Gold	B-B	**0**	0	0	0	0	0	0	0	0
	B-I	1	**956**	11	0	152	0	0	0	0
	B-O	0	0	**0**	0	0	0	0	0	0
	I-B	0	0	0	**0**	0	0	0	0	0
	I-I	0	71	0	4	**16363**	78	59	77	872
	I-O	0	0	0	0	83	**1109**	0	0	74
	O-B	0	4	0	10	131	0	**958**	17	144
	O-I	0	0	0	0	0	0	0	**0**	0
	O-O	0	129	7	1	1285	157	139	87	**5550**

Table 3: Confusion matrix opposing the number of gold BIO labels of pairs of consecutive tokens in the essays corpus to those predicted by our best-performing method, the Bi-LSTM using all features. The correct predictions (on the diagonal) are marked in bold.

Furthermore, although the results of our reimplementation of the approach of Stab (2017) are lower than those reported by the author, our own CRF approach performs comparably well in almost all cases using simple linguistic features.

5.2 Improvement by Second Output Layer

A side effect of predicting the BIO label of each token separately is that two consecutive tokens can be labeled as *Arg-O* and *Arg-I*. This is not reasonable, since it corresponds to a unit without beginning. Without the second output layer $Output_2$, our neural network method produced about 400 such pairs. However, when we added the layer, the number dropped by half to 200 pairs. While the effect on the F-score is small, using the second output layer therefore produces more comprehensible results. We thus only report the results with $Output_2$.

5.3 Error Analysis

To learn about the behavior of our best-performing Bi-LSTM model, we carried out an error analysis. Table 3 presents the confusion matrix of the gold BIO label pairs and the predicted pairs on the essays corpus. While it is not possible to discuss all errors here, we observed a few typical cases, as discussed in the following.

In particular, some wrong predictions result from cases where the Bi-LSTM combines several units into one. For instance, the two units in *"... [the criminal is repeated second time]; also, [it is regarded as the "legalized revenge"...]"* are predicted as one unit. This produces errors of the types *(I-O, I-I)*, *(O-B, I-I)*, and *(O-O, I-I)* (gold vs. prediction). Conversely, the Bi-LSTM also sometimes chops one unit into several units. For instance, the unit *"Crimes kill someone which is illegal; nevertheless, the government use law to punish them..."* is chopped into *"[Crimes kill someone which is illegal]"* and *"[the government use law to punish them...]"*. This will create *(I-I, I-O)*, *(I-I, O-O)*, and *(I-I, O-B)* errors, despite noticing that it may also make sense for some annotators.

Finally, some *(I-O, I-I)* errors occurred a number of times, because of the delimiter of units (such as ",", "." or ";") were not included in the gold data but predicted as being part of it by our Bi-LSTM.

6 Discussion

Given our experimental results, we come back to the three research questions we initially raised, and then turn our head to ongoing research.

6.1 Major Parameters of Unit Segmentation

Our study aims to provide insights into three major parameters of unit segmentation: features, models, and domains. Each of them is reflected in one of our guiding research questions from Section 1.

Research Question 1 *What features are most effective in unit segmentation?*

According to the results of the in-domain experiments, the semantic features are the most effective. The models employing these features, achieve the highest F-scores, except for the SVM on *editorials*, where structural features perform better. However, there is no feature type that dominates the cross-domain experiments. At least, the structural features seem rather robust when the training and test sets are from different domains.

Corpus	Label	Sentence			Clause			Phrase		
		B	I	E	B	I	E	B	I	E
Essays	Arg-B	0.30	-0.19	-0.05	0.23	-0.13	-0.06	0.04	0.04	-0.08
	Arg-I	-0.30	**0.44**	-0.30	-0.23	0.34	-0.22	0.04	0.03	-0.08
	Arg-O	0.18	-0.37	0.33	0.14	-0.29	0.25	-0.06	-0.04	0.11
Editorials	Arg-B	**0.75**	**-0.51**	-0.05	**0.57**	-0.38	-0.07	0.15	-0.09	-0.09
	Arg-I	**-0.53**	**0.74**	**0.48**	**-0.44**	**0.58**	-0.33	0.02	0.12	0.11
	Arg-O	0.05	**-0.50**	**0.64**	0.09	**-0.41**	**0.47**	-0.10	-0.09	0.21
Web Discourse	Arg-B	**0.48**	-0.33	-0.03	0.32	-0.22	-0.04	0.10	-0.06	-0.05
	Arg-I	-0.12	0.09	0.00	-0.09	0.07	0.00	-0.02	0.01	0.01
	Arg-O	0.18	0.01	-0.01	0.01	0.01	0.08	0.00	0.00	0.00

Table 4: Pearson correlation between argument unit boundaries and structural features. Values range from -1.00 (total negative correlation) to 1.00 (total positive correlation). Absolute values above or equal to 0.40 can be seen as moderately correlated and are marked in bold.

While the results of the semantic features across *essays* and *editorials* — two domains that are comparably similar — remain high, the performance of the models employing them dramatically drop when tested on *web discourse* after training on either of the other. The intuitive explanation for this decrease in the domain transfer is that important content words are domain-specific. Thus, the learned knowledge from one domain cannot be transferred to other domains directly. In contrast, structural features capture more general properties of argumentative text, which is why we can use them more reliably in other domains.

As shown in Table 4, the sentence, clause, and phrase boundaries correlate with the boundaries of argument units. Especially in the editorials corpus, the boundaries of sentences and clauses show high Pearson coefficients. This reveals why we can still achieve reasonable performance when the training and test set differ considerably.

Research Question 2 *What is the best machine learning model to capture the context of a unit that is relevant to segmentation?*

Comparing the different models, the SVM performs worst in most experiments. This is not surprising, because the SVM model we used utilizes local information only. In a few cases, however, the SVM performed better than the other models, e.g., when evaluating pragmatic features on *essays* that were learned on *web discourse*. One reason may be that such features rather have local relevance. As a matter of fact, adding knowledge from previous and preceding tokens will add noise to a model rather than being beneficial.

Overall, the models employing sequential features turn out stronger. Among them, the Bi-LSTM achieves the best results in most cases regardless of the domain or the features. This suggests that context information from the tokens around a token to be classified is generally useful. In addition, using neural networks seems to be a better choice to encode those features.

Another advantage of using a Bi-LSTM is that this model can utilize all features related to tokens from the beginning to the end of the document. This allows the Bi-LSTM to capture long-distance dependencies. For a CRF, such dependencies are hard to encode, requiring to increase the complexity of the model dramatically and thus making the problem intractable.

Research Question 3 *To what extent do the features and models generalize across domains?*

From the results and the previous discussion, we conclude that our structural features (capturing the boundaries of phrases, clauses, and sentences) and the Bi-LSTM model are the most domain-robust. Other features, especially the semantic ones tend to be more domain-dependent. The ability to model long-distance dependencies and a more advanced feature encoding indicate why the Bi-LSTM apparently learns more general, less domain-specific features of the given argumentative texts.

6.2 Major Challenges of Unit Segmentation

The drastic effectiveness loss in the domain transfer suggests that the notion of an argument unit is not entirely the same across argumentative text corpora. This hypothesis is supported by the high variance in the size of argument units, ranging from clause-like segments (Al-Khatib et al., 2016) to partly multiple sentences (Rinott et al., 2015). At the same time, it seems reasonable to assume that there is a common concept behind argument units that connects their different notions and that distinguishes argument units from other types of segments. Under this assumption, a general question arises that we see as fundamental in research on unit segmentation:

Open Question about Argument Units *What makes argument units different from syntactic and discourse units, and at what point do they deviate?*

The difference between argument units and elementary discourse units is discussed by Stede et al. (2016). The authors claim that the boundaries of the more coarse-grained argument units clearly are also boundaries of discourse units. While this may be the case in their corpus as a result of their annotation scheme, no reason is given why the claim should generally be true. Accordingly, for other corpora such as the essays corpus studied in this paper, the claim simply does not hold.

In principle, it is possible to more generally study the raised question based on a matching of argument units with the syntactic and/or discourse units in different datasets. A generally satisfying answer might not exist, though, because we expect the segmentation into argument units to be task-specific to some extent. Similar observations have been made for discourse units (Taboada and Mann, 2006). In case of argument units, some annotations, for example, model the hierarchical structure of a text primarily (Stab, 2017), whereas others aim to capture self-contained evidence (Rinott et al., 2015). Even for a given task, however, unit segmentation remains challenging, though, as underlined by the limited effectiveness we observed in some experiments. As a result, the notion of an argument unit is a topic of ongoing discussion in the community. This brings up another question:

Open Question in Unit Segmentation *What knowledge is needed to effectively perform unit segmentation?*

In particular, it has been discussed controversially in the community as to whether unit segmentation should actually be tackled as the first step of argument mining. When doing so, no knowledge about the main claims of an argumentation, the applied reasoning, and similar is given, making the feasibility of distinguishing argumentative from non-argumentative parts doubtful. Of course, other orderings might lead to analog problems, which would then suggest to jointly approach the different steps. We plan to explore the best ordering and decomposition of mining steps in future work.

7 Conclusion

Most existing research on argument mining either ignores the task of argument unit segmentation, assuming the units to be given, or considers an argument unit to simply span exactly a sentence or a clause (Teufel, 1999; Palau and Moens, 2009; Mochales and Moens, 2011; Rooney et al., 2012). Recently, the task of argument unit segmentation was tackled on persuasive student essays by casting the problem as a sequence labeling task, classifying each token as being either at the beginning, inside, or outside an argument unit (Stab, 2017; Eger et al., 2017). Both approaches perform comparably well while employing different sequential models and different feature types: Stab (2017) uses local linguistic features whereas Eger et al. (2017) capture the global semantic and argumentative context.

In this work, we adopt the approach to frame argument unit segmentation as a sequence labeling task. We conduct a systematic comparison of three machine learning models that encode the context and the linguistic features of a token differently. Among these, our new Bi-LSTM neural network model utilizes structural, syntactic, lexical and pragmatic features, and it captures long-distance dependencies for argument unit segmentation. In in-domain experiments and cross-domain experiments on three different corpora, we study what model and feature set perform best.

Our experiments show that structural and semantic features are the most effective for argument unit segmentation across domains, while semantic features are the best for detecting the boundaries of argumentative units within domains. We also find that a sequential model capturing a wider context (i.e., our Bi-LSTM) tends to perform better within and across domains. Nevertheless, the results reported in Section 5 show the insufficiency of the employed linguistic features and machine learning models for a domain-robust argument unit segmentation. We therefor conclude that further research is needed in order to clarify the difference between argument units and other types of units as well as to find out what knowledge is best to segment argumentative texts into these units.

References

Khalid Al-Khatib, Henning Wachsmuth, Johannes Kiesel, Matthias Hagen, and Benno Stein. 2016. A News Editorial Corpus for Mining Argumentation Strategies. In *Proceedings of the 26th International Conference on Computational Linguistics.*

M. Azar. 1999. Argumentative Text as Rhetorical Structure: An Application of Rhetorical Structure Theory. *Argumentation* 13:97–114.

Michael Collins. 2002. Discriminative Training Methods for Hidden Markov Models: Theory and Experiments with Perceptron Algorithms. In *Proceedings of the 2002 Conference on Empirical Methods in Natural Language Processing.* Association for Computational Linguistics, volume 10, pages 1–8.

Steffen Eger, Johannes Daxenberger, and Iryna Gurevych. 2017. Neural End-to-End Learning for Computational Argumentation Mining. *Proceedings of the 55th Annual Meeting of the Association for Computational Linguistics* In Press.

Nancy L. Green. 2010. Representation of Argumentation in Text with Rhetorical Structure Theory. *Argumentation* 24:181–196.

Ivan Habernal and Iryna Gurevych. 2015. Exploiting Debate Portals for Semi-Supervised Argumentation Mining in User-Generated Web Discourse. In *Proceedings of the 2015 Conference on Empirical Methods in Natural Language Processing.* Association for Computational Linguistics, pages 2127–2137.

Ivan Habernal and Iryna Gurevych. 2016. Argumentation Mining in User-Generated Web Discourse. *Computational Linguistics* .

Dan Klein and Christopher D Manning. 2003. Accurate Unlexicalized Parsing. In *Proceedings of the 41st Annual Meeting on Association for Computational Linguistics.* Association for Computational Linguistics, volume 1, pages 423–430.

John Lafferty, Andrew McCallum, Fernando Pereira, et al. 2001. Conditional Random Fields: Probabilistic models for Segmenting and Labeling Sequence Data. In *Proceedings of the Eighteenth International Conference on Machine Learning.* volume 1, pages 282–289.

John Lawrence, Chris Reed, Colin Allen, Simon McAlister, and Andrew Ravenscroft. 2014. Mining Arguments From 19th Century Philosophical Texts Using Topic Based Modelling. In *Proceedings of the First Workshop on Argumentation Mining.* Association for Computational Linguistics, Baltimore, Maryland.

Ran Levy, Yonatan Bilu, Daniel Hershcovich, Ehud Aharoni, and Noam Slonim. 2014. Context Dependent Claim Detection. In *Proceedings of COLING 2014, the 25th International Conference on Computational Linguistics: Technical Papers.* Dublin City University and Association for Computational Linguistics, Dublin, Ireland.

Nitin Madnani, Michael Heilman, Joel Tetreault, and Martin Chodorow. 2012. Identifying High-level Organizational Elements in Argumentative Discourse. In *Proceedings of the 2012 Conference of the North American Chapter of the Association for Computational Linguistics: Human Language Technologies.* Association for Computational Linguistics, Stroudsburg, Pennsylvania.

William C. Mann and Sandra A. Thompson. 1988. Rhetorical Structure Theory: Toward a Functional Theory of Text Organization. *Text - Interdisciplinary Journal for the Study of Discourse* 8.

Raquel Mochales and Marie-Francine Moens. 2011. Argumentation Mining. *Artificial Intelligence and Law* 19(1):1–22.

Naoaki Okazaki. 2007. CRFsuite: A Fast Implementation of Conditional Random Fields (CRFs) .

Raquel Mochales Palau and Marie-Francine Moens. 2009. Argumentation Mining: The Detection, Classification and Structure of Arguments in Text. In *Proceedings of the 12th International Conference on Artificial Intelligence and Law.* ACM, pages 98–107.

Andreas Peldszus. 2014. Towards Segment-based Recognition of Argumentation Structure in Short Texts. In *Proceedings of the First Workshop on Argumentation Mining.* Association for Computational Linguistics, Baltimore, Maryland.

Andreas Peldszus and Manfred Stede. 2013. From Argument Diagrams to Argumentation Mining in Texts: A Survey. *International Journal of Cognitive Informatics and Natural Intelligence* 7(1):1–31.

Andreas Peldszus and Manfred Stede. 2015. Joint prediction in MST-style Discourse Parsing for Argumentation Mining. In *Proceedings of the 2015 Conference on Empirical Methods in Natural Language Processing.* Association for Computational Linguistics, Lisbon, Portugal.

Jeffrey Pennington, Richard Socher, and Christopher D. Manning. 2014. GloVe: Global Vectors for Word Representation. In *Proceedings of the 2014 Conference on Empirical Methods in Natural Language Processing.* pages 1532–1543. http://www.aclweb.org/anthology/D14-1162.

Isaac Persing and Vincent Ng. 2016. End-to-End Argumentation Mining in Student Essays. In *Proceedings of the 2016 Conference of the North American Chapter of the Association for Computational Linguistics: Human Language Technologies.* Association for Computational Linguistics, pages 1384–1394. https://doi.org/10.18653/v1/N16-1164.

Rashmi Prasad, Eleni Miltsakaki, Nikhil Dinesh, Alan Lee, Aravind Joshi, Livio Robaldo, and Bonnie L Webber. 2008. The Penn Discourse Treebank 2.0. In *Proceedings of the Sixth International Conference on Language Resources and Evaluation.*

Ruty Rinott, Lena Dankin, Carlos Alzate Perez, M. Mitesh Khapra, Ehud Aharoni, and Noam Slonim. 2015. Show Me Your Evidence — An Automatic Method for Context Dependent Evidence Detection. In *Proceedings of the 2015 Conference on Empirical Methods in Natural Language Processing*. Association for Computational Linguistics, pages 440–450. https://doi.org/10.18653/v1/D15-1050.

Niall Rooney, Hui Wang, and Fiona Browne. 2012. Applying Kernel Methods to Argumentation Mining. In *Proceedings of the Twenty-Fifth International Florida Artificial Intelligence Research Society Conference*.

Christos Sardianos, Ioannis Manousos Katakis Katakis, Georgios Petasis, and Vangelis Karkaletsis. 2015. Argument Extraction from News. In *Proceedings of the Second Workshop on Argumentation Mining*. Association for Computational Linguistics, Denver, Colorado.

Mike Schuster and Kuldip K Paliwal. 1997. Bidirectional Recurrent Neural Networks. *IEEE Transactions on Signal Processing* 45(11):2673–2681.

Christian Stab and Iryna Gurevych. 2014a. Annotating Argument Components and Relations in Persuasive Essays. In *Proceedings of the the 25th International Conference on Computational Linguistics*. Dublin City University and Association for Computational Linguistics, Dublin, Ireland.

Christian Stab and Iryna Gurevych. 2014b. Identifying Argumentative Discourse Structures in Persuasive Essays. In *Proceedings of the 2014 Conference on Empirical Methods in Natural Language Processing*. Association for Computational Linguistics, pages 46–56. https://doi.org/10.3115/v1/D14-1006.

Christian Matthias Edwin Stab. 2017. *Argumentative Writing Support by Means of Natural Language Processing*. Ph.D. thesis, Technische Universität Darmstadt.

Manfred Stede, Stergos Afantenos, Andreas Peldszus, Nicholas Asher, and Jérémy Perret. 2016. Parallel Discourse Annotations on a Corpus of Short Texts. In *Proceedings of the Tenth International Conference on Language Resources and Evaluation (LREC 2016)*.

Maite Taboada and William C. Mann. 2006. Rhetorical Structure Theory: Looking Back and Moving Ahead. *Discourse Studies* 8(3):423–459.

Simone Teufel. 1999. *Argumentative Zoning: Information Extraction from Scientific Text*. Ph.D. thesis, University of Edinburgh.

Stephen Toulmin. 1958. *The Uses of Argument*. Cambridge University Press.

Kristina Toutanova, Dan Klein, Christopher D Manning, and Yoram Singer. 2003. Feature-rich Part-of-Speech Tagging with a Cyclic Dependency Network. In *Proceedings of the 2003 Conference of the North American Chapter of the Association for Computational Linguistics on Human Language Technology*. Association for Computational Linguistics, volume 1, pages 173–180.

Henning Wachsmuth, Benno Stein, and Yamen Ajjour. 2017. "PageRank" for Argument Relevance. In *Proceedings of the 15th Conference of the European Chapter of the Association for Computational Linguistics*. volume 1, pages 1117–1127.

Author Index

Association for Computational Linguistics
209 N. Eighth Street
Stroudsburg, Pennsylvania 18360